Television Journalism

Journalism Studies: Key Texts

Journalism Studies: Key Texts is a new textbook series that systematically maps the crucial connections between theory and practice in journalism. It provides the solid grounding students need in the history, theory, 'real-life' practice and future directions of journalism, while further engaging them in key critical debates. Drawing directly from how journalism is studied and understood today, the series is a full-service resource for students and lecturers alike.

Series Editors: Martin Conboy, David Finkelstein, Bob Franklin

Published Titles
Radio Journalism Guy Starkey and Andrew Crissell
Alternative Journalism Chris Atton and James Hamilton
Newspaper Journalism Peter Cole and Tony Harcup
Magazine Journalism Tim Holmes and Liz Nice
International Journalism Kevin Williams

Television Journalism

Stephen Cushion

Los Angeles | London | New Delhi
Singapore | Washington DC

First published 2012

Apart from any fair dealing for the purposes of research or private study, or criticism or review, as permitted under the Copyright, Designs and Patents Act, 1988, this publication may be reproduced, stored or transmitted in any form, or by any means, only with the prior permission in writing of the publishers, or in the case of reprographic reproduction, in accordance with the terms of licences issued by the Copyright Licensing Agency. Enquiries concerning reproduction outside those terms should be sent to the publishers.

SAGE Publications Ltd
1 Oliver's Yard
55 City Road
London EC1Y 1SP

SAGE Publications Inc.
2455 Teller Road
Thousand Oaks, California 91320

SAGE Publications India Pvt Ltd
B 1/I 1 Mohan Cooperative Industrial Area
Mathura Road
New Delhi 110 044

SAGE Publications Asia-Pacific Pte Ltd
33 Pekin Street #02–01
Far East Square
Singapore 048763

Library of Congress Control Number: 2011926242

British Library Cataloguing in Publication data

A catalogue record for this book is available from the British Library

ISBN 978–1–4462–0740–6
ISBN 978–1–4462–0741–3 (pbk)

Typeset by C&M Digitals (P) Ltd, Chennai, India
Printed and bound by CPI Group (UK) Ltd, Croydon, CR0 4YY
Printed on paper from sustainable resources

CONTENTS

LIST OF TABLES

ACKNOWLEDGEMENTS

I would like to thank colleagues at the Cardiff School of Journalism, Media and Cultural Studies for their support whilst researching and writing the book. In particular my gratitude goes to Justin Lewis for collaborating on several of the research projects that are explored in some of the chapters that follow and to Bob Franklin for encouraging me to write *Television Journalism*. I would also like to thank Mila Steele, Sarah-Jayne Boyd, Imogen Roome and the rest of the Sage team for helping with the production of the book.

INTRODUCTION

Introducing television journalism: sustaining its influence into the twenty-first century

For all the hype of the digital, interactive, multimedia era, television news remains the most viewed, valued and trusted source of information in most countries around the globe. Whether at election times, in moments of tragedy or joy, as matter of routine, most of the time television is where people will turn to first to make sense of what is happening in the world. Major national bulletins both nationally and internationally are watched by many millions each day. Network and cable evening news in the United States (US) is watched by over 24 million viewers (Pew Project for Excellence in Journalism 2010), while the terrestrial nightly bulletins in the United Kingdom (UK) reach 15 million (Ofcom 2010a) and the Australian Networks' Seven, Nine and Ten reach extends to five million viewers (Ward 2008: 349).

Even in so-called developing countries (where a television, let alone a multi-television channel culture, is less ubiquitous), television news covers huge swathes of the population; 42 per cent of Brazilian households, for example, tune into the country's evening newscast, *Jornal Nacional* (Porto 2007). In mass populated regions, television news viewing can be enormous: Al-Jazeera is watched by more than 50 million people in the Arab world (Black 2008) and despite only 120 million Indian households having television sets India's AAJ TAK has 45 million regular viewers (Lakshmi 2007). However, these figures are dwarfed by China's CCTV's evening news bulletin audience, which currently stands at 200 million (Hayes 2010). Today, international news channels are racing to capture their piece of the global market. BBC World News, CNNI, Euronews, Deutsche Welle, Al-Jazeera, NUK World, Press TV, France 24 and Russia Tonight are dedicated television news channels that broadcast in many languages and attract hundreds of millions of viewers world-wide every day. India alone has more than 70 dedicated news channels that broadcast in 11 different languages, making up a combined audience of many hundreds of millions (Mehta 2010). Most national 24-hour news channels, of course, will never reach these epic proportions, but rolling news is becoming a more familiar part of the media landscape. When a major news story breaks audiences are increasingly reaching for the remote control and seeking out these news channels (Cushion and Lewis 2010).

And yet despite television's continued reach and penetration of the global market, the pace in which social media has risen and the changing nature of how online journalism is consumed are what fascinates most. Since Internet penetration levels continue apace worldwide and globally binding sites like Twitter and Facebook have caught the imagination, this is perhaps under-standable. Launched in 2006 Twitter now boasts (as of October 2010) 176 million users and signs up seven million new people a month, with the aim of having one billion global members (MacMillan 2010). Meanwhile Facebook, at just seven years old, remains the most celebrated, with more than 500 million users worldwide (Sweeney 2010a) and boasts a Hollywood feature film – *The Social Network* – released in 2010 about its inventor, Mark Zuckerberg. It is hard not to be impressed with the breathless speed of Facebook's global dominance.

And yet while new media continue to penetrate global markets and soak up the acclaim it is easy to lose sight of *television's current and continued worldwide penetration and influence,* for it remains the most globally ubiquitous medium. Its penetration rate is 98 per cent in developed countries compared to 66 per cent for those with Internet access (ICT 2010). In developing countries the difference is much starker; just 16 per cent are online in devel-oping countries whereas 72 per cent of households have televisions (ICT 2010). At the same time global media habits show how, irrespective of the Internet, television watching continues to rise year-on-year (Lindsay, cited in Kerwin 2010). For example, on average, an American's daily diet of television is typically four and a half hours per day (Lindsay, cited in Kerwin 2010), while for European Union citizens it is three and a half hours (Ofcom 2009) and for viewers worldwide three hours and 12 minutes (Lindsay, cited in Kerwin 2010). During the 2010 football World Cup 400 million people would typically tune in for most games; close to half of all American house-holds watched the 2010 Superbowl (Deloitte's TMT 2010); and more than a billion people worldwide witnessed the Chilean miners being rescued in the same year (CBC News 2010). Meanwhile the UK's 2010 Christmas day television schedule achieved its highest viewing figures for more than a dec-ade with an average of 15.8 million; figures that show, according to the *Media Guardian,* that 'despite the distractions of the Internet and video games and growing ways to watch programmes, including the iPlayer, families are still gathering on the couch for the festive season' (Deans 2010a). Television, in short, continues to be a place where millions if not billions worldwide invest much of their time and attention.

The narrative of 'the future' encourages a play-off between television and the Internet. The latter is seen as progress but television less so, unless its sets are bigger, wider, in High Definition (HD) or a three dimensional (3D) format. But for many years now television sets have been integrating with computers – widescreen TVs were, after all, bought as much for Nintendo consoles as live sports and action films – and broadband is increasingly replacing digital or cable receivers. 'Old' and 'new' media, in this context, are not mutually exclusive. For Twitter and Facebook are not supplanting television, they are being used on computers, laptops and mobile phones to *accompany* viewing. A representative poll found that close to eight in ten 18–24 year olds in the UK use social media whilst watching the box (Mason 2010).

For news audiences, a similar pattern is emerging. Online news is used as a supplement to rather than a substitute for competing forms of journalism. A longitudinal audience study in the US by the Pew Research Center for the People and the Press (2010: 2) concluded that: 'Instead of replacing traditional news platforms, Americans are increasingly integrating new technologies into their news consumption habits'. Likewise, Brubaker (2011: 298) found that 'In seeking political information, audiences use Internet and television in conjunction as supplements or complements, rather than substitutes'. But old media platforms can prove to be resilient beasts, refusing to wither and die after years of dominance. Take the 2010 UK General Election for example: it was not the 'Internet wot won it', it was the widely watched televised leaders' debates and Gordon Brown's campaigning *faux pax* – calling an old-age pensioner a 'bigot' whilst entirely unaware that his microphone was still on – that were television events that shaped the wider campaign agenda (Wring and Ward 2010). Far from being cannibalised by new and exciting telecommunication and online multimedia, television news continues to be the port of call for most people when they wish to understand what is happening in the world today.

Because television is part of everyday life its journalism connects more regularly and compellingly with audiences than that produced by most other news media. This has long been acknowledged by many countries in advanced democracies where – with the exception of the US – television news has grown up with robust public service requirements and regulatory structures that have ensured its journalism, unlike many newspapers', has remained relatively balanced and in many countries more valued and trusted by its news' audiences.

Even in countries that routinely starve news media of their independence and subject them to considerable state interference, television news bulletins can retain a special significance. With varying degrees of control and manipulation at play, countries with huge populations such as China, Egypt, Iran, North Korea and Russia will carefully script and structure their daily state broadcasting, well aware of the mass reach television has relative to other media. When hundreds of thousands of Egyptians were protesting against the government in Cairo in early 2011, Nile News – a state-run television news service – largely ignored the demonstrations and concentrated on how order was being restored in the city (Fahim 2011). Similarly, in North Korea television news routinely avoids anything controversial or critical of the state. The *Guardian* critic, Mark Lawson (2010a), has observed how semiotic displays of North Korean power are sustained in television news: 'The vivid colour schemes make us think of children's telly – appropriately, because this is current affairs with the bad news left out – while the absence of a video screen behind the anchor, reminds us that North Korea's television service is unusual in proceeding largely without pictures, for security reasons'. With one eye on international viewers, North Korean state television is reluctant to expose the country to the outside world. At the same time, state television can be a powerful global diplomatic tool as well. In March 2010 Georgia's state controlled Imedi TV station featured a fake report claiming the country was under attack from Russia. With echoes of Orson Welles' notorious hoax radio broadcast in the US where the Martians were said to have landed the Georgian people understandably went into panic mode, with mobile phone networks crashing and chaos on the streets (Harding 2010). Knowing the significant immediate impact state television can have, the Georgian government's manipulation of its news operations was designed to convey the real possibility of Russian military action not just to the country itself but also to the wider international community.

While television news shares many characteristics with competing journalisms it still has a unique history and, as the chapters that follow explore, continues to exert its influence not just in a conventional sense but also in how new media are shaping up. And yet within media and communication studies, journalism research, theory and practice can at times skate over the broader context as to why and how news media are so comparatively different. As journalism studies has established itself as a global discipline in recent years (Löffelholz and Weaver 2008), this book addresses the need to provide more sustained interpretations of particular types of journalism. After all, television news agendas differ locally, nationally and internationally, operating under different broadcasting structures and regulatory frameworks (Curran and Park 2000). This book explores these differences and more, making sense of how television news can be understood within the broader forces that help shape its journalism production, practice and reception.

'Death of TV news ... much exaggerated': a story of declining television audiences but signs of a revival?

Television journalism, of course, is not without its faults nor immune from some of the broader challenges that similarly face the radio (Starkey and Crisell 2009), magazine (Holmes and Nice 2011), online (Allan 2006) or newspaper industries (Cole and Harcup 2010). While television news may remain the most consumed form of journalism, as has been the case with other news media it has broadly seen its audiences decline over previous decades. Figures from the State of US News Media by the Pew Project for Excellence in Journalism (2010) demonstrate just how far the power of network news has diminished in the last 30 years (see Table 0.1).

On average, audiences for the evening newscast on ABC, NBC and CBS have declined by a million year on year. This decline slowed up in 2008 and 2009 to 300,000 and 565,000 respectively, but the bigger picture indicates that the era when the three networks dominated television journalism is over. However, US television news audiences are not abandoning ship

Table 0.1 Evening network (ABC, CBS, NBC) news viewers in the US from 1980 to 2009

Year	Millions of viewers
1980	52.1
1985	48
1990	41
1995	35.7
2000	31.9
2005	27
2009	22.3

(Source: Pew Project for Excellence in Journalism: The State of the News Media 2010 http://stateofthemedia.org/2010/network-tv-summary-essay/audience/)

Table 0.2 Evening cable news (Fox News, MSNBC and CNN) viewers in the US from 1998 to 2009

Year	Millions of viewers
1998	1.3
2000	1.5
2002	2.4
2004	2.8
2006	2.5
2008	4.1
2009	3.8

(Source: Pew Project for Excellence in Journalism: The State of the News Media 2010 http://stateofthemedia.org/2010/cable-tv-summary-essay/audience/)

completely; the advent of new cable channels and programming in recent years has seen the numbers for television news viewers increase (see Table 0.2). Chapter 4 explores the broad decline of US network audiences and the revival of television news in the form of new cable rolling news channels and comedy-news formats.

In the UK, audience figures for national television news declined throughout the 1990s and into the new millennium. From 2004 to 2009, however, where take-up of multi-channel increased from 61 per cent to 91 per cent of the population, the average size of evening television bulletins remained broadly at the same level (Ofcom 2010a). In 2009 figures for the flagship evening bulletins stood at 4.3 million viewers for the BBC's *Six O'Clock News*; 4.7 million for the BBC's *Ten O'Clock News*; 3.2 million for ITV's *Early Evening News*; 2.5 million for ITV's *News at Ten*; 791,000 for *Channel 4 News*; and 768,000 for *Five News*. For Stuart Purvis, a former ITN chief executive, who oversaw the review of flagship news programming for the Office of Communication (Ofcom), these figures showed the 'death of TV news on linear channels turns out to be much exaggerated. In fact, these programmes [flagship UK news bulletins] remain the main source of news for most of the population' (cited in Ofcom 2010a).

Yet this should not gloss over the underlying trends that trouble the future of television news. Television news viewers are disproportionately older – the median age is sixty two for US network news – putting them in a precarious position since online news and cable competition attracts far younger audiences. If commercial broadcasters cannot reach out to more advertiser-friendly demographics, the long-term future for TV news looks even more perilous. Of course, history might repeat itself and the audience figures for television news viewers may be sustained as news audiences get older. However, for the time being future engagement does not appear promising; studies have shown television news is not engendering itself to a new generation of audiences or to the wider viewing public.

In the UK many young people and ethnic minorities in particular are tuning-out of the main national television news bulletins (BBC Trust 2009; Ofcom 2007; Ofcom 2010a; Wayne et al. 2010). Wayne et al's (2010) study of young people's relationship with television journalism found a deep-rooted disconnection in evidence since many felt alienated from much of its news agenda and approach to reporting politics. The same was uncovered by Ofcom's (2007) *New News, Future News*, where young audiences were finding television news increasingly irrelevant. They had carried out a representative poll of the UK population in 2002 asking if they agreed whether much of the news on TV was not relevant to them and had discovered less than half of 18–24 year olds agreed: by 2006, over two thirds did so. Ethnic minorities, by contrast, appeared turned off by the mainstream generally and many had switched over to international news channels for relevant news

(Ofcom 2010a). The national news channels have in turn attracted a greater share of viewer numbers having doubled their audience size from 2004 to 2009. But unless a huge news story breaks, their reach remains marginal (16 per cent) when compared to that for evening television bulletins (50 per cent) (Ofcom 2010a).

There is no easy answer as to why television news audiences have broadly declined. This book explores many possibilities but the reasons why less people are watching TV news remains elusive and multilayered. Over the last decade or so news sources have proliferated and the competition has intensified, not least from emerging online news provision (Allan 2006). At the same time newspapers have got bigger (Lewis et al. 2008), radio spectrums have been extended, and more digital stations have gone on air (Starkey and Crisell 2009). Meanwhile television has moved into a multichannel era, with hundreds of channels now readily available via cable and digital packages (Chalaby 2009). Audience loyalty, in this context, may have simply been diluted, as people turn toward new online material or to the assorted array of entertainment, film, sports and other lighter programming. Indeed television viewing does continue to increase, even reaching record highs in some countries.

In an attempt to win back or at least prevent audiences from declining further, television journalism has been accused of going 'downmarket', appealing to a wider audience by adopting what might be labelled a tabloid or 'soft' news agenda (Franklin 1997; Patterson 2000). While these terms may, in one sense, prove unhelpful in interpreting changing news practices and conventions (explored in Chapter 1), studies increasingly show (and will be examined throughout this book) that many countries, in different ways, have reassessed what counts as 'news'. There are, of course, many possible explanations as to why news values have shifted in recent years and these need to be carefully understood in the context they are produced (addressed in Chapter 3 and Chapter 4). However, what no television station can avoid, even the many subsidised by licence fees or taxpayers, is the increasingly commercial market that television news operates within. As competition has increased, in some countries – most notably the US – it has been suggested that journalism has entered a period of hypercommercialism (Cooper 2004; McChesney 2000, 2004), forcing newsrooms to scale back their operations and adopt news values that are motivated, above all, by capturing a larger share of the audience.

These shifting news agendas and values, it should be pointed out, are not uniformly found in different parts of the world nor are they evenly distributed across national or regional television news and current affairs. We can, nonetheless, draw on systematic content analyses studies that have identified repeated trends and patterns of coverage. Broadly speaking, over many years studies have generally shown that 'hard news' – politics, business, economics and international affairs – has declined while 'soft news' – crime, sports, royalty and celebrity gossip – has increased. At the same time hard news may be treated in a soft way (e.g., politicians pictured embracing celebrities) while soft news can be treated in a hard way (e.g., exposing the actions of corporate crime). In a UK study examining news bulletins from 1975–1999, for example, it was found that, almost across the board, what the authors' defined as broadsheet topics – politics, business and economics – was making way for what they labelled tabloid coverage – on crime, sports, royalty and celebrity issues (Barnett et al. 2000).

In characterising the changing nature of news and current affairs, notions of 'quality', 'hard', 'broadsheet' and 'serious' on the one side must be carefully (and not simply pejoratively) compared with terms such as 'popular', 'soft', 'tabloid' and 'trivial'. Like the 'dumbing down' thesis (explored in Chapter 1), these values can often obscure rather than enlighten our understanding of contemporary television journalism. As Lehman-Wilzig and Seletzky (2010: 43) have pointed out, the dichotomy of 'hard' and 'soft' categories in news studies can often be artificial and 'ambiguous', failing to 'uncover statistically significant findings and/or their conclusions'. The use of hard and soft distinctions can also, at times, encourage a form of cultural relativism that either dismisses or sidesteps around the evidence that demonstrates news agendas have shifted from hard to soft news. Stephen Harrington (2008: 279), in this respect, has rightly suggested that disagreeing 'over what counts as a worthy way of informing the public' is somewhat misleading since popular forms of journalism – like *The Daily Show* or Michael Moore's documentaries – blur the lines between entertainment and news (see Chapter 4). While these new forms of programming should not be dismissed for drawing on popular conventions, by the same virtue traditional news bulletins should also not be for choosing to remain tied to their more formal practices. Since television news is being increasingly hybridised Chapter 1 situates the competing ways by which the genre is understood and introduces the focus of television journalism that will be critically examined in subsequent chapters.

For television journalism is diverse in how it operates locally, nationally and internationally. Indeed in many countries it does not conform to some of the wider trends already identified here. Much of the contemporary lament about increasingly tabloid news agendas (Langer 1998; Thussu 2007), hypercommercial instincts (Cooper 2004; McChesney 2000, 2004, 2008) and declining audiences (Wayne et al. 2010) can be exclusively linked to Westernised journalism trends. But in many developing countries television journalism operates under different pressures and challenges. This book, where the evidence is available (e.g. Curran and Park 2000), will look towards 'de-Westernising' the interpretation of television journalism, examining its economic uncertainties in different parts of the world, the changing nature of its news agendas and the shifting patterns in which news is consumed and understood. All of which can potentially spell trouble for the future of television journalism. Note that 'future' is used cautiously here since the book argues that television journalism can sustain its position as the most valued and significant source of news if what made it so successful in the twentieth century can be safeguarded. The chapters that follow make clear what needs to be included for this to happen and why. Readers, in this sense, are invited to reach their own conclusions based on the relative merits of the evidence and analysis that together inform the arguments advanced.

In doing so the book's intention is to reawaken an interest in studying television news. For making sense of what is often the *potential* impact of 'new' media/journalism studies has meant, in recent years, that emerging mobile and online communications have pushed, in some scholarly areas, the *continued* and *present* influence of television news agendas toward the sidelines (an argument advanced in Chapter 7). This is not to discourage making sense of the online world or even to deny the transformative impact the WWW has had on journalism and communication more generally. But for all the democratic promise and revolutionary predictions associated with the Internet, television news overwhelmingly remains the most consumed form of journalism today, still exerting its influence on how the new media landscape has unfolded and continues to into the future.

In this context, television news should arguably be the lead protagonist in journalism studies if understanding the primary medium that most advanced democracies rely on to understand the world is what motivates research and scholarship. After all, while television journalism may be 'old' news to many scholars it remains remorselessly up to date for many viewers who still tune in most days of the week in order to find out what is happening in the world.

The scope of the book

The aim of this book is to explore television journalism in depth, examining its history from radio to television, unravelling how its political economy has evolved, asking how the cultures of television newsrooms have been shaped by education and training, and establishing the challenges that television journalism faces in a more crowded and competitive news environment. While it is important to situate the television news genre historically and explain some of the broader shifts within the industry, a central aim here is to draw on detailed empirical endeavours into television news journalism.

In doing so, not all areas of television journalism or the differences between nations can be explored at length or scrutinised in detail. The book will focus on five globally emerging trends, drawing on empirically-led studies that principally compare the UK and the US: the impact that 24-hour news values and conventions are having on television news culture and audiences

(Chapter 3); the increasingly partisan approach to television news and political journalism in the US (Chapter 4); the tension existing between national and local television journalism in an increasingly devolved UK (Chapter 5); the shifting demographics of journalists working in the industry now and in the future (Chapter 6); and, finally, the past, present and future of television news studies within the broader disciplines of journalism, media, sociology, cultural and communication studies (Chapter 7). At the risk of sounding like a mere empiricist, these trends will not be examined in isolation. For changing news values and audience expectations, (de) and (re) regulatory shifts and emerging forms of journalism, market forces and public service interventions, editorial pressures and occupational values will be discussed and more in order to understand how and why television journalism is evolving well into the twenty-first century.

At the same time, questions about where media power resides, how it operates, what conditions it thrives under or is suppressed, and most importantly whether this is for the public good or private self-interest will be critically interrogated. For television journalism's broader impact on citizenship and democracy will remain central to understanding contemporary – and future – television journalism. Democracy, after all, relies on an informed and vibrant citizenry and television news remains vital to the acquisition of public knowledge and citizenship engagement. To explain the democratic importance of television journalism Chapter 1 begins by situating television's place in the public sphere and asking where television news is scheduled in an increasingly entertainment-driven, multi-channel and multi-media environment. It will, furthermore, critically examine television journalism's changing news values and conventions and, in the context of a so-called post-broadcasting culture, explore how much impact media convergence has had on television news and its journalists.

Having examined the broad changes and challenges currently facing the television news industry, Chapter 2 turns to the past to make sense of the present. It charts the rise of radio and the structures that shaped how it was developed and regulated for since television has largely inherited its broadcasting legacy. The histories of UK and US television news will be compared to demonstrate how the pursuit of different broadcasting pathways could cultivate distinctive political economies of television news with profound implications for the health of a democracy. The chapter will also explore these implications in light of the wider trends – media commercialisation, concentration and deregulation – that threaten many of the public broadcasting structures that are safeguarded in the UK but have been largely diminished in the US.

The book then turns to address more contemporary trends in television news and examines the various implications these pose for the future of journalism. Chapter 3 begins by critically assessing the news values that are exclusive to television and rolling news journalism. The arrival and development of 24-hour news channels on a global scale are explained in three phases. First, when rolling news 'came of age' with the arrival of CNN. Second, when a global race for transnational reach and influence began with international news channels being launched. Third, when an ongoing phase then emerged where 24-hour news channels are regionalising and commercialising the rolling news conventions. More detailed empirical studies on 24-hour news are engaged with to explore how conventions such as breaking news or live journalism are impacting on the way rolling news operates. For rolling news values appear to be editorially shaping not just 24-hour news but also television journalism more generally.

Chapter 4 explores another broader shift in television news that is evident in the US – the creeping partisan nature of television journalism and the polarisation of its audiences. Whereas objectivity was once a mainstay of US network television journalism, the emergence of cable television and the popularity of channels such as Fox News has politicised television news agendas. The chapter looks at when television news became more partisan in nature and why this happened by examining the wider culture of journalism, the (de)regulation of television news, and the incursion of comedy-news formats such as the *The Daily Show* on television. As a conclusion it assesses whether a partisan approach to television news will be imported to other countries and, if so, the impact this would have on news culture more generally.

Attention then turns to local as opposed to national television news. Chapter 5 begins by briefly comparing why local and state-wide television seems to flourish commercially in the US but not in the UK. It then charts the demise of commercial local and regional broadcasting in the latter and the reliance on public service broadcasters to cover an area of journalism the market has increasingly withdrawn itself from. Since the UK government devolved much of its powers in 1999, the importance of localised political news in the nations and regions has become a more significant democratic resource. A detailed empirical study is drawn on to compare how far public and commercial television news reflects the UK and covers the world of devolved politics. By exploring two contrasting broadcasting structures and the regulatory requirements that shape the kind of journalism that is produced the reporting of devolved politics is a useful case study which goes beyond the parochial concerns that are relevant to the UK alone. In doing so, the chapter also demonstrates how interventionist regulation can enhance rather than impede the quality of journalism.

The final two chapters focus on journalists and journalism scholars. Chapter 6 puts television journalists under the spotlight, making sense of who they are, what backgrounds they come from, how much they are paid, the kind of education or training they have received and, above all, how far they are trusted and valued amongst viewers and within the news industry. Chapter 6, in other words, examines the sociology of journalists, exploring how distinctive television journalists are compared to those working in other news media. Behind the shifting demographics of television journalists in recent years are many structural obstacles that shape the sort of journalism that is produced and how this is done, thereby posing many challenges for aspiring journalists in the future.

The final chapter situates the academic discipline of journalism within the related fields of media, communication, sociology and cultural studies. It then explores television news studies within the discipline of journalism studies, combining a further reading guide with a critical interrogation of the past, present and future of television journalism scholarship. The chapter charts the rise and fall of television news studies as academic attention has moved increasingly towards uncovering the new media landscape and emerging online cultures. In doing so, it will argue that while it remains important to make sense of journalism in this multimedia age television news studies needs to make a decisive return to centre stage. The future of television news studies is examined in the context of two wider trends. First, how the more collaborative relationship the media industries have cultivated with scholars in recent decades can be enhanced to inform journalism practice. Second, how internationally comparative television news studies can be used to expose the ways in which broadcasting systems and regulatory structures can shape different television news cultures.

1

THE ROLE OF NEWS IN TELEVISION CULTURE: CURRENT DEBATES AND PRACTICES IN CONTEMPORARY JOURNALISM

Television and the public sphere: journalism in a multi-channel environment

In making sense of television journalism, it is important to look beyond a particular headline or breaking news story in order to situate whatever purpose it serves more generally in society. Since television is where most people turn to understand what is happening in the world, what news is – and what is not – routinely included in an increasingly crowded and multi-channel environment matters. It constitutes, like other media, a space that is commonly identified as the public sphere, a normative theory used widely in journalism studies to understand the role the media could (or should) play in society.

This theory was developed by a German scholar, Jürgen Harbermas, in *The Structural Transformation of the Public Sphere*, which was originally published in 1962 and translated into English in 1989. It has, over the years, received comprehensive treatment (Calhoun 1992; Dahlgren 1995) and been related to far grander political, economic and philosophical arguments than the scope of this book can include. This is not the place to rehash or flesh out those debates. The public sphere is briefly summarised here as a means of characterising what television journalism can democratically make possible rather than something it can tangibly achieve. What the public sphere represents, in other words, is a normative rather than an empirical aspiration.

Put simply, Habermas (1989) charted an historical journey of how citizens, in post-feudal times between the seventeenth and mid-twentieth century, reached an understanding of the world that was independent of state forces.

At the beginning of this period, when the early symbols of democracy (parliaments, newspapers) began to take shape, citizens met and exchanged ideas by drawing on sources that were largely reliable and free from any commercial agenda or political corruption. These meetings were not pre-scheduled events but organic moments in social spaces such as salons and coffee bars. Engaging in a form of deliberative democracy citizens had a range of factual information at their disposal. In Habermas's view, this constituted an idealised site – a public sphere – where citizens could participate, at length, to form (and reach) a rational consensus on the prevailing issues of the day.

As societies became more modern and industrial, mass production opened up the opportunities for media (at this point primarily newspapers) to reach a far wider audience and, importantly, to generate healthy profits for the rich and corporate minded. This triggered, in Habermas's thesis, the decline of the public sphere. When society reached a more advanced stage of industrialisation in the mid-twentieth century, capitalism was in full flow and a corporate culture had taken control. The mass media (at this point newspapers, magazines, radio and the early years of television) had become more factually dubious and politically motivated. A wider communication crisis had also engulfed societies with the rise of the public relations and advertising industries. For Habermas, these pernicious industries wielded considerable influence over the kind of mass media that would be produced and fostered a more trivial and commercially motivated public sphere. No longer publicly meeting to deliberate at length on the burning issues of the day, citizens instead were fast becoming private consumers: passively watching, reading and listening to information in their own homes, much of it entertainment-based, on television, radio and print media. The mass media, in short, had become the public sphere but one that fell considerably short of the idealised site Habermas had envisaged happening centuries ago.

Before we start to untangle the complicated economic, social and political forces that shape television journalism today we must recognise that Habermas's public sphere captures what is democratically possible (and for some even desirable) from mass media. As a normative theory the public sphere reflects a mythical time and idealised space, a benchmark for assessing whether the conditions for sustaining a healthy democratic culture and vibrant citizenship are being met. Television, of course, was still in its early days when Habermas's book was first published in 1962. As Hallin (1994: 2) has noted, Habermas's 'account of the later history of the public sphere is extremely thin. He jumps abruptly from the salons of the eighteenth century to the mass culture of the 1950s'. Since then television has grown into a complex and fragmented beast, the most significant and consumed medium in many countries, representing 'the major institution of the public sphere in modern society' (Dahlgren 1995: x). Across many regions of the world, it has 'been essential to the experience and practices of citizenship for five decades or more' (Gripsrud 2010: 73).

While news and current affairs is not the only genre to experience and practise citizenship on television (Stevenson 2003; Wahl-Jorgensen 2007), it is what best captures the kind of public sphere Habermas imagined centuries before. The genre of television journalism today, of course, stretches well beyond conventional evening bulletins or serious current affairs programming. From afternoon chat shows like *Loose Women* in the UK to *View* in the US (which featured the first ever daytime television interview with an American President, Barack Obama, in July 2010), Michael Moore documentaries such as *Bowling for Columbine* and *Fahrenheit 9/11* to comedy news like *The Daily Show* in the US or *10 O'Clock Live* in the UK, television journalism has become an increasingly hybrid genre. In what some might call a postmodern development, conventions from a range of genres have been spliced together to form new ways of informing, engaging and entertaining viewers about politics and public affairs (Jones 2005, 2009). Chapter 4 weighs up the relative merits of new television journalism formats and asks how much of a contribution they have made to rejuvenating the television news genre.

When compared to other forms of journalism, television news and current affairs operate on a medium where their consumption is deeply ingrained in everyday life and culture (Hart 1994; Silverstone 1994). While newspapers may conveniently fall through the letterbox, magazines can be religiously purchased each week or news delivered at the touch of a button online, none of these media are utilised with the same degree of routine as watching television. Ethnographies of media use have shown how the television set is strategically placed at the centre of people's social living space (McKay and Ivey 2004). And in more recent years, television sets have moved beyond the living room. As a result, multiple televisions shape not only the layout of a living room, but also increasingly the bedroom, kitchen, garage and, for those lavish enough (to afford it), the bathroom. Television, in this sense, is more than part of the furniture: it is part of the family home, invited into every room and engaged with at any given opportunity. In pubs and clubs, gyms and health spas, libraries and waiting rooms, trains and planes, a television screen – often showing a rolling news channel – will never be far from people's view. Indeed, apart from sleeping and working, surveys show watching television is what occupies most people's time and energy. As Briggs has put it, television viewing is

> utterly ubiquitous in Western societies, part of the fabric of our everyday lives, a common resource for storytelling, scandal, scrutiny, gossip, debate and information: always there, taken for granted ... Television, both as a communicator of meanings, and as a daily activity, is *ordinary*. (2009: 1; original emphasis)

Television, then, is a one-stop-shop for information, education and entertainment programming.

While the rise of dedicated 24-hour news channels over the last decade or so (see Chapter 3) has made information and education services more widely available, most of the time it is entertainment channels that are most desired. Soap operas, football games, reality game shows, films and other popular programming are what dominate television schedules. Towards the end of the last millennium this was exacerbated by the arrival of multi-channel television that was able to broadcast a plethora of new programming around the clock.

But, as Chapter 7 illustrates, the actual diversity of television schedules can often be related to the level of public and private broadcasting provision within nation states. While many countries have increasingly moved towards the highly commercialised US model of broadcasting (Gripsrud 2010), there is resistance still being shown in some nations who remain proud of their public service traditions and are unwilling to let an unfettered market power dominate and state control diminish. In Europe, where an infrastructure of public service remains relatively strong, this has been difficult to withstand (Cushion 2012). As a result of the commercial media market being liberalised in the late 1980s and 1990s, it is today possible to access hundreds of channels via cable and digital platforms (Chalaby 2009). Rather than fuelling a more diverse television culture, however, systematic studies of television schedules have found these tend to rely on cheap, populist programming – imported shows (usually US in origin), Hollywood films, light entertainment, low-budget shopping channels – to make up the vast majority of what appears on screen. While there are some highly valued cultural and arts channels it has been observed that, in a European context over the last two decades, 'unashamedly commercial television was on the offensive and conquered large parts of the viewing audiences' (Gripsrud 2010: 81).

In this increasingly populist and crowded multi-channel television culture, then, how much priority is given to television news journalism?

Scheduling wars: locating television news in an increasingly entertainment-based medium

Most striking, for news and current affairs journalism in the multi-channel era, is the abundance of dedicated 24-hour news channels that have sprung up over the last decade or so (Cushion and Lewis 2010). For many viewers rolling news channels have become a familiar and accessible part of cable and digital television packages. Different packages make it possible to access a range of international, national and local stations, not just from their own countries but also from different regions of the world (Rai and Cottle 2010). In the UK, it is not uncommon – with even a basic cable Freeview package – to tune into English-language versions of BBC World News, Russia Today, Fox News, Sky News, CCTV and Euronews, amongst many more, without paying any subscription charge. While the international news channels can attract millions of viewers around the world, the audience size for some national 24-hour news channels can be relatively low. Moreover, rolling news channels tend to be watched by media, business and political elites (Garcia-Blanco and Cushion 2010; Lewis et al. 2005). Rolling news, nevertheless, has extended the menu of journalism on television and – as argued in Chapter 3 – has had a broader impact on the conventions and practices of television journalism.

Notwithstanding the contribution made by 24-hour news channels, television journalism is most regularly consumed on terrestrial or free-to-air channels. But these channels, such as BBC1 and ITV in the UK, are not genre specific: they offer up a range of programming throughout the day. Within the UK, the free-to air channels are required by law to run a quota of public service programming in their schedules. In this respect news and current affairs are seen as being synonymous with public service commitments (a point returned to in a moment). At the same time, the quota of programming legally imposed on channels operating within a public service framework includes balancing out the genres beyond news such as children's programming, the arts and religious affairs. The rest of the time they are free to run more preferred (since they are more popular and advertiser friendly) entertainment and sports programming. In balancing these genres, the priority placed on news and current affairs can be assessed by examining *where* they appear in television schedules.

Television schedules, for the most part, tend to be ignored by scholars (Ellis 2000). Instead it is the advertisers and programme makers who pay most attention to them since these are used to generate revenue or capture the largest slice of the audience. In our multi-channel era, however, scheduling has perhaps become even more important. With so many channels to choose from, now more than ever a routine relationship with viewers needs to be forged in order to cultivate consumer loyalty. For John Ellis, television schedules are 'the locus of power in television' (2000: 134), revealing much about how programming is prioritised across different channels. If we examine television journalism in this context it can be observed that news and current affairs plays an important role in the schedule but one that, in more recent years, appears to be second best to other television genres. Apart from breaking news stories (such as the terrorist attacks of 9/11 and 7/7 which, in the UK, were broadcast live on terrestrial channels), news and current affairs programming seems to be scheduled *outside* of prime time. The peak viewing hours – broadly 7pm–10pm in most countries – tend instead to be reserved for more popular, light-hearted entertainment.

A quick glance at the UK's, Australian and US's evening television news (see Tables 1.1–1.3) time slots indicates that the free-to-air bulletins avoid, for the most part, prime-time scheduling. While it would be misleading to suggest these bulletins represent a complete picture of news and current affairs on television in each country, they nonetheless usefully demonstrate where television journalism routinely features in the prime-time schedule.

Table 1.1   Time slots for the evening news bulletins on UK terrestrial television channels

Television channel	Time slots for UK national news and in the nations and regions opt outs (for Scotland, Wales, Northern Ireland and regions across England)
BBC1	6–6.30pm (national) and 6.30–7pm (nations and regional opt-outs)
	10–10.30pm (national) and 10.30–35pm (nations and regional opt-outs)
ITV	6–6.30pm (nations and regional outputs) and 6.30–7pm (national)
	10–10.30 (national) and 10.30–10.35 (nations and regional outputs)
Channel 4	7–7.55pm (national)
Channel 5	5–5.30pm (national)

Table 1.2   Time slots for the evening news bulletins on Australian terrestrial television channels

Television channel	Schedule for national
Seven Network	6–6.30pm (Seven News) and 6.30–7pm (Today Tonight)
Nine Network	6–6.30pm (Nine News) and 6.30–7pm (A Current Affair)
Network Ten	5–6pm (Ten News at 5pm), 6.30–7pm (6.30 with George Negus) (repeated at 11.11–11.39pm) and 11.39pm–0.06am Ten Late Night News/Sports Tonight
ABC1	7–7.30pm (ABC News), 7.30–8pm (The 7.30pm Report) and 10.30–11.05pm (Lateline)

Table 1.3   Time slots for the evening news bulletins on US terrestrial television channels

Television channel	Schedule for national
CBS	6.30–7pm CBS Evening News with Scott Pelley
NBC	6.30–7pm NBC Nightly News with Brian Williams
ABC	6.30–7pm ABC World News with Diane Sawyer and 11.35pm–12.00am (Nightline)

Apart from ABC1 in Australia, television news across the three countries is scheduled either before 7pm or after 10pm. While there is some variation in Australia and the UK, it is noteworthy that many rival television channels routinely schedule their bulletins against each other. This is most obvious in the US where the three big networks all provide news *at the same time* – namely 6.30–7pm – with each emphasising the role of the anchor to brand its own identity. In one sense, this may reflect when television news is most likely to be consumed. It can, however, also be viewed as a highly strategic move on the part of the broadcasters concerned: if each one runs news and current affairs at the same time, no one station will suffer a dip in ratings (and thus 'take a hit' from lost advertising revenue). Either way, it reduces pluralism in television news since viewers are not able to routinely watch the day's events from a variety of perspectives. There is, however, more pluralism in the Australian and UK schedules – where a stronger public service culture exists – compared to the US which is more commercially orientated (Cushion 2012).

If scheduling is sometimes overlooked in academic circles this is not the case within the industry. In the UK the rescheduling of the BBC1 and ITV evening news bulletins that took place at the end of the last millennium was to generate considerable publicity. Since both channels were legally required to air television news as part of their routine schedules, ITV requested permission to move its late night bulletin from 10pm to 11pm in 1999 on the basis that it wanted to run more entertainment programming and screen films uninterrupted (having previously had to break for the *Ten O'Clock News*). While this was accepted by the then regulator, the Independent Television Commission (ITC), audiences rapidly declined within a year and ITV was asked to schedule its nightly bulletin at an earlier time. Returning to its 10pm slot, ITV was then faced with competition from the BBC who had also requested whether it could move the nightly bulletin from 9pm to 10pm. This decision, in the words of BBC1's controller, was to allow 'us to open up our schedule to show more quality programmes at 9pm, including new drama such as *Crime Doubles* and *Clocking Off* and strong documentaries like *Blue Planet*' (cited in BBC News 2001). Having enjoyed a 30-year stint at 9pm, television news had ceded its prime-time slot for more entertainment genres.

A scheduling war soon broke out between ITV and the BBC. The latter believed, in a multi-media and online age with rolling news channels, that it would not impact on news audiences overall. ITV, meanwhile, argued the BBC's move to 10pm reflected 'a major abdication of the corporation's public service responsibilities' (cited in BBC News 2001). In the years following the BBC has attracted a greater share of the audience than ITV and the news slot has remained on the schedule at 10pm. ITV, however, never settled on a regular slot and has struggled to sustain consistent viewing figures. While it agreed initially to a 10pm slot with the ITC for three days of the week, this was subsequently renegotiated to a more permanent time of 10.20pm during the week and then moved again to 10.30pm a year later. In 2008 it returned to 10pm, but has struggled to compete with BBC1's 10pm news. A McKinsey review into the future of ITV news for the Chief Executive, Adam Crozier, in November 2010, reportedly recommended ITV's national news (and its regional 6pm service) should be reduced from 30 minutes to 15 and replaced by a quiz show (Brown 2011). At the time of writing no decision had been made about ITV news's scheduling future, but McKinsey's proposal alone suggests commercial television news is under threat from more populist programming.

More importantly, the squabbling over scheduling reveals much about the politics behind news provision in an increasingly entertainment-based multi-channel age. For while ITV and the BBC can be (and were at the time) criticised for prioritising populist genres above news, compared to other countries (see Table 1.1–1.3), both currently maintain early evening *as well as* evening news bulletins. This is not something that can be entirely credited with either organisation however. Enshrined in UK law, television programming remains subject to a larger broadcasting ecology that values news and current affairs as a key public service requirement (Cushion 2012). Since broadcast models of television news impact not only on scheduling but also on its journalism's news values and conventions more generally, public and commercial television systems need to be introduced.

(Re)shaping television journalism: public and commercial models of broadcasting

Television channels operate under broadcasting models that differ from one country to the next and relate to wider social, cultural economic traditions. While the history of television journalism will be explored in more depth in the subsequent chapter, for now it is vital to recognise that the political economy of broadcasting is an important aspect of understanding how news and current affairs are made and shaped (Cushion 2012). What must be taken into account, in other words, is a range of external factors that may impact on why television journalism is produced and how this happens.

In one sense, explaining broadcast models is a question of economics. For commercial broadcasters the primary goal is to generate revenue. Since this is most productively achieved by advertising, delivering large, or better still, affluent audiences is what sustains commercial broadcasting systems. Answerable to shareholders, commercial broadcasting is largely scheduled through financial decision making: which market will it appeal to and how many viewers will watch it? Public service broadcasting, by contrast, is funded either directly or indirectly via public subsidy. In theory, this means public service broadcasting is immune from market forces, making programming that appeals beyond the largest possible demographic or those groups with the most disposable incomes. While its purpose is to remain universally accessible, a key aspect of public service broadcasting is making programmes for minority tastes and cultures (Tracey 1998). This means embracing those genres which are typically marginalised by commercial broadcasters, such as children's programming, science, religion, the arts and, importantly for this book, current affairs and news journalism, and are invested in by public service broadcasters without (again, in theory) the pressure of attracting large audiences.

The reality of how broadcasting systems operate, however, is somewhat more complicated (Cushion 2012). While the US represents a fully fledged commercial system with a minimal public service television infrastructure

(McChesney 2004, 2008), across many regions of the world broadcasting ecologies have been pushed in different directions and developed hybrid broadcast models and systems of regulation (Hallin and Mancini 2004). As a result, in some countries public and commercial operations now overlap, creating what might be termed duopolistic broadcasting environments (Corner 2010). In the UK, for example, while the BBC has always remained an entirely public service system, ITV, a commercial broadcaster, was launched in the 1950s under the proviso that it would shoulder some public service responsibilities including scheduling news and current affairs programming. From the 1980s onwards a new multi-channel broadcasting environment challenged – or, some might say eroded (Tracey 1998) – the traditional model and concept of public service broadcasting. This has prompted debates into how public service communication should be 'reinventing' (Iosifidis 2010) itself for the digital age and in the face of greater commercial competition. Since the rise of multi-channel television, a new tripartite broadcasting system has evolved in countries where channels have either no, some, or fully blown public service broadcasting responsibilities. As broadcasting ecologies have shifted and overlapped somewhat, how then has television news and current affairs been reshaped?

Despite the commercial competition faced by publically-funded broadcasters in recent years, many have defied free market critics and risen to the challenge of remaining relevant in a digital and interactive environment (Debrett 2010). As Chapter 6 shows, many public service broadcasters have maintained a brand identity as a trusted and valued source of information in many countries because of their commitment to impartial and accurate news and current affairs provision. Those values associated with well resourced and high quality journalism lie at the heart of public service values, informing not only public but also some commercial broadcasters in this new millennium. So, for example, in the UK, even the relatively 'light touch' regulator (meaning it will not impose heavy regulations on broadcasters), Ofcom – which monitors, amongst other media, commercial television provision – places great value in ensuring news and current affairs remains central to broadcasters' schedules. In an introduction to a report into the state of the UK's broadcast journalism, *New News, Future News*, Ofcom stated:

> For the last 50 years the UK's public service broadcasting tradition has ensured high quality news provision on the BBC and independent television channels. It has been a clear policy objective of both government and broadcasting regulators to maintain and support plurality in the supply of high quality PBS news. (2007: 1)

The report raised many questions and concerns about the future of news that are also explored throughout this book, such as the challenges presented by the Internet, the consequences of relaxing the regulation of broadcast journalism, and the demise of regional and local news content. But what is important to emphasise here is how necessary a healthy provision of television journalism is to the regulators of *commercial* television.

It would be wrong, of course, to suggest news and current affairs on commercial channels share the same level of importance across many other regions around the world. Indeed in later chapters the key differences between countries with varying degrees of public service and commercial media are explored and compared to the kind of journalism produced and the wider audience knowledge of public affairs (Aalberg et al. 2010; Curran et al. 2009, 2010). But neither would it be right to suggest that public service journalism – in the UK and beyond – has not been influenced by the increasingly competitive commercial environment within which it now operates (Cushion 2012). It would be difficult, for example, to interpret the decision by the BBC to move its flagship 9pm news bulletin to 10pm as anything other than attempting to capture a larger share of the audience with drama and entertainment genres in a prime-time slot, since both bulletins have been described as 'seemingly immovable journalistic objects, fixed forever in their slots as symbols of British public broadcasting's commitment to the provision of quality news for a mass audience' (McNair 2003: 42).

Far from public service broadcasters being immune to market forces, at times it is possible to detect commercial factors exerting their influence on editorial agendas. This paradox confronts many such broadcasters: how can their programming remain relevant and popular at the same time as being distinctive and able to cater to those areas neglected by the market? After all, if viewers are not regularly tuning in and out of a channel it could be treated like one amongst many specialist stations, with tiny audiences hidden away in a multi-channel environment. By ghettoising public service channels the concern is that they will no longer reach a critical mass and, by extension, also no longer justify the licence fee or other means of public subsidy. Thus in an age of multi-channel choice news and current affairs on public service channels have to pull off no mean task: remaining distinctive from what the market already supplies while also continuing to be relevant and popular with the masses.

It is perhaps inevitable, in this context, that some publicly-funded broadcasters have been accused of encroaching on commercial television's territory by adopting populist news values and going 'down-market' in order to remain competitive news outlets. This criticism tends to be most frequently voiced by the BBC's competitors and most notably by certain right-wing newspapers such as *The Times, Daily Mail, Daily Express, The Daily Telegraph* and *The Sun*. But while such carping from the BBC's competitors can be viewed as somewhat predictable there has also been criticism from within the organisation itself. One example of this came from Kate Adie, a BBC correspondent, who suggested in 2002 that BBC news had become 'increasingly tabloid. Health scares, education crises … it's far more tabloid than it used to be' (cited in Jury 2002). And more recently, in 2010, a current affairs journalist for BBC1's *Panorama*, John Ware, provided another instance of this by stating that the BBC1 Controller, Jay Hunt, was 'as shallow as a paddling pool' when commissioning programming. BBC1's schedule, he claimed, should have 'more depth and boldness' (cited in Revoir 2010).

It is not unusual, of course, for the BBC or any other public service broadcaster to be taken to task about their news values and journalism. As far back as the reporting of the miners' strike in 1922, the history of the BBC has been marked by arguments with the government of the day or its commercial competitors from print, television and, increasingly, online sources (Curran and Seaton 2010). But beyond such industry rivalry and quarrels what is more significant here is why journalism is currently being critiqued in the way it is. While terms such as 'soft news', 'dumbing down', 'tabloidisation' or 'commercialisation' are often pejoratively invoked to describe an approach or style of journalism, it is less clear what these values actually encapsulate or tell us about the changing nature of television journalism.

Changing times, changing values: television news's shifting values and conventions

Accusations of 'dumbing down' are not reserved for television news or journalism more generally. Even some lifestyle programming, such as the BBC's *Gardener's World*, has not escaped unscathed, with the term being applied in this instance after the show was accused of 'patronising' viewers over its approach to gardening. A spokeswoman for the Chelsea Flower Show, for which the BBC holds a contract for exclusive coverage, said 'I will certainly … see if we can get a bit more quality. I think they're making a mistake in dumbing down' (cited in Jamieson 2010). This notion of 'quality' is important since it often appears to drive debates about the nature of television journalism. So, for example, the UK's Media, Culture and Sport Secretary, Jeremy Hunt, has argued that the BBC should 'concentrate on producing great TV programmes at the quality end of the spectrum. One of the things I think we get from having a BBC is that there is competition in British broadcasting at the quality end and not just at the mass end of the market' (cited in Watt 2010). While the 'quality end' of television is often reflected in Shakespearian dramas or arts programming, for television journalism its conventions and values are not as clearly defined and have historically been subject to much pejorative speculation about how the form and style of news have changed.

Towards the end of the nineteenth century, Matthew Arnold, a famous literary figure, suggested that a decline in 'quality' journalism was increasingly becoming apparent in British print media. Arnold is credited with coining the phrase 'The New Journalism', which Hampton (2008) describes as representing

> controversial changes, some influenced by American practice, including formatting innovations, such as headlines, and new types of content, such as interviews, human interest stories, celebrity features, and a shifting emphasis from opinion to news ... Lengthier columns were replaced by paragraphs, often derisively called "snippets", and the tone grew more personal.

On the face it, it is difficult to distinguish much of this critique of down-market print journalism from contemporary interpretations of 'dumbed down' news television and current affairs. In response US journalist Danny Schechter (2007) has observed that

> TV News comes alive when celebrities or former presidents die. That's the time when news ghouls come out to play ... Programmers look for 'hooks' – and try to generate interest for lowest common denominator stories, stories that will keep viewers coming back ... Increasingly, the avalanche of dumbed-down news and reality shows shapes the media environment with more celebrity chatter and viewers encouraged to partici-pate on shows they often have no influence in organizing ... The effect of all of this, of course, is to further limit and reduce our attention spans, to distract and divert us from what matters, and to give us a distorted view of the world ... Clearly, if you want news these days, 'THE NEWS' on TV is the last place to find it.

Several years before similar concerns were voiced in an editorial for *The British Journalism Review*:

> Do we hear a distant voice whispering, once again: 'Beware the Ides of Dumbing Down'? ... There is little doubt in the minds of many serious journalists that there has been a growing superficiality in television news reporting; that the 'quick-fire', in-and-out tendency is in command; that this leads to a vulgarisation of the message because background material is so thin or often completely absent. (Goodman 2000)

In each of these accounts there appears to be an arbitrary yardstick by which to measure journalism from a previous era, a time where news was more serious in its tone and content. Brian McNair (2009: 69) has labelled this the 'narrative of decline' whereby a romanticised, 'golden age' of jour-nalism is unfavourably compared to the contemporary news culture. McNair (2009: 69) suggests this 'cultural pessimism' is espoused by 'jour-nalists and politicians as often as academic observers in newspaper columns, television and radio talk shows, and debates in Parliament'.

While the 'dumbed-down' tag is certainly well-used journalistic shorthand for characterising trends in modern life – from lowering educational standards to (re)interpreting Shakespearian plays, and even for patronising viewers on gardening shows – academic observers, in more recent years, have arguably been more critical of the term and the values it represents. Shirley Harrison

(2006: 20) for one has put forward that 'at times the charge of dumbing down is too often wistful or nostalgic and in both cases wrong ... the history of news does not support the charge'. Likewise, Hugo de Burgh (2005: 39) has observed that 'many current anxieties about "dumbing down", commercialisation and the like can be found in discussions of journalistic evaluation going back centuries'. For Elizabeth Bird (2010: 13), the all-encompassing 'notion that "tabloidization" was a negative process that was "dumbing down" journalism and discouraging rational discourse' must be understood in the cultural context it was produced. In 'Mexico and the former Eastern Bloc', she has observed, 'apparently similar trends in journalism – a loosening of controls, snappier, more accessible writing, concerns about engaging the reader – were acting as positive forces for social change and democratic participation' (2010: 13). In a similar vein, Mick Temple (2006) has argued that 'dumbing down is good' and suggests scholars should look beyond a Habermasian model of constructing audiences as rational and critical actors since many people engage with news that is trivial or emotionally driven. The 'dumbing-down' thesis, in this context, is caught up in intellectual snobbery, informed by an elitist and highbrow sense of what news and current affairs should be as opposed to an accessible form of journalism that audiences can understand or participate in.

Within journalism studies, then, the 'dumbing-down' slogan has arguably generated more heat than light about the changing nature of television news agendas and values. It represents, in itself, a lazy means of approaching media and journalism scholarship, since it provides a somewhat vague and impressionistic narrative of how news has evolved over time (McNair 2009). After all, while the notion of 'dumbing-down' can be contested (since it remains, at best, an imprecise category – see Sparks and Tulloch 2000), what the term broadly encapsulates – a shifting of news conventions and practices, or news agendas and values – can, from a variety of perspectives, be explored by empirical means. Thus, scholars invoking the 'dumbing-down' charge to characterise news and current affairs will arguably undercut what journalism research has achieved in recent decades. Since journalism studies has grown up and internationalised the discipline (Löffelholz and Weaver 2008), there is an increasing range of global sources that demonstrate how television journalism has changed. The chapters in this book engage with this material to explore evidence-based changes and more broadly evaluate what it is that contemporary news values and conventions can tell us about the present and future of television journalism.

Towards a post-broadcasting culture? Television news and media convergence

In order to understand contemporary television journalism the wider culture of news delivery and consumption cannot be ignored, for no news media text can exist in isolation, nor can it operate in a vacuum shielded from the larger world of competing journalisms. The history of television news makes this clear since its development has been closely intertwined with the broadcast culture it inherited. Struggling in its early years to be distinctive from radio's many decades of dominance and adapt to the visual demands of the medium (see Chapter 2), television news also evolved with one eye on newspapers breaking news which broadcasters found hard to resist reporting. In a twenty-first century media landscape, television news competes beyond the familiar world of broadcasting and newspapers. The emergence of the Internet and mobile phone technology has brought new pressures and chal- lenges since these can constantly update news audiences who now no longer have to wait for an evening bulletin to catch up on the day's events.

In making sense of an increasingly crowded marketplace for news, schol- ars have suggested we live in a 'post-broadcast democracy' (Prior 2007; c.f. Cohen 2010). Whereas broadcasters once monopolised what was seen and heard in family homes and by mass audiences, today our mediated experi- ences have become fragmented and highly individualised. In Turner and Tay's (2009) edited book, *Television Studies After TV: Understanding Television in the Post-Broadcast Era*, many of the chapters expose how television – or the TV – has redefined itself in the face of more intense competition. Turner and Tay (2009: 2) have stated that television's

> content has migrated onto the web through the conventional media's branded websites, but more significantly through video aggregators like YouTube; the circulation of televi- sion increasingly occurs through viral, rather than broadcast, networks such as those available through blogs or the social networking sites Myspace or Facebook.

Which television content is watched and when this happens, it is argued, are no longer entirely under the control of major broadcasters. For audiences, this is interpreted as empowerment since they can tune in and out, pick and choose, email-on or delete in a flash the 'vast swampland' of progamming that Newton Minow once defined as being typical of American television in the 1960s. Since the arrival of multi-channel culture television has moved away from a time of 'scarcity' to an 'era of plenty' (Ellis 2000), ostensibly making far more choice available to viewers. In an American context this has been described as the 'Post-Network' era, where new cable operators have challenged the monopoly that was once firmly in the grasp of just three major networks (this is explored further in Chapter 2 and Chapter 4).

It would, viewed in this light, be hard to empirically contest a Post- Network era. After all, US network audiences have fragmented and increas- ingly turned to new cable channels for news, films, sports and entertainment (even if these offer more of the same as opposed to radically extending the nature of programming available). Viewed in a different light, prefixing post *before* broadcast more generally appears somewhat premature since it implies something has ended – the end of television? – and something entirely new has begun. Of course, as with the arrival of any new media, the digital era has impacted on how 'old' media operate. Television – and television news – is an increasingly interactive medium, and its journalism has spent much time and energy on integrating the salient features of the Internet to harness 'user generated content' (UGC). Whether texting or tweeting, building interactive websites or Facebook pages, many television news formats have attempted to enter into a real-time dialogue with their viewers.

While this has encouraged audiences to interact with each other and programme-makers, it remains open to question if anything meaningful has changed in a post-broadcasting era. In Wardle and Williams's (2010: 792) observatory study of the BBC's use of UGC, they argued that there was 'no radical upheaval in the way they work, and no great change in the structural roles played by traditional producers and consumers of news'. Rather than citizen journalism leading to an audience revolution in newsrooms, Williams et al. (2011: 85) suggest it is 'business as usual at the BBC', in that audience contributions have been dealt with by using 'long-standing routines of traditional journalism practice'. Nonetheless, audiences themselves have more power since remote controls now allow them to record simultaneous programmes, live pause, or go active at the press of a button. But while the potential for enhanced interactivity is open-ended, most of the time television viewers will continue to watch in 'real time' (OFCOM 2009). Television viewing, in other words, still remains largely within the 'flow' that was once conceived by Raymond Williams (1974) as characterising how programming could seamlessly shift from one programme to the next.

Of course this is not to deny that one day the Internet will reign supreme. In the UK a free to-air, web-connected television service – YouView – is due to be launched in 2012 and this will enable viewers to access programming via the WWW. Television is thus becoming a more integrated online service, with higher definition enhanced and on-demand facilities also becoming more sophisticated. Scholars are right, in this sense, to interpret how television is evolving and reshaping its technology, format and style to meet the demands of the interactive era (Turner and Tay 2009). However the 'post-broadcast era' has become embroiled in debates about Media Studies 2.0, where the enthusiasm and potential for new, multi-media, online technology have not matched what it is empirically delivering. Chapter 7 explores Media Studies 2.0 in the context of television news studies and suggests, within journalism studies, that 'old' broadcasting questions about media power, ownership and deregulation should not be marginalised even if the transformative potential of the Internet can potentially challenge and resist previously omnipotent gatekeepers.

From another perspective, the post-broadcast era has also been part of wider debates into media convergence. As Tay and Turner (2008: 71) have observed, it is in the 'post-broadcast era where the convergence of media platforms has challenged conventional understandings of how the mass media work'. Since new and old media have collided, convergence culture has been explored from a wide range of perspectives (Jenkins 2006). Media convergence is seen to represent how new technologies have become 'accommodated by existing media and communication industries and cultures' (Dwyer 2010: 2). But it must also critically examine the impact converged industries have had on the autonomy of media workers to operate the creative pathways that may have evolved.

For journalists this has meant increasingly sharing job descriptions, technical equipment and media platforms. In order to fill the many hours of television news journalism, new cable and digital channels have created more employment prospects. The number of freelance journalists – without permanent contracts or security behind them – has risen in recent years and, according to Ryan (2009: 648), 'can be found in a variety of markets and television operations' in a US context. A survey of freelance US journalists found that some had become accustomed to being casual workers in a convergent culture, adapting to new technologies and revelling in the autonomy they might not otherwise would have been able to enjoy working under tighter contractual agreements (Ryan 2009). In *Media Work*, Deuze (2007) has argued many journalists have forged new professional identities in converged newsrooms. In the 'daily interaction of creativity, commerce, content and connectivity', he writes (2007: 83), new meanings and values have been shaped by journalists in fast-changing multi-media environments.

At the same time, media convergence has had many implications for the role and status of television journalists, making it a more precarious profession to enter. As working environments have evolved into multimedia newsrooms, staff time and resources have been stretched and the required demands of multi-skilling have not corresponded with substantially improved pay or contractual conditions. An IFJ report – *The Changing Nature of Work* (2006) – surveyed 38 countries and found journalists' pay and conditions across the world were diminishing. The report suggested that as more state-owned media were privatised, employers were looking to cut costs by recruiting younger staff at lower rates of pay. In a global marketplace, where the budgets for news have become tighter in the face of increased competition, cost-cutting exercises now include employing more casual and freelance journalists at the expense of more experienced journalists in long-term positions. The report labels these positions as 'atypical workers' – journalists on short-term rolling contracts, subcontracted work, casual work, temporary work, and freelance work. And while journalists may have creatively adapted to these new working conditions and converged newsrooms, many remain dissatisfied with diminishing employment rights and the demands imposed on them by news organisations (IFJ 2006; Ursell 2003).

Örnebring (2009) has identified four trends in the working environment of news production that potentially threaten not just the editorial content but also the professional values of journalism. These overlapping areas include: the deregulation of labour markets as union power diminishes; new forms of employment, such as the use of temporary or freelance staff; the changing use and purpose of technologies; and finally, possible de-skilling, where technical skills are valued above the creative impulses of journalists. All of which, Örnebring (2009) concluded, should not be assumed but empirically assessed within the context of shifting working routines and practices. This is because new technologies are not to blame for 'dumbing' journalism 'up' or 'down'; rather, the impact of employment conditions on the autonomy of journalists needs to be understood and evaluated against the quality of news produced (Ursell 2001, 2003). Chapter 6 takes a close look at the status of television journalists, exploring their employment conditions, rates of pay and what kind of training journalists receive to cope with the demands of converged and integrated newsrooms.

For within multi-media newsrooms, the role of a television journalist does not start and end on the small screen; it may involve radio broadcasts, online blogs and mobile tweets. Tanner and Smith's (2007) study of 51 television markets in the US found close to 70 per cent of journalists surveyed carried out a range of convergent tasks. They argued new training was urgently required for new journalists to cope with the fast-changing profession. Multi-skilling has become part of the professional jargon to encapsulate the range of demands contemporary journalists are now facing. In the midst of this there has, according to Palvik (2004: 21), been a 'sea-change in journalism' since the relationship journalists have with sources, audiences and producers has been compromised by the demands and pressures that exist in the production of instant news on multi-platform journalism. Ryan et al. (2008) compared the US television news network's use of its talented journalists from 1987 and 2007 and found, by drawing on comparative content analyses studies, that reporters were used in many more newcasts per day than twenty years ago and that the same content was oft-repeated.

While the empirical value of a 'post-broadcast' era was questioned in this section, the convergence of 'old' and 'new' media nevertheless holds many challenging prospects for television journalists: on the one hand, converged newsrooms appear to breed healthy creativity and new professional spirit and resolution, while on the other, integrated staff and technology pile the pressure on already strained time limits and resources and have also pushed many journalists into the realms of freelance work, thereby weakening their job security and employment conditions. In the chapters that follow the stresses and strains journalists routinely face in converged newsrooms should not be divorced from how contemporary trends in television news are identified and understood.

However, before we attempt to understand the present we must turn to the past to interpret the wider context in which television developed and how its journalism has evolved within different broadcasting structures, cultures and regulatory arrangements. The next chapter shows how the political economy of television in many countries was shaped by the national broadcasting cultures it inherited. In doing so, this demonstrates why contemporary television journalism can differ from one country to the next and, in more recent years, how various trends in media ownership and deregulation are pushing television journalism in a new direction.

PART I

HISTORY AND CONTEXT

2

FROM RADIO TO TELEVISION: MAKING SENSE OF BROADCASTING HISTORY

In order to understand the history of television we must first turn to the medium of radio, for in the first half of the twentieth century radio was the most widely used source of information for most people. At the flick of a switch, radio could connect to millions of people without the need to physically transport or distribute any media products (like newspapers, say, or magazines). It marked a significant technological leap forward and forged a new relationship with media audiences. As Crisell (1997: 4–5) has observed:

> broadcasting was the first genuinely live mass medium since 'theatre' because it was instantaneous: its messages were received by its audience at the very moment they were sent; they were not fixed messages in the form of printed texts and photographs or recordings of sounds or moving images.

No longer reliant on media retrospectively telling audiences about the world, radio worked in real-time and soon established itself as a vital means for knowing what was happening in the world. As Chapter 3 shows, the discourse of 'live' news has become more prominent throughout the twentieth century, representing the impact wireless technology initiated and reflecting the wider influence broadcast culture would have on journalism more generally.

The wireless technology that enables radio communication to be instant and broadcast over large areas was developed towards the end of the nineteenth century. There are fascinating histories, beyond what is immediately relevant here, about how the medium was developed by its use in the US navy and British army and how it evolved, years later, into a commercial vehicle (Crisell 1997: 13–26; Crook 1998; Hilmes and Loviglio 2001; McChesney 1993; Rosen 1980). However, the history of radio broadcasting, at this stage in its development, remains a little murky. There is evidence that radio broadcasts did take place before the 1920s (Crook 1998), but broadly speaking it was in this decade that radio became a more formally institutionalised medium. So, for example, governments began to issue licences to broadcast organisations and transmitters were sold in countries such as the UK, Holland, the US, Australia and South Africa (Crook 1998: 57–62). Unbeknown at this time, each nation set in train broadcasting models that would shape the future of television news provision in the many decades to follow.

The birth of broadcasting: creating national broadcast ecologies

In what follows, the birth of radio and the development of television are introduced in a US and UK context. By only comparing the US (with its primarily market-driven system) and the UK (with its mixture of a public- and market-driven model) this does not do full justice to the many possible shapes and sizes of broadcasting ecologies that operate internationally (Cushion 2012). Market and public broadcast models have both evolved over time (indeed many now overlap and co-exist) and in many countries more complicated funding mechanisms and organisational structures have been adopted to sustain a broadcasting industry: for example, while Australia or the Scandinavian countries followed a similar *national* structure to that of the UK, Spain's and Germany's (post-war) broadcasting ecology was organised along more *regional* lines. Meanwhile, Canadian broadcasting developed public service operations with private radio stations and advertising revenues were used to sustain these. Of course, examining the US and UK broadcasting operations and regulatory requirements could be likened to comparing apples and oranges. But in tracing the *starting point* of broadcasting, we can explore how broadcasters developed over time in different environments and relate this to contemporary trends in television journalism.

What the formative years of radio represent are the different paths each country pursued in building a future broadcasting system. While there have been monumental changes to national broadcasting ecologies since the advent of radio, in order to understand the structures that shape contemporary television journalism today it is still necessary to trace back the decisions made about how national broadcast ecologies evolved almost a century before.

The birth of US radio: towards a market-led broadcast culture

If we look first at the US, its broadcast infrastructure was shaped by the free market spirit embodied more widely in the country's political, cultural and economic identity. While most European states shared a relatively strong *national* political culture, many US citizens were hostile to and suspicious of a Washington-based government that at times appeared distant and over-controlling. Since the 50 states that make up the US share fragmented identities (most notably between north and south), creating a national broadcasting ecology – like the one developed in the UK for example – would have been difficult to promote let alone put into practice. As a result, the US's broadcast ecology has been developed regionally, with national stations affiliating to local or state television channels supplying much of its programming. With the US government stepping back from the delivery of broadcasting, its television culture has been driven by commercial investment rather than state sponsorship.

Histories of broadcasting culture in the US demonstrate that, as with other commodities, radio was treated as something that could be bought and sold to the highest bidder (Douglas 1987; Hoynes 1994; McChesney 1993). Within this market-driven model, advertising played a key role in sustaining the production of radio, helping to shape the type and nature of programming pursued. Radio shows quickly became associated with individual sponsors to the extent that brands began appearing in the titles of programmes. In a short space of time, advertising had become a familiar part of broadcasting culture and audiences had also become accustomed to their programmes being rubber-stamped by sponsors.

It is difficult, in this context, to imagine or propose an alternative model of broadcasting. As a way of organising and funding radio stations, advertising appeared to be the accepted wisdom for sustaining the industry, quickly naturalising the relationship between US broadcasting and consumerism. This was no accident, McChesney (1993) has argued, and attempts to make broadcasting less commercially reliant and more educationally driven between 1928–1935 were met with fierce opposition by the radio industry. Under intense pressure not to lose their grip on the broadcast market, commercial broadcasters lobbied with all their might (Crook 1998). A 1934 Communications Act marked a key turning point in the debate and established a long-standing legacy in the broadcast ecology of the US. A 'light touch' regulatory system, the Federal Communications Committee (FCC), was established and this has remained in place ever since. With a minimal interventionist mandate programming was left to the mercy of market forces, meaning commercial broadcasters were free to make whatever listeners demanded. 'Market' is the operative word here since audiences were seen less as a diverse mix of 'listeners' and more as key demographics for advertisers to appeal to.

Developing a market-led model of broadcasting had important consequences for the type of programming being pursued. While the FCC was set up to regulate, in its own words, 'without discrimination on the basis of race, color, religion, national origin, or sex', inevitably commercial programming was tailored to meet key demographics – the 'shopaholic' house-wife, say, or the 'impressionable' younger listener – since they had greater access to disposable dollars compared to other sections of society. Against the back-drop of the Great Depression in the late 1920s and 1930s, the economic inequalities inherent in the country were significant at this point. Poverty was on the march and huge disparities existed between different social groups, most notably amongst ethnic communities. To ensure advertisers hit their demographics, popular entertainment type shows trumped the more highbrow educational endeavours which many had campaigned for in the early years of radio.

This did not mean, however, news was not part of radio's daily schedule. In what has been described as a 'press–radio war', radio journalism competed intensely with that of newspapers (Allan 1999). Radio, of course, had the advantage of breaking the latest unfolding news story to its listeners or at least updating them. And without having to abide by any formal impartiality regulations, radio did not need to balance a story or conform to an imposed news agenda of politics and social affairs. As Allan (1999: 35) has pointed out, in these early years of radio

> boundaries of journalistic 'impartiality' were thus being defined, in part, by a conception of the audience not as citizens in need of a public forum for argument and debate, but rather as potential consumers in search of entertaining diversions from everyday life.

While this somewhat loose system of regulated journalism has been chal-lenged at various points in US history (most notably in the 1960s, a point returned to later), the initial formation of radio broadcasting had laid the foun-dations for the market-driven news environment television was to inherit.

The birth of UK radio: towards a public service broadcast culture

By contrast, in parts of Europe – and the UK in particular – the formative years of radio established a strikingly different broadcasting model and regu-latory system. Once again it is necessary here to understand the wider political, economic and cultural environment in which broadcasting arrived. While the US had a fractured political and cultural identity, European coun-tries had far smaller economies of scale and thus a more nationalised and centralised system of governance. In addition, Europe was dealing with the aftermath of World War I and fears about the use of media propaganda were widespread. In this sensitive political environment, the arrival of broadcast-ing and its possible impact was viewed with some suspicion. Existing popular media – films, newspapers, comic books – were already held in great con-tempt by politicians and the wider intelligentsia for debasing culture and promoting salacious values (Springhall 1999). With the ability to instantly connect to a mass audience radio represented a more optimistic medium, a potentially powerful antidote to a diet of cheap and trivial media content.

There remained, of course, a battle between state powers and commercial interests. For radio transmitters to sell entertainment based programming offered the widest possible appeal. But with the government keen to exercise control, a range of official reports on radio broadcasting was carried out. In sharp contrast to the US, a 1923 Report of the Broadcasting Committee chaired by Sir Frederick Sykes warned against organising and financing a commercially self-sustaining system. It concluded:

> We attach great importance to the maintenance of a high standard of broadcast programmes, with continuous report to secure improvement, and we think that advertisements would lower the standard ... the operating authorities, who would want revenue, would naturally prefer the big advertiser who was ready to pay highly, with the result that only he would get a chance of advertising. This would be too high a privilege to give to a few big advertisers at the risk of lowering the standard of broadcasting. (Report on the Broadcasting Committee, Sykes Committee 1923, para. 41)

There are many ways to analyse and interpret the long-standing significance of the Sykes Committee's efforts (Scannell and Cardiff 1991). Above all what stands out in this paragraph are the repeated values of 'high' and 'low' ascribed to programming. Broadcast content, in other words, was subject to regulatory standards that were imposed not by audience demand but by what the state and its legislators valued. These values, it was argued, would be adversely compromised if commercial operations were able to shape the type and nature of broadcasting.

What emerged, between 1922 and 1927, was the first ever nationally established radio station under the aegis of British Broadcasting Ltd that was owned and developed by British and American electrical companies. While it was a privately run organisation, unlike the situation in the US it was closely monitored by state regulators. Its significance to state affairs and public life was soon recognised by its reporting of the 1926 General Strike. Under pressure to take a sympathetic line on government policy, the corporation had to negotiate how independent its journalism should be from state intervention – or, more accurately, could be. According to Williams (2010: 95), during the 1926 strike the BBC 'did not publicly take sides but it did operate within a particular understanding of the political and moral order which led it to support the government'. If we compare that stance to how a former BBC television news editor, Ian Hargreaves, described BBC impartiality in the next millennium – 'BBC journalism is magnificent in its range, carefulness, and resources, but it does tend towards an establishment view of the world' (Hargreaves 2003: 27) – the 1926 General Strike perhaps represents the limits of the BBC's impartiality both then and ever since.

Nonetheless, just months later, in January 1927, the BBC came under public ownership and was more formally recognised – via Royal Charter – as an independent state broadcaster. Under the direction of the BBC's first

General Director, Sir John Reith, the corporation developed its mission to 'inform, educate and entertain'. This brief mission statement many years on has remained a much used sound-bite to describe what it is that public service broadcasting represents. In what is often characterised as a Reithian tradition, the BBC strove to deliver highbrow programming of a religious and highly moralistic bent. In the form of a radio licence fee the public contributed to a service that, in theory, was to be universally accessible, serving all its listeners as opposed to satisfying commercial needs. Having reflected on its reporting of the General Strike and accrued more confidence since it had been made more independent from state forces, the BBC, according to Curran and Seaton (2010: 117), 'imposed new criteria of selection on the news. Journalists stopped being passionate advocates, saw themselves rather as independent professionals, and their writing as a negotiated product of conflict between partisan views'. The arrival of television, however, brought new challenges for news reporting since the use of pictures encouraged a different form and style of journalism.

Making sense of television: reshaping news journalism

While television's dominance is sometimes broadly interpreted as a post-war story, its origins and rise in popularity actually lie both *before* and roughly a decade *after* the Second World War. Like the history of wireless technology, the transmission of visual images had been experimented with for many decades before the medium of television grew popular. With sales of radio sets burgeoning in the 1930s, companies such as RCA in the US and the BBC in the UK decided to invest in experimental television broadcasts in New York (Spigel 1993) and London (Crisell 1997). However, before they were able to establish a reliable television service or a network to distribute equipment World War II began and in Europe at least resources were to be focused elsewhere (Curran and Seaton 2010; Williams 2010).

The development of US television news: sustaining a commercial model

It was in the US that television was to grow most rapidly, not just because the networks had perfected the technology but also because, unlike parts of Europe, its economy was buoyant and consumerism was on the march. Lyn Spigel, in her detailed book *Make Room for TV: Television and the Family Ideal in Postwar America*, has summarised this well:

> Over the course of the 1950s, television was rapidly installed into American homes. National penetration rates for television rose from .02 percent in 1946 to 9 percent in 1950. After that, penetration rates inclined fairly steadily so that by 1955 about 65 per cent of the nation's homes had television. (1993: 32)

For Spigel, the television set became synonymous with an increasingly middle-class America, one that was eager to buy houses, get married, have kids, and watch television (1993: 32–33). Television, in this sense, soon became part of the increasingly consumer-driven culture of American life. Since the market-driven broadcast system was already at full throttle with radio sales booming, there was scant debate about creating a different set of structures to shape the way television was organised. In a detailed history of the early years of broadcasting, *Telecommunications, Mass Media and Democracy*, McChesney (1993: 3) has shown that by 1935 the capitalist radio 'system was entrenched economically, politically and ideologically, and it would provide the eventual development for television in the 1940s and 1950s'. Three radio stations – the National Broadcasting Company (NBC), the Columbia Broadcasting System (CBS) and the American Broadcasting Company (ABC) – quickly established themselves, in this respect, as the dominant television networks. Building on the success of popular radio genres – soap operas, dramas, quiz shows, weather reports and, importantly for this book, news bulletins – the networks began making sense of programme-making *visually* as well as aurally.

In the early years of television news it was widely viewed as being second-best to the more polished and reliable sounds of radio bulletins. For Barkin (2003: 28), 'The Evening newscasts of CBS and NBC were hardly the flagships of their news divisions. Perhaps they were the tugboats'. Conway (2009), by contrast, has more favourably interpreted the origins of American television news, giving credit to CBS News as the first 'visualizers' of television journalism. Despite being much lampooned by the radio industry in the 1940s, the station innovated and developed a new set of generic conventions in order to meet the challenge presented by television news. Faced with a new medium by which to understand the day's events, Conway (2009: 331) has highlighted that 'CBS television news staff would not settle for long stretches of the newscaster reading a script on camera' like radio journalism allowed for. Instead, they chose to generate what he labels 'visualization techniques such as maps, animated graphics, artwork, cartoons, drawing … designed to hold the viewer's attention and make each story more understandable' (Conway 2009: 331). While the use of a personality-driven news anchor dominated television bulletins from the mid-1950s, in the early years CBS was reluctant to over use them since in their view they did not command on-screen confidence. From 1944 to 1948 a dozen or so regular anchors were used compared to just three (Dan Rather, Walter Cronkite, and Douglas Edwards) at CBS News over a 57-year span (Conway 2007).

It was to be at least a decade before the conventions adopted (the use of two-ways, lead anchors, more polished editing and voice-overs) began to reassemble the form and style of news bulletins today. And while news bulletins had become a routine service in the 1950s it was not until the 1960s, after an initial agreement with an under-threat newspaper industry had been loosened, that they could last longer than 15 minutes. But perhaps most significantly, as with other programming, television news was driven by the needs of advertisers. So, for example, early evening newscasts included NBC-sponsored programmes such as *The Esso Newsreel* (the oil giant) and *The Camel Newsreel Theater* (the tobacco giant) (Barkin 2003: 28). Unlike most other television programmes, however, watching news was not always consistent with the tone or mood which advertisers wanted the context of their products to be viewed in. As Lawrence Samuel (2001: 178) has pointed out in *Brought to You: Postwar Television Advertising and the American Dream*, potential advertisers 'shied away from sponsoring news shows because of their notorious fear of controversy, and the belief that their brands would somehow be associated with the tragedies that were being reported'. News, after all, can be bland, depressing and serious when compared to more fun and pleasurable genres like quiz shows or soap operas.

To make news bulletins more appealing for viewers – or, perhaps more accurately, for advertisers – according to Allan (1999) television news started to select and structure its journalism strategically around pre-scheduled events: 'An emphasis was routinely placed on staged events, primarily because they were usually packaged by the news promoters behind them (whether governmental or corporate) with the visual needs of television in mind' (1999: 45). From an early age, then, the commercially-driven approach to television journalism has had to interpret its viewers not only as curious news audiences tuning in to be informed about the world but also as potential consumers who are not averse to being sold products in between the news segments. Since television news has had to shape an environment where viewers are able to remain upbeat and adopt a tone advertisers would want to associate their products with, editorial agendas have had to balance their professional and commercial news values. And with the three big television networks competing to capture the largest slice of the news audience, each has also had to tread carefully when deciding what is 'newsworthy'.

Faced with the pressure to succumb to commercial influence, questions about the impartiality of television news increasingly began to surface. This was to be particularly pertinent since television news, by the end of the 1950s, had overtaken radio as the primary source of information. As an increasingly familiar and conventionalised part of television it was subjected to more critical attention and federal intervention. To ensure broadcasters remained impartial, in a 1949 FCC report, *Report on Editorializing*, the concept of the Fairness Doctrine was introduced. This asked those broadcasters with a licence to 1) devote a reasonable percentage of airtime to the coverage of public issues, and 2) to be fair in their coverage by providing an opportunity for the presentation of contrasting viewpoints (Chamberlin 1978: 361). On the face of it the Fairness Doctrine appeared to be, to coin a well-used phrase since, 'fair and balanced'. However, tacitly encouraged by its sponsors many broadcasters were to adopt a risk-averse strategy of steering clear of contentious issues or events. Television news, in other words, increasingly retreated from the controversial and adopted a middle-of-the-road form of journalism.

Sharpening up its regulatory tools, under the authority of the Fairness Doctrine in the 1960s, the FCC provided perhaps the most sustained period of intervention into television journalism. It encouraged commercial television networks to enhance the volume of their journalism and more robustly policed the kind of coverage that it judged to be lacking in balance. Most famously in 1969 a US Supreme court decision, *Red Lion Broadcasting Co. v. FCC*, was to strengthen the authority of the Fairness Doctrine after a Federal decision was challenged. The concept lasted until 1987, disappearing as a consequence of a more deregulatory spirit sweeping across not only the US but also global media policymaking. Nonetheless, it remains conspicuous by its absence and its legacy for US journalism is taken up in Chapter 5.

Yet even as the commercial networks dominated US television in the 1950s and 1960s, there remained at the fringes continued support for a more publicly subsidised broadcast system. Against the backdrop of more rigorous FCC intervention, the movement to set up public service broadcasting had gathered momentum. This culminated in the 1967 Public Broadcast Act, which in turn led to the creation of both radio and television public service stations. Reflecting on the Act forty years after it was passed, one close observer at the time suggested its very arrival was nothing short of a miracle (Avery 2007: 359). With minimal federal funding, an advertising market reluctant to sponsor its programming, sustained political attacks from conservative groups (Croteau et al. 1996; Douglas 1987; Hoynes 1994), and several re-branding exercises since it was launched as PBS (the Public Broadcasting Service) in 1970 (Hoynes 2003), the conditions for public service broadcasting to thrive were, in truth, significantly handicapped.

Pitted against heavyweight contenders, public broadcasters were always going to be hard-pushed to compete with commercial television resources. However, this did not mean public service television was not possible or sustainable. In much of post-war Europe an infrastructure was being built that could sustain public service broadcasting and television journalism played a central role in its development.

UK television news: from public service monopoly to a tripartite model of public and commercial broadcasting

The UK and Germany had aired some broadcasts before World War II had started and many thousands of television sets had been sold in both countries, but it was not until well after the war when a routine service was established that sales of televisions would run into the millions. Coping with the immediate aftermath of the conflict, television had to wait until the economy was able to bounce back and affluence could grow. As had been the case in the US, television represented a new-found consumerism, even if what was to mark this shift remains quintessentially British. In most media history books the coronation of Queen Elizabeth II in 1953 was when television came of age and witnessed its 'first ever "media event"' (Crisell 1997: 81). With millions choosing television ahead of radio, many watched with family, friends and neighbours. In what has since been recognised as a seminal broadcasting experience, television was to bind a nation together and cultivate a shared sense of national identity. The event appeared to act as a catalyst, triggering a rise in the number of television sets bought and convincing a nation that television – not radio – was the future of broadcasting. As Williams (2010: 149) has noted in *Get Me A Murder A Day*, 'In 1950, only 4 per cent of the adult population owned a television set; by 1955, this had risen to 40 per cent and in 1960, it had doubled to 80 per cent'.

Radio, nevertheless, remained a highly valued source of information. During the war the BBC had cultivated a trusted relationship with its listeners in the UK and beyond. Television managed to inherit some of this good will. Having laid the foundations for broadcasting, the BBC, at least initially, picked up the baton and carried on running a public service television agenda. As Crisell (1997: 79) has pointed out, 'To a considerable extent television gave a renewed opportunity to those Reithian principles of public service which the corporation still espoused'. While the BBC had experimented with perfecting television signals, many senior programme makers – most notably Reith himself – remained hostile to the medium. Privileging the visual over the aural, television represented a more superficial form of communication than radio. In this context, it is perhaps understandable why the BBC's transformation from providing radio to television news is not as celebrated as the origins of American networks (Conway 2009). From 1946 to 1954, BBC television news bulletins did not feature an anchor or any continuous images. Instead a voice-over read out the day's stories and, for visual effect, a clock-face was superimposed on the screen that was interrupted only when a photograph was available. Television journalism was, for just a short period at least, made to fit with the medium of radio.

The story of television journalism in the 1950s, however, does not centre on BBC news. For a Beveridge Broadcasting Report, commissioned in 1949 by a Labour government but published shortly before a Conservative one gained power in 1951, set out plans that would permanently alter the UK's broadcast ecology. There was more or less a general agreement that the BBC should remain a public broadcaster funded by a licence fee, but competition was needed to challenge its monopoly on television. A campaign for commercial television was thus launched, led by Tory backbenchers but championed by a range of pressure groups (Crissell 1997). The BBC, it was argued, was an overly-centralised, too nationalised and top-down cultural institution. To democratise broadcasting, it was further argued, television could be a more regionalised experience, one that reflected the views and opinions of 'ordinary' folk. Perhaps most persuasively, even if it was not voiced that loudly at the time, there was increasing industry pressure on the government to introduce advertising. With affluence rising television opened up a lucrative space for consumerism to flourish. Nonetheless there remained much resignation about the relationship broadcasting would have with advertising and the direction in which this would push programming. Most famously, John Reith, speaking at the House of Lords in 1952, was to leave a lasting impression on the debate: '... somebody introduced smallpox, bubonic plague and the Black Death. Somebody is minded now to introduce sponsored broadcasting into this country' (Reith 1952).

Fears that a full blown commercial broadcaster was about to appear over the horizon were overstated. What emerged – and has remained more or less ever since – was a 1954 Television Act that established a hybrid television channel (Independent Television or ITV) which could balance commercial and public service broadcasting responsibilities. While it had a national news service, ITN (Independent Television News), 14 separate regional networks developed their own mix of commercial programming. Unlike the US, however, ITV was not free to air whatever its advertisers demanded. ITV had to include a healthy provision of regional programming and, moreover, a not-for-profit, impartial news service that was policed by the regulator, the Independent Television Authority (ITA). ITV represented, in short, a commercially sustainable television channel but one that, at least in the short term, was regulated and shaped by public service values. The next section suggests ITV has, over time, gradually had its public service commitments loosened and, in 1990 and 2003, appeared to become a more commercial vehicle, first under the 'light touch' regulator, the ITC, and then Ofcom.

Even if BBC journalism had already begun to reshape its news bulletins to meet the television age (Curran and Seaton 2010: 161), it was ITV journalism that defined the genre, quickly establishing a new set of generic conventions. All of a sudden television news had a single face – a newscaster – who presented each story, and a more personalised mode of address was installed. Whereas BBC journalism reluctantly carried visuals in its news bulletins, ITN embraced the potential of the medium. Informed by an American brand of television news, it 'employed two newcasters to develop pace and variety within the bulletin with the newscasters increasingly playing off each other journalistically and stylistically' (Conboy 2004: 203). The legacy of post-war television journalism, however, cannot only be explained by shifting styles or the adaptation of more sophisticated newsgathering techniques. ITN reacted and responded to an increasingly consumer-driven society, favouring, for example, 'the spontaneity and human interest of "vox pops", informal interviews with people in the street' (Crisell 1997: 99). The BBC, in this respect, appeared to be an elitist institution, deferentially treating politicians and pushing a relentlessly serious news agenda. ITN interviews, by contrast, were more adversarial when interviewing the ruling class and topics, whilst remaining serious, appeared more in tune with 'the people's' anxieties.

The 'swinging sixties' brought with them a new set of social values and ITN journalism encouraged the BBC to relinquish some of its Reithian pomp and ceremony in order to compete with and fit into an expanding commercialised media sector. Thus, as society became less deferential television journalism had to change its coverage of politics and public affairs. Once the preserve of newspapers, television began to provide more satirical interpretations of politicians which, for the first time, pushed the boundaries of how television journalists treated the political class. While we today have become familiar with television programmes such as *The Daily Show* in the US or *Have I Got News For You* in the UK, at the end of the 1960s it was the BBC's *That Was The Week That Was* that first subjected politicians to a new era of political satire. Without being pressured by competition from ITV, it would be difficult to imagine the BBC pursuing an alternative approach to its typically high-brow interpretation of politics quite so rapidly.

And yet if the BBC had begun to adopt some of ITV's popular conventions, the political establishment was less than enthused by the impact of commercial television. When a 1962 Pilkington committee report concluded television 'had abused its power, and failed to realise its possibilities', this comment was directed at ITV's relatively short-lived contribution to the medium. Pilkington chastised ITV for subscribing to an overly-Americanised approach to its programming, and the Independent Broadcasting Authority (IBA) for not policing the boundaries of what was, the report said, a channel with serious public service obligations. The IBA soon after had its regulatory powers strengthened and ITV post-1964 appeared to take its public service duties more seriously. It carried heavyweight current affairs programming and its flagship 10 o'clock bulletin routinely won awards for its innovative journalism (Curran and Seaton 2010: 173).

Television journalism was to mature in the 1960s and 1970s. Even when a new channel, BBC2, was introduced in 1964 it failed to dislodge the relatively harmonious relationship – or what Williams (2010) terms the 'cosy duopoly' – which ITV shared with the BBC. The introduction of Channel 4 in 1982, however, and advances in satellite and cable technologies (explored in a moment) brought an end to what is sometimes known as the 'golden age' of UK television. Television journalism, meanwhile, was busy interpreting the boundaries of impartial news reporting. A series of complicated political and military matters in the 1970s and 1980s – notably the political turbulence in Northern Ireland and the Falklands war – put BBC news, in particular, on a collision course with the government of the day. In each context, the state argued public broadcasters should not remain impartial and sought, at various points, to intervene and encourage a more patriotic spin on events. Balancing both sides of the story, in most cases, was the journalistic norm in how impartiality was delivered. But in matters when the state was militarily involved with another, the broadcasters' independence appeared to be threatened. To use Margaret Thatcher's oft-repeated phrase, broadcasters should starve the state's enemies of 'the oxygen of publicity'. Thus impartiality became an increasingly contested notion, a point developed in Chapter 4, with the US abandoning its legal enforcement of the Fairness Doctrine in the 1980s and a relaxation of the 'due impartiality guidelines' in the UK becoming the source of much debate in recent years.

Despite some occasions when ground was indeed ceded on how particular events, individuals or stories were to be reported, for the most part the independence of television journalism in the UK remained largely intact by the end of the 1980s. Even repeated threats to the purpose, values and costs of public service broadcasting under Margaret Thatcher's right-wing Conservative government could not dismantle an institution that had by then, over many decades, established a close rapport with UK listeners and viewers. Thatcher's broadcasting legacy, however, was to lay the foundations for the arrival of cable and satellite technology and initiate a process of deregulation that has continued ever since. These decisions profoundly transformed the UK's broadcast ecology. For television journalism, a new national news service, Sky News, was established in 1989. But more broadly, in this decade a more globally competitive marketplace was to emerge after cable and satellite technologies paved the way for a more commercialised and inter-connected news environment.

Deregulating broadcast structures: towards a commercial news environment

Before the 1980s, television journalism had primarily evolved in national contexts. As we have seen so far national broadcast ecologies developed systems and regulatory bodies that reflected the broader political, economic and cultural characteristics of each nation. But throughout the 1980s technological advancements, first in cable and then satellite communication, transformed broadcasting into an international arena. No longer restricted by national boundaries, images could be beamed around the world. Broadcasting, in short, had entered the age of globalisation. But it is worthwhile to remember that the extent to which information could flow transnationally remained, for the most part, a responsibility held by nation states. Many countries, of course, were concerned about the volume of 'foreign' television being aired. With more channels operating, it was feared that cheap entertainment programming, primarily from the US, would clog up the airwaves.

To allow commercial markets to flourish many countries sought to deregulate the media industries, thereby making broadcasting less reliant on the state and creating an infrastructure where new television channels could be launched and more consumer-driven programming could be developed. In doing so, debates about the impact of media deregulation on a global scale have been ongoing (see Bennett 2004 for a review). This section explores deregulation in the context of television news produced primarily in the US and UK.

Deregulatory overdrive: the rise of populist US television journalism in the 1990s

Within the US, the largest and most lucrative global media market-place, the television industry grew substantially in the 1980s. Since the US had a commercially-driven television system with minimal regulatory obligations, it openly embraced the advent of technology that moved its television culture into the multi-channel era. With their grip on the market weakened, the three big American networks were joined by new players, eager to cash-in on more of the population watching even more television than ever before. Rupert Murdoch's Fox Network, for example, soon penetrated the entertainment market with a succession of popular shows, most famously *The Simpsons*. But by opening up broadcasting's floodgates it has been argued that, by the end of the decade, American television had been infused with tabloid genres, from hyper-reality TV-programmes, outrageously scripted soap operas and, in the case of television journalism, sensationalist pseudo-news shows (Glynn 2000). According to John Caldwell (1995) in *Televisuality: Style, Crisis, and Authority in American Television*, towards the end of the 1980s the genre of television news had increasingly begun to resemble the visual excesses and stylistic forms of populist, entertainment formats. All of which, it has been argued, adversely impacted on how network news made sense of key political crises. For Hallin (1994: 110), 'Since 1985 … we have witnessed the supreme example of "populist" TV news'. This, he has argued, represents a distinct '"tabloid" style: the push to cancel critical distance, to plunge viewer and "journalist" into the emotion of the moment' (1994: 110).

The advent of cable and satellite technology shoulders only some of the responsibility for the shift in America's television culture. For what is sometimes air-brushed out of media and journalism textbooks – when the form and style supersede questions about media ownership and regulatory structures – is the role that American legislators and regulators played in encouraging more television channels to flourish. The political economy of American television, of course, has always embraced a market-driven approach to broadcast news and a minimalist form of regulation. But throughout the 1970s and 1980s deregulation was moved up a gear and, to complete the metaphor, television culture and news journalism accelerated away commercially, off-loading many of their previously minor public service obligations in the process.

So, for example, while television licences had previously been granted on a three year basis in 1981 this rose to five years. And since licences did not need to be renewed as frequently there was less pressure to conform to the FCC's regulations. Likewise television ownership regulations were liberalised in 1985, with the effect that an organisation could own up to 12 stations. In doing so media pluralism soon diminished. Television stations were increasingly bought up by a small group of wealthy companies, leading to a concentration in media ownership. Guidelines on the volume of advertising for licence payers were also dropped in 1985. Television stations, in other words, could advertise as much as they wanted. At the same time where once a minimal level of non-entertainment programming was mandatory for licence-holders the FCC abolished this stipulation. Thus television could pump out as much popular programming as it wished to without fulfilling previously imposed commitments such as news and current affairs programming. Finally, and as previously mentioned, the Fairness Doctrine – which ensured a relative balance in how journalism was covered politically – was terminated in 1987. Considered an affront to free speech, television journalism no longer had to conform to federally-imposed rules of impartiality. The effects of this decision, in particular, are subjected to a far lengthier treatment in Chapter 5, since it will argue that this move triggered a new direction in US journalism and raised debates about the future of impartiality in television news in the UK.

Television journalism, moving into the 1990s, rapidly expanded. Keen to break apart the network monopoly, a proliferation of cable and local/state television stations emerged. By the end of the 1980s the network share of television audiences had declined from 90 per cent to 60 per cent (Hallin 1994: 177). Facing stiff competition, television journalism was swept up in a ratings war between channels. According to Hallin (1994), commercial values further infused an already increasingly tabloid television news culture, changing the character of its journalism and embracing new story-telling conventions. Hallin has stated that television news in the 1990s resembled

more closely the pace of the rest of commercial television, with 10 second soundbites and tightly packaged stories. The agenda of news has changed, with fewer traditional political stories and more stories that 'tug at the heart strings'. And the pressure is far greater today for the stories to have high 'production values', both narrative and visual: drama, emotion and good video. (1994: 177)

While Hallin (1994: 178) does suggest not all these changes have uniformly diminished the quality of television journalism, he concludes that an increasingly deregulated culture of television and proliferation of news sources encouraged, above all else, a commercially-driven system of television journalism.

We should be cautious, however, when interpreting the impact of deregulation and the 'quality' of television journalism. For Pippa Norris (2000), this media deregulation has cultivated a media environment where viewers have far more choice and greater access to information. While much of this might be 'soft' news – as Chapter 1 explored – journalism should not be judged entirely by simplistic 'hard' or 'soft' news distinctions, or tabloid and broadsheet formats, or 'low' and 'high' cultural values. The rise in commercial television news, in this context, has been interpreted along with the supply of more democratic choices, since viewers are able to pick and choose from more entertaining programming that has been driven by their needs as opposed to the more top-down, high-brow world of public service journalism (Baum 2003a; Zaller 2003). Zaller (2003) has argued that soft news has the potential to reach a far wider range of viewers than the serious brand of hard news. What Zaller and other scholars, most notably Michael Schudson (1998) have claimed, is that citizens do not need a heavy supply of hard news to satisfy their information needs in a democracy. Instead viewers can be viewed as savvy 'Monitorial citizens' (Schudson 1998) with television news being used like a 'Burglar Alarm' (Zaller 2003) to alert them to those issues that are directly relevant to their everyday concerns. Interpreting the impact of commercial television news should, in other words, be critically assessed within the context of the wider informational environment that is necessary for democracies to flourish.

In the early 1990s, broadcast television stations had tended to be the significant players during key regulatory changes. By 1996 a new Telecommunications Act had been introduced to cover the increasingly wide range of communication industries – radio, television, telephone, cable, satellite and, about to take off, the Internet – which the FCC regulated. In what has been described as 'arguably one of the most important pieces of US legislation' (McChesney 2004: 51), the entire infrastructure of US communications was given a renewed deregulatory zeal. In Barkin's (2003: 176) view, 'The new law emerged as a compact between Big Government and Big Business. The outcome was a pro-market document that invoked the public interest while relaxing public-interest standards'.

The Act, of course, has proved far reaching and its impact on different communication industries needs to be carefully reviewed (see Aufderheide 2000), most notably for removing significant layers of radio ownership laws. But for television channels, and television news stations, it perpetuated the consolidation of media ownership and encouraged cross-media ownership, both of which, as Barkin (2003) has argued, diminished media pluralism. So where companies had not been able to own more than 12 television stations to prevent companies from dominating the market, this limit was now gone. It was also possible to own a television station and a cable operator. And likewise, while previously no one company could own stations that, between them, accounted for more than 25 per cent of audience share, this was increased to 35 per cent of the market. Television licence renewals – when the FCC evaluated whether a station had abided by its public interest criteria – were also relaxed from every five years to every eight. While much of the legislation was already in place, the 1996 Act put the deregulation of television into overdrive.

Within this 335-page piece of legislation, many complicated regulatory agreements are contained. But what is striking is that if we compare the 1934 Act that stated the public owns the airwaves with the 1996 Act 62 years later is how far American television had been deregulated by the end of the twentieth century. Not only were broadcasters allowed to interpret their own rules of impartiality, the rules prohibiting a concentration of media ownership had also been relaxed to the extent where just a handful of major conglomerates owned the major television channels in addition to other news media sources. Notwithstanding the consequences of the bill to the communications industry, what has also captured the attention of some academics is how saliently the Act was passed without any wider public consultation other than that to be found in the business pages of broadsheet newspapers. According to a systematic content analysis of coverage of the 1996 Communications Act in 14 US newspapers,

> very different pictures of the likely effects of this legislation were being painted by the different newspapers examined, pictures that served to further the interests of the newspapers' corporate owners rather than the interests of their readers in fair and complete coverage of an important public policy issue. (Gilens and Hertzman 2000: 383)

What is perhaps ironic, given the main thrust of the 1996 Act, is that the findings of the study demonstrated what the legislation further encouraged – a promotion of cross-media ownership and the creation of an infrastructure that would allow powerful conglomerates to further consolidate their existing power. All of which, in short, has led to less diversity in news reporting and a public sphere constrained by the financial conflicts of the interests involved. Subsequent chapters will explore the consequences of further media deregulation when examining the type and nature of US television news in the twenty-first century.

But while the US had cranked up media deregulation to a new level in the 1990s, it was not alone in pursuing a more commercialised broadcasting ecology. Much of the media landscape of Europe had embraced the new cable and satellite technologies. Terrestrial public service broadcasting, as a result, was on the retreat and television journalism was to enter a new era of commercial competition. Many other countries, including the UK, had begun to reshape their system of broadcasting using an American model with television journalism adopting new conventions and stylistic formats.

Towards an increasingly market-orientated broadcasting culture: reshaping UK television news in the 1990s

Running parallel with the US, the 1980s laid the groundwork for a dramatic period of change for television journalism across much of Europe. The political economy of television was radically shaken up by the combined forces of new technologies, globalisation and an Americanised approach to deregulation. Globally binding technologies also opened up opportunities for transnational media markets to develop (Collins 1998; Chalaby 2009). Lured by the promise of new and highly lucrative streams of revenue, many governments began a process of deregulation, stripping back any legislation that might impede growth and spark competition such as liberalising media ownership laws (Humphreys 1996). By deregulating the media industries and promoting commercial enterprise, it was argued that the media market-place would be sufficiently stimulated to foster media pluralism.

In much of Europe, of course, public service broadcasting remained an instrumental part of national television culture. Allowing national airwaves to be opened up and freed from regulatory requirements as well as developed within a commercial market had been, prior to the 1980s, almost impossible to envisage. However, at that point in time many key European states had elected right-wing governments – most notably, the UK, France and Italy – and each was united in a shared political drive to deregulate the media land-scape and encourage a free marketplace for television and its related indus-tries. Each country, Williams (2005: 47) has stated, 'committed themselves to liberating broadcasting from the "nanny-state" and ensuring that consumer choice, as determined by audience tastes and preferences, would prevail. They embarked on the process of deregulation and liberalization which represented a direct challenge to public service values'. This process was by no means uniform. In Italy, for example, it had begun in the late 1970s with powerful commercial channels being launched that over time significantly weakened public service provision. What this period represents, more broadly, is the end of the broadcast state monopoly and the emergence of national variations in the direction television journalism would take.

In the UK, for instance, it was not only new technologies that con-tributed to a new broadcasting ecology. A powerful right-wing press/lobby (including influential think-tanks such as the Adam Smith Institute) and a new UK government with strong free market instincts under the leadership of Margaret Thatcher sought repeatedly to abolish or at least significantly erode the BBC's broadcasting presence during the 1980s. Incensed by news coverage and documentaries that challenged government policy – whether about the miners' strike, the Falklands war, security in Northern Ireland or other politicised events – historians have recorded many anecdotes about the Thatcher government's disapproval of (as they saw it) unfavourable state-sponsored journalism (Crisell 1997; Curran and Seaton 2010; Williams 2010). Likewise, there are many examples of orchestrated attacks by right-wing newspapers such as *The Times, The Sun* and *The Daily Telegraph* that not only undermined the BBC's credibility but also questioned the justification for funding a public service broadcaster in an increasingly consumer-driven environment.

Thus the path was suitably paved for the Thatcher government to dismantle the BBC. However, a government-appointed review into broadcasting, chaired by Alan Peacock in 1986, provided a more complicated set of recommendations. Ruling out disbanding the licence fee or introducing advertising as a means of funding, Peacock suggested that the BBC brought cost efficiencies with its brand of quality programming. Nonetheless, whereas previous broadcasting reviews had explicitly linked television with Habermasian notions of citizenship and democracy, Peacock developed a more economic rationale with consumer choice and market growth. This is well explained by O'Malley (2009: 9), who has suggested that the Peacock report put 'an idealistic stress on the value of consumer sovereignty, which assumes that it is both the guarantor of freedom and the best way of organising the economics of a future communications system'. Television provision, in other words, was being increasingly defined as a commodity that could be bought and sold. Plans to develop a satellite station with multiple channels, for example, were gathering pace. In 1989 this came to fruition with the establishment of BSB (later to be renamed BSkyB after Rupert Murdoch acquired greater control). It launched four new channels, with a sport, entertainment and movie channel, but most importantly for television journalism the UK and Europe had launched their first dedicated news channel, Sky News (see Cushion 2010a). The significance of the channel's contribution to broadcast journalism will be addressed in the following chapter, but for now it is important to recognise how the UK's broadcasting ecology was fast becoming redefined.

The Broadcasting Act of 1990 further shook the broadcast foundations. Since attempts to directly downsize the BBC had been counter-productive, attention turned to marketising the main commercial channel ITV. To generate a competitive market for television programming, ITV became a network channel with 14 regions bidding to supply programming across the UK. With Channel 4, the second terrestrial commercial channel, required to start selling its own advertising in 1993, in a short period of time the infrastructure of the UK broadcast ecology had strategically changed. Apart from the BBC, terrestrial channels – including the introduction of Channel 5 in 1996 – had become more commercially driven operations. As in the US, a more competitive television culture, in other words, had been created and sustained by advertising. In addition, the existing regulatory structure of the IBA was replaced by the Radio Authority and the ITC. The latter not only had responsibility for commercial terrestrial television, it also oversaw cable and satellite channels, with a mandate to intervene less in policing television content. According to Negrine (1994), this reflected the prevailing regulatory mood of the 1980s which was moving into the 1990s. He suggested that the ITC had been set-up

> to apply the 'lighter-regulatory' touch across all … delivery systems in line with the sorts of philosophies of broadcasting developed under conservative governments. In practice, this meant that so long as services complied with the ITC's code of practice, they were free to operate as they wished without too many burdens. (1994: 192)

Since broadcasters now had to compete in a commercial market for advertising, the public service 'burdens' ITV shouldered were 'lightened' in the 1990 Broadcast Act. While it still had more obligations than the minimalist requirements which satellite or cable competitors had to abide by, 'the old ITV system was subtly pushed partly out of the public service ring' (O'Malley 2001: 36). Most notably, for example, more entertainment programming could now be aired in the much coveted prime-time slot. With less public service obligations and a loosened regulatory structure, according to a range of seasoned observers, the impact of ITV's television journalism was soon evident.

This was partly the case because a previously not-for-profit ITN was now a money-making television news service that was answerable to shareholders. Facing new financial pressures, its television news agenda succumbed to commercial values in a bid to capture a greater share of television audiences. For Crissell (1997: 247), 'A predictable consequence of ITN's need to become competitive was that during the 1990s its approach to the news became rather more populist, more concerned with "human interest" stories'. Cutting costs as well as its newsgathering structures, Williams (2010: 174) has argued, meant ITN moved 'away from serious news towards a more tabloid, human interest format'. Former BBC journalist and maverick politician, Martin Bell, suggested that while it was 'once a proud name in journalism … In hock to the advertisers, ITN set the trend by its decision, early in the 1990s, to promote an agenda of crime, celebrity and miracle cures – and to downgrade foreign news to a couple of slots a week on Tuesdays and Thursdays, unless anything more sellable happened closer to home. The judgements were not editorial, but commercial' (Bell, cited in Harcup 2009: 117). The arrival of *Channel 5 News* in 1997 also introduced some commercial news conventions and reinforced the widespread belief that UK television was increasingly resembling television journalism in the US. Anchored by a female presenter who was standing rather than sitting formally behind a desk the news bulletin was being redefined to capture a younger audience, with a faster pace of editing and a less serious news agenda than its terrestrial counterparts.

Perhaps the most convincing and evidenced-based account of UK television news by the end of the decade was Jackie Harrison's (2000) *Terrestrial TV News in Britain* and Steven Barnett, Emily Seymour and Ivor Gaber's (2000) *From Callaghan to Kosovo: Changing Trends in British Television News 1975–1999*. The latter study draws on a systematic content analysis of all television news bulletins over 15 years. While they conclude that UK television journalism offers a more balanced and international agenda than that of the US, Barnett et al. (2000: 12) found that 'there has undoubtedly been a shift in most news bulletins towards a more tabloid domestic agenda … This shift has been particularly apparent over the last 10 years in the two ITN bulletins'. Combining content analysis with a detailed examination of production practices, Harrison (2000) broadly identified the important differences between public and commercial television news bulletins. Over the course of the 1980s, she concluded that:

> The BBC has introduced a variety of entertainment format changes (such as a new studio set, and other devices such as graphics to help tell and sell the story), and will continue to do so; but the content of BBC news (especially the *Nine O'Clock News* and BBC2's *Newsnight*) in the main still avoids an excessive coverage of human interest or people-centred stories, although this may be changing. In contrast, ITN's Channel 3 news programmes, *GMTV News*, Channel 4's *Big Breakfast News* and Yorkshire Tyne-Tees Television's *Calendar News* programmes all show a strong commitment to a high percentage of human interest coverage … The current trend is towards the maintenance of mainstream mass audiences through introducing a faster tempo to the news programmes and providing interesting and entertaining news stories. (2000: 207)

What this suggests, overall, is that the 1990 Act triggered a shift in the nature of television news. Television's political economy not only pushed commercial broadcasters towards adopting a more market-led approach to television journalism, there were also signs that it had a knock-on effect on public service news bulletins that were eager to sustain their audience share.

Similar to the 1996 US Telecommunications Bill, the UK's 1996 Broadcasting Act created structures that would further develop a commercialised television market. With globalisation on the march and satellite technology improving, legislation was passed to foster more internationally competitive television companies. This, in effect, meant smaller media organisations were bought up by bigger companies and cross-media ownership was relaxed. Even if this was not to the same extent as in the US – where conglomerates had cumulatively built up media empires – a similar trend was beginning to take shape in the UK. But perhaps most significantly, the Act laid the foundations for the birth of digital and terrestrial channels in 1998. While a multi-channel television culture had alreadycommenced, it was from this point onwards that via Sky hundreds of channels became available at the touch of a button.

From public service to public value: the changing political economy of television journalism in the 2000s

In the previous decade or so, further legislative action in the US and UK had been taken that was to exacerbate the trends of deregulation and concentration of media ownership. At the same time, since the broadcasting environment has changed with the expansion of multi-channel television, re-regulation has taken place where new requirements had been imposed on broadcasters in order to maintain programming standards. Interventions into how cable television operated in the US in the 1980s and 1990s, for example, were brought about to protect consumers (Hazlett 1997). However, as Graham Murdock has pointed out, re-regulation on 'public interest' grounds can often be misleading since much legislative action has primarily benefited private, corporate power. 'The balance between public and private enterprise', he argued at the end of the 1980s, has 'tipped permanently in favour of the market in a growing number of countries' (Murdock 1990: 9). Julian Petley, a decade on, has similarly suggested re-regulation has been used to propagate economic competitiveness and not public service goals. In the context of the UK's 2001 Communications Bill, Petley (2003: 140) has stated that 'regulations designed to protect and enhance citizens' communicative rights are, under the patronizing and weasel-like guise of "giving people what they want", being replaced by those designed to further the economic interests of vast global media corporations'. Re-regulation, in other words, has not necessarily brought about a more robust policing of television's content or safeguarded minority programming. Chapter 5 draws on a case study to explore where re-regulation has enhanced the quality of local journalism in the UK on public service television while deregulation has diminished it on commercial channels.

While assessing the longer-term impact of legislation is a job best left to media historians, it can still be observed that in recent years trends of 're-' or 'de' regulation or the further concentration of media ownership have brought about key changes in the make-up of the broadcast ecology, particularly in the UK. More specific legislative decisions and their implications will be traced in subsequent chapters, such as the gradual erosion of regional public service requirements for ITV in the UK (Chapter 5) or the cumulative impact of the relaxation of the Fairness Doctrine in the US which spanned several decades (Chapter 4). The most influential Act since the new millennium occurred in the UK and this is worth reflecting on in detail since it represents an important shift in the political economy of television and the values ascribed to its journalism.

After six years in power, in 2003 New Labour followed the US in introducing a Communications Act that swept aside existing regulatory structures by establishing what was hailed as a 'super-regulator', Ofcom. It not only held responsibility for the regulation of the telecommunications and commercial broadcasting industries, it also had a mandate to monitor – without regulatory power – whether public service broadcasters were adversely encroaching on commercial territory. For the most part it was established in order to help stimulate a communications market (Freedman 2008) and thus was less concerned with what it should regulate and more with what it should not. As a result of this, in a Communication Bill in 2002, it was stated that Ofcom should 'not involve the imposition or maintenance of unnecessary burdens' (cited in Shaw 2004). And in a press release announcing Ofcom's launch, its new chief executive, Stephen Carter, stated 'When Ofcom is fully formed our statutory responsibilities will include the importance of creating and promoting a dynamic communications market, underpinned by limited and effective intervention through a constructive and mutually respectful relationship with stakeholders'. Its market-orientated ethos and minimal approach to intervention resembled, more so than ever before, the US's FCC that many previous broadcasting Acts and commissions (pre-Peacock) had worked hard to try and avoid.

But while Ofcom may share some characteristics with the FCC, it continues to be shaped by the values of public service broadcasting even if these are being increasingly redefined. Ofcom has undertaken several reviews into public service broadcasting, producing myriad data on how much time is spent on different types of programming as well as what audiences are watching and what they value. Thus, public service broadcasting, on the face of it, has remained a much championed concept and television news, even for commercial broadcasters, remains central to this ethos. So, for example, in an Ofcom commissioned review, *New News, Future News*, the foreword to the report stated 'The prospects of television news in a fully digital era are a central element in any consideration of the future of public service broadcasting' (Ofcom 2007).

In this Ofcom era the regulation of television news has become more transparently policed, with impressive quantitative data sets about its content and the attitudes audiences have towards journalism. At the same time, the technocratic nature of Ofcom's approach does invite some criticism. Thus in *New News, Future News*, there are chapters which are tellingly labelled 'UK Television – A Market Analysis', 'DSO [digital switch over] and Plurality – Economics and the Views of the Stakeholders', and 'Disengagement, Trust and Impartiality'. In each of these what counts as 'value' is often motivated by economic questions or market-driven imperatives. Of the limited scholarly attention paid to Ofcom's impact, this has been the central critique. Harvey (2006: 91), for instance, acknowledged Ofcom's 'ability to assemble and publish a wide range of statistics about the industry'. But at the same time she also argued, 'it [Ofcom] may plausibly be accused of knowing "the cost of everything and the value of nothing"'. For Harvey (2006: 91), Ofcom's 'ethos is predominantly neoliberal, and its language and organizing concepts are suitable for an analysis of markets and of competition, but not of social significance and cultural value'. John Corner (2010: 146) has likewise suggested that the liberal use of 'citizen-consumer' in Ofcom's mission statements suggested an 'unresolved argument' about its role in enhancing democratic culture, on the one hand, and championing the market on the other. Where once broadcast policy referred to viewers primarily as citizens (certainly in many Acts and commissioned reports pre-Peacock), in today's language audiences appear to be interpreted more as consumers in a marketplace (Livingstone et al. 2007).

Moreover, what both Harvey and Corner are suggesting is that Ofcom produces public 'value' as opposed to public 'service' tests as a way to monitor commercial television's content. In doing so, while the broad principles of public service television regulation remain in place, commercial television is increasingly being policed less from a citizen's perspective and more from a cost-effective, consumerist one in order to demonstrate public 'value'. The distinction here may appear small, but it has important consequences for television journalism. Chapter 5 explores these implications in relation to the gradual loosening of ITV's public service requirements. This will be compared to the BBC's regional coverage which has a more robust system of regulation. For BBC television is policed more vigorously by a body called the BBC Trust which, according to its mission statement, describes itself as having 'considerable power to wield on your behalf – and when we need to, we act quickly and decisively in your interests' (BBC Trust website). It is, in other words, more interventionist than a light-touch regulator, but it often faces pressure both for intervening too much in television journalism and, in some contexts, not robustly enough.

But despite being challenged by the multi-channel commercial era and an increasingly relaxed approach to television regulation, at the turn of the century the UK's broadcast ecology, overall, has continued to maintain a relatively strong public service presence. While it could be argued that the model of public service funding is fraying at the edges somewhat, compared to the US the UK's public service infrastructure remains relatively secure. Indeed, the values of public service broadcasting continue to shape the wider culture of commercial television journalism, such as the strict broadcast impartiality guidelines that have remained in place for all UK broadcasters. Nonetheless, since the publication of Peacock, a more commercialised broadcast ecology has evolved with deregulation encouraged at a faster rate and the concentration of cross-media ownership, if not openly accepted, tacitly tolerated in order to allow internationally competitive media corporations to develop. While the UK has not endorsed wholesale the US broadcast model, it has inched some way forward in a little over two decades towards replicating its political economy.

In this sense, on both sides of the Atlantic, and perhaps more so than ever before, television journalism is facing similar challenges. The UK's regulatory structures increasingly resemble the US's laissez-faire approach to the policing of the communications industry, and the further expansion of commercial media and the values they bring with them – similar to the US in the 1980s and 1990s – are changing the nature of television journalism in the UK. Locked into a battle that is no longer just with terrestrial rivals or their print and radio counterparts, television news faces unprecedented market competition from a rise in domestic and international news channels (see Chapter 3) and government structures that favour a deregulation of television journalism (Chapter 4 and Chapter 5). Meanwhile the growing popularity of the Internet is significantly redefining journalism (see Chapter 5 also) and thus also reshaping what it means to be a journalist in a converged, multi-media newsroom (see Chapter 6). The wider context to these trends and the evidence of what impact they are having on television journalism will be taken up in the chapters that follow.

PART II

TRENDS IN TELEVISION JOURNALISM

3

REDEFINING WHAT'S NEWSWORTHY: TOWARDS 24-HOUR NEWS VALUES AND CONVENTIONS?

News values: what makes television journalism distinctive?

For many journalists and media professionals, deciding 'what's news' is something they learn on the job. Journalists often suggest they are able to 'sniff out' a good story as opposed to following a set of guidelines or an instruction manual. In the fast-paced environment of journalism, practitioner accounts tend to apply 'gut feeling' to make sense of their news gathering (Marr 2004; Scruton, cited in Peak and Fisher 2000). If this is taken at face value it implies the selection of news is somehow 'discovered' by journalists on a daily basis. The reality, of course, is altogether different.

News is far from being an arbitrary selection of events and issues that are chosen on a whim by the editor of the day. Indeed for many decades, the concept of news values has generated much debate amongst scholars about the kind of criteria journalists will unconsciously use to select a story or reject it (Brighton and Foy 2007; Gans 1979; Harcup and O'Neil 2001; O'Neil and Harcup 2008; Schlesinger 1978/1987; Tuchman 1978). Journalists have often been reluctant to enter into this sociological exchange since in doing so it diminishes their news-gathering autonomy. If journalism is reduced to a set of predictable rules and conventions it fails to identify the routine conflicts *between* journalists about what is – and is not – newsworthy. Newsrooms, after all, are typically awash with disagreements about the relative merits of particular stories or events.

And yet while differences about individual stories will always be part of the competitive world of newsrooms, scholars have long established a broad pattern for the kind of news which most of the time is identified as being 'newsworthy'. Galtung and Ruge's much cited (1965) taxonomy of news values systematically demonstrated, for the first time, that news was a more formulaic than a spontaneous pursuit. Needless to say, in the close to 50 years since Galtung and Ruge published their study, news values have been subject to much contestation and revision. Despite a vast amount of empirical and theoretical enterprise in previous decades, when summarising competing taxonomies by a range of scholars, O'Neil and Harcup (2008: 62) have suggested that news value remains a 'slippery concept'. Nonetheless, by examining what is routinely selected in journalism scholars have demonstrated news values are prioritised on the basis of many competing and inter-related factors. While many of Galtung and Ruge's (1965) criteria still remain relevant to most news media today, key differences did emerge when the different systems of media were compared (public with private broadcasters, say) or different types of media (television with radio). As Brighton and Foy (2007: 29) have put it: 'The approach to the delivery and packaging of news has altered with the passage of time, and the shape of the media in the 21st century is quite different from how it was ... [news] values will vary from medium to medium, and from each individual package to the next'. Deciding what's newsworthy, in other words, is as much a function of the medium as it is the message.

For in the case of television news, compared to other news media – with radio, again, being the most striking point of comparison – the delivery of moving, live or still images will trump many other news criteria. As previous ethnographies of television news production have found, the availability of moving pictures, to a large extent, will shape the editorial selection and the priorities of much of its journalism (Schlesinger 1987; Tuchman 1978). As a result, there are signs that the delivery of live, moving picture-led journalism has had a knock-on effect on journalism more generally. According to Harcup and O'Neil (2001), newspapers have been reluctant to keep up with the fast-paced medium of television since it can deliver news almost instantaneously. Newspapers, in this context, appear to have taken on a more editorialising role, with less emphasis on the reporting of 'hard' journalistic facts (Franklin 2006). Unable to compete on the same terms as electronic news outlets, the former editor of ITN, Richard Tait (2007), has likewise argued cross-media competition has forced newspapers to become 'viewspapers'. The influence of rolling news, in this sense, has moved print journalism away from supplying news and information towards the promotion of ideas and opinions. News values are thus increasingly subject to renegotiation and reinterpretation and can be shaped externally by their relationship with rival news outlets and competing media.

Television news, moreover, has been distinguished from different forms of journalism by a range of scholars from a variety of perspectives. Less attention, though, has been paid to how television news's own values have evolved in recent years. Of course the various dramatic changes in the 1950s and 1960s – when television 'came of age' and developed over several decades (see Chapter 2) – have been well documented (Conway 2009; Curran and Seaton 2010; Williams 2010). But the more contemporary rise of 24-hour news channels and the impact which rolling news culture has had more broadly on television news values is less clear. As O'Neil and Harcup (2008: 172) have pointed out, the 'continuing study of the news values of 24-hour broadcast news ... will help shed further light on the changing journalistic environment of the 21st century'. There have, at newsworthy times, been moments when 24-hour news television has hogged the academic limelight. The emergence of CNN and its global impact during the first Gulf War prompted much scholarly enquiry (Livingston 1997; Robinson 2002, 2005; Volkmer 1999). And, more recently, the Middle Eastern rolling news station Al-Jazeera gained much notoriety as a result of its live reporting of the war in Afghanistan, with several scholars exploring its role in military and wider diplomatic affairs (Ayish 2010; El-Nawawy 2003; Miles 2005; Thussu and Freedman 2003; Zayani 2005, 2010). But beyond the novelty factor of rolling news's arrival and putting aside globally significant events, the *day-to-day role and purpose* of 24-hour news channels has not been subjected to quite as much critical attention.

And yet, with cable and satellite penetration on the rise in most advanced democracies, dedicated news channels have become an increasingly familiar part of the television landscape (Cushion and Lewis 2010). Viewers, at any given time, can tune into an update of the news or a breaking news story and 24-hour news channels have played a vital public service role by informing viewers about fast-breaking events like a terrorist attack, where concerned families and friends will be glued to their TV sets frantically trying to find out about the latest development or to locate follow-up sources of information. Reflecting on his role during moments of high public drama, a former UK Home Secretary, Jack Straw, for example, has written that: 'When the news of an outrage comes through, information about it will inevitably be incomplete. Some of it will be inaccurate. Communication systems will be overloaded. Decision-makers use every available source of information – including the rolling news programmes, which do a remarkable job in these circumstances' (Straw 2010).

Where once television news was exclusively a pre-packaged event, today it is continuous and delivered on-demand. In this sense, 'television constitutes itself – particularly in an era of 24-hour broadcasting – as an apparently endless flow, always available and never pausing' (Mariott 2007: 51). In doing so, television news screens have become a hive of activity, littered with on-screen news digests and flashy graphics. If the latest FTSE figures are down or NASDAQ's numbers are up, if a football or baseball transfer has just gone through, or if a court case has been decided or a legislative act passed, a steady stream of on-screen headlines will keep viewers up to speed. And while these may be just the merest snippets of information, what 24-hour news channels are promoting is the instant and continuous news update.

This quick-fix news diet is reflected in how 24-hour news audiences will watch rolling news journalism. Despite 24-hour news channels being a dedicated, always on service, viewers routinely dip in and out of rolling news programming. As will be suggested elsewhere in this chapter, the style and structure of rolling news channels appears to discourage sustained viewing. Thus while most television audiences will have access to a range of sometimes local, certainly national, and international news channels, day-to-day rolling news coverage is watched by just a tiny proportion of audiences. Of course, at those times when a significant breaking news stories develops the viewing figures will rise dramatically (during terrorist attacks, say, or critical moments in wars or elections). Otherwise 24-hour news channels, at any given time, account for a relatively meagre share of the total television audience (approximately 0.7 per cent or 1.1 per cent in April 2011 for the leading rolling news channels, Sky News and the BBC News Channel respectively).

Given its routinely low reach, a 24-hour news channel's direct impact on television news audiences should not be oversold. However, since new technologies have enabled dedicated news channels to be launched the genre of rolling news has arguably had a wider and more subtle and systemic impact on television news's values and conventions in the last decade or so. This is not to suggest, of course, that prior to the arrival of 24-hour news channels journalism was not caught up in a race to deliver the fastest headlines or driven by the urgency to scoop a rival. Classic ethnographies by Gans (1979), Schlesinger (1978/1987) and Tuchman (1978) all paint pictures of chaotic newsrooms, with journalists working flat-out in order to reach their deadlines and break news first. Nor are the fast-paced conditions of rolling news culture the exclusive preserve of television journalism. The promotion of instant, rolling news has been accelerated since the birth of the Internet and the creation of multi-media newsrooms. With the technology at their fingertips to break news almost immediately, online – as much as 24-hour television news – journalists share the journalistic need for speed even if, as Juntunen (2010) has shown, it may compromise their own ethical standards. Journalists, in this sense, are caught up in what Barbara Zelizer (1993) calls 'interpretive communities'. Sharing a broadly held conventional wisdom on news conventions and practices, it is difficult to resist let alone openly challenge a dominant culture where pace, above all, will shape journalism's end-product. All of which means, as this chapter will suggest, that the urgency to delivery breaking journalism is a more systemic issue, infusing not just the values of 24-hour news channels but also much of contemporary journalism. However, since this book is primarily concerned with television journalism, the focus of this chapter must be on examining how the genre of 24-hour news has developed and which dominant news conventions have emerged as a result. Towards the end of the chapter, the impact that rolling news has had on television news more generally will be explored.

Before examining the style and approach of rolling news journalism more specifically, gaining a wider context to the rise of 24-hour news television is necessary. For while 24-hour news channels may seem a familiar part of the television news landscape, the presence of rolling news stations remains a relatively short-lived phenomena.

The arrival and impact of 24-hour news channels: three phases of global television journalism

The history of the rolling news genre and the way its conventions have evolved over time can be interpreted within three overlapping phases. However, not all countries have conveniently followed this narrative. In France (see Khun 2010) and Australia (see Young 2010), for example, 24-hour news channels are little over a decade old. Nor do all 24-hour news conventions pursue a uniform pattern. Euronews – a European news channel – operates at a far slower pace with less breaking news action than many of its competitors (Garcia-Blanco and Cushion 2010). Nevertheless, each phase can be seen to broadly mark out key turning points in the genre of 24-hour news television. These have been explained in greater detail elsewhere (Cushion 2010b), but for now a shorthand version for making sense of the growth and development of 24-hour television news channels is warranted. The first stage can be viewed as *a coming of age*, with the arrival of CNN and its live reporting of the first Gulf War. Its global impact triggered the second phase of rolling news, one that could be characterised as *a race of transnational reach and influence*. The third ongoing phase can be seen as *the regionalisation and commercialisation of rolling news conventions*.

The first dedicated news channel was launched by CNN in 1980. With cable penetration low and limited resources, the pressure was on for CNN to make an immediate impression that would justify the existence of a news channel and reach out to more viewers. A failed assassination attempt on Jimmy Carter within minutes of CNN's launch was quickly exploited. Live pictures rolled in of the American President in some distress. For the first time, a channel did not have to interrupt its programming: immediacy and presence could be taken for granted in an ongoing rolling format. The delivery of live, breaking news soon became a 'talking-point' in journalistic circles as other events – a failed assassination attempt of Ronald Reagan in 1981 and the launch of the space shuttle *Challenger* in 1986 – appeared to be pushing television journalism in a new direction. Compared to the conventions on nightly news bulletins – on ABC, CBS and NBC – that most viewers had grown up with, rolling news production appeared to be rather messy and amateurish. Since 'live' news was less predictable and polished than that to be found on the nightly television packages, CNN's credibility was lampooned by rival broadcasters. The 'Chaos News Channel' and the 'Chicken Noodle Network' (Huntzicker, 2002: 293) were just some of the derogatory labels the channel had to work hard to shake off.

With advancing cable technology an international version was launched. Reaching many countries around the world, CNNI made it more possible to imagine a global public sphere (Volkmer, 1999: 2). Since CNNI was an American-constructed 'window on the world', it triggered a significant amount of concern about American imperialism and Western supremacy (Sreberny-Mohammadi et al. 1997; Thussu, 2007). The reporting of the first Iraq/US Gulf War (1990–1991) demonstrated the impact of CNN and its hegemony when defining a military conflict. By building diplomatic ties with the Iraqi forces, it exclusively provided live commentary of the opening military conflict. The war turned into a global event with a single broadcaster communicating what was happening to a worldwide audience. This could, in a sense, be defined as a 'coming of age' moment in the life-time of 24-hour television news television.

The second phase of 24-hour news's history was thereby triggered because television news channels were racing one another to emulate CNN's transnational reach and influence. While there had been other news channels in existence beforehand – Sky News in the UK, for example, was launched in 1989 – many more international news channels were now launched. A post-national broadcasting ecology was beginning to take shape. With cable and satellite communication improving rapidly, news channels were able to reach international audiences. The impact of CNN also caught the attention of aspiring media barons. Rupert Murdoch, for example, launched several Sky News channels in different regions around the world and the soon-to-be-highly-influential Fox News channel also saw the light of day (see Chapter 4). As a result, scholars began to recognise the impact 24-hour news television could have. The so-called 'CNN effect' gained academic currency in the 1990s after the channel appeared to have encouraged military responses from western governments when they intervened in the Iraqi (1991) and Somali (1992) conflicts. CNN, it was argued, was shining a light on areas of the world that had been typically overlooked by the mass media. With news channels having raised levels of consciousness, governments were being forced to sit up and take action.

As other news channels emerged, the 'CNN effect' was invoked to describe the role and impact of globally spanning communication on diplomatic matters. Under greater academic scrutiny, it was subsequently argued that its interventionist role was something of a myth (Robinson 2002). For rather than news channels playing a decisive role in diplomatic disputes, a whole host of variables – the role of aid agencies, political lobbying, political decision making, and much more – were proving to be significant factors that had perhaps been overlooked (Gilboa 2005; Robinson 2002, 2005). In other words, if there was indeed a 'CNN effect', its influence was less tangible than had originally been conceived. However, for television journalism generally, and 24-hour news channels in particular, their role and profile in politics and public life had risen considerably.

Heavyweight international news channels emerged with global aspirations about what they could democratically achieve. Having had a well-established BBC World Service on the radio for many decades (Walker 1992), a BBC World News Channel was launched in 1991 (known today as World News). With clear public service objectives, it has since become a highly influential and much watched source throughout the world. Two years later Euronews was launched, with more politicised motives. Under the auspices of the European Union, a news service had been created in order to assist with cultivating a stronger European identity and to challenge the hegemony of American journalism (Garcia-Blanco and Cushion 2010). A transnational battle then continued from another part of the world with the launch of Al-Jazeera in 1996. Reminiscent of CNN's transformation on the world stage, Al-Jazeera played a significant role in the reporting of the Afghanistan conflict in 2001. With noticeable gusto, it challenged the Western interpretation of the war and led with the human suffering element of the conflict. Taking a Middle-Eastern perspective it has since become credited with opening up a more diverse global public sphere: it is now broadcast in many languages (Miles 2005; Zayani, 2005, 2010).

The transnational battle for 'hearts and minds' during conflicts like those in Afghanistan and Iraq in the past decade has perhaps diluted anything like a 'CNN effect'. With many syndicated stations pooling resources around the world – CNN being the operative example – there is some debate about how far the agenda of many news channels diverge. But towards the end of the 1990s it was not only international channels launching new services, national and regional ones also began to open up audiences to more localised rolling news journalism. Twenty-four-hour news television thus entered a more competitive era, marking a third and ongoing phase that would be characterised by a more commercially-led set of journalism conventions.

Today, rolling news channels appear to be a familiar part of the television landscape. Tuning into Sky – the dominant satellite provider in the UK – television viewers are able to access a News Section on the menu. Subject to different levels of subscription, they can then (in the order Sky lists channels) have a choice of 15 dedicated channels, including Sky News (and Sky News High Definition), Bloomberg, BBC News, BBC Parliament, CNBC, CNN, Euronews, Fox News, CCTV News, NDTV 24x7, Russia Today, France 24, Al Jazeera English, Press TV and NHK World TV. According to Rai and

Cottle's systematic (2010) review of news channels around the globe, this is just the tip of the iceberg. They mapped hundreds including 'commercial, public and non-profit broadcasters, at global, regional, national and even sub-national levels'. What is most striking is the regionalisation of news channels in recent years. This is especially the case in highly populated parts of the world such as India, where it is estimated 70 stations are in operation (Vasanthi, cited in Magnier 2009). From this perspective, it might be concluded that 24-hour news stations have diversified their news agendas from more global to localised journalism. However, on closer inspection many regional channels are not as localised as they might appear. New Zealand's Sky News, for example, is more of a glorified version of Australia's Sky News broadcasting with just a couple of hours of rolling New Zealand content per day. Likewise, there is evidence CNN syndicates such as CNN TÜRK, CNN-IBN, CNNj and CNN Chile arguably do not pursue as localised an agenda or mode of address as rival broadcasters based in that locale (Boyd Barrett and Boyd Barrett 2010). In short, there may be more news channels but there remain globally binding influences that prevent the plurality of news agendas.

The plurality of news agendas is also threatened by the increasingly competitive environment within which 24-hour news channels operate. In countries like India there is evidence to suggest rolling stations are adopting more market-led conventions. The Mumbai terrorist attacks in 2008 prompted, according to P.N. Vasanti (cited in Magnier 2009), 'extraordinary pressure to sensationalize, claim specious "exclusives" and do almost anything else to attract attention' amongst Indian news channels. Thussu (2007) has suggested many television stations are turning to the US model of rolling television journalism in a bid to remain as competitive. As Chapter 4 demonstrates, this is most strikingly the case with the rise of the Fox News channel and its adoption of commercially conceived television conventions. An apparent 'Foxification' – whereby rival channels mimic its market-led style and approach – has arguably cast a spell on American television journalism and other parts of the world.

But as the previous chapter explored, the commercialisation of television journalism has not spread uniformly world-wide. There are, in many countries around the globe, regulatory structures in place that would prevent a Fox-style approach being replicated as well as a broader journalistic culture of objectivity that would be difficult to challenge (Cushion and Lewis 2009). From a global perspective, moreover, it can be observed that the architecture shaping 24-hour news channels and the boundaries policing its journalism are diverse, making broad generalisations about rolling news coverage problematic (Cottle and Rai 2008). It remains important, in other words, to empirically interrogate 24-hour news channels. The next section draws on a range of studies that have explored the content and nature of

24-hour news channels, most notably in the UK and US. In doing so, it asks whether rolling journalism is meaningfully different from terrestrial television news bulletins.

Live, rolling news drama: empirical endeavours into 24-hour news conventions

Since the turn of the millennium, the analysis of news has increasingly moved beyond academic circles. A 2007 BBC series, *Broken News*, satirised contemporary news culture by poking fun at the fast-paced world of 24-hour news and some of its journalistic conventions. In the words of one of its writers, John Morton, *Broken News* was designed to show

> the frenetic world of news isn't about news anymore. It's about predictions, speculations, recap ... each episode mirrors how we, as consumers of continuous news, surf the infinite choice of networks, pressing the button immediately an item loses our interest, desperate for something to hold our interest, moving as soon as we are bored.

Likewise, Charlie Brooker, in another BBC comedy sketch, *Newswipe*, repeatedly attacked the culture of rolling television journalism. Writing about coverage of the US presidential election in the *Guardian*, Brooker suggested:

> When you stand at a distance and survey the level of nitpicking idiocy, taking in the full landscape of stupidity and meaningless analysis, it's hard not to conclude that 24-hour rolling news is the worst thing to befall humankind since the Manhattan Project. The focus on conjecture and analysis has reached an insane degree that pundits are chasing some kind of meaning in the way a presidential candidate scratches his face ... News networks are supposed to offer news. Instead they serve little but loops and chatter. (Brooker 2008)

Both accounts are not lone voices. When a major story receives continuous news coverage (most notably the disappearance of Madeline McCann in 2006 – see Jenkins 2007), 24-hour news conventions are often the object of parody and belittlement within the media industry. Michael Jackson's sudden death in 2009, for example, or the reporting of Raoul Moat being tracked down live on air by police in 2010, have formed the basis of several pejorative commentaries about the nature of 24-hour news journalism in the UK national press (Brooker 2009; Lawson 2010b). Like CNN in its very early days, 24-hour news channels appear to be increasingly susceptible to criticism about their approach to television journalism. However, while there is some mainstream disapproval of rolling news coverage (the BBC's *Broken News* being the most prominent), closer scrutiny of 24-hour news channels tends to be reserved for moments of high breaking news drama rather than day-to-day routine 24-hour news coverage.

The same is true in a more scholarly context, where major breaking news such as the 9/11 terrorist attacks will grab most attention (c.f. Nacos 2003; Reynolds and Barnett 2003). More generally, however, the critique made against 24-hour news channels is relatively well rehearsed. A body of evidence has shown that the rolling format of 24-hour television news journalism adversely diminishes the content of the 'news' being communicated (see Brighton and Foy 2007; Harrison 2000; Lewis and Cushion 2009; Lewis et al. 2005; MacGregor 1997; Thussu and Freedman 2003; Tuggle and Huffman 2001). However, not all of these have been subject to much critical review or reflection. So, for example, in summarising critiques made of 24-hour news channels, Brighton and Foy (2007: 94) have stated:

> The criticisms most frequently levelled at rolling news are that it is repetitive, that it is too speculative, that it relies too much on the two-way between presenter and reporter, and that it puts more emphasis on speed than on accuracy. On the evidence of our brief analysis, and of much more extensive viewing, this is a partial and rather inaccurate picture of the output. It is arguably a justified commentary on 24-hour news at times of large breaking stories. Here, the output is often characterized by two-ways long on speculation and short on hard facts. In more normal times, however, the criticism is not especially relevant. Our own sample and a more extended viewing of 24-hour news channels actually reveals extensive packaging and shows evidence of the same diary-driven and planning-based news agenda that we find in terrestrial television news.

The main thrust of Brighton and Foy's analysis is difficult to argue against. However, a series of empirically driven content analysis studies – some of which are co-authored by this author – suggests part of their assessment glosses over some striking differences in how rolling news routinely operates. Moreover, because some of these studies are longitudinal in scope they are able to cast more light on the prevailing trends of rolling news coverage over the previous decade (Cushion and Lewis 2009; Lewis and Cushion 2009; Lewis et al. 2005; Tuggle et al. 2010). Many of these studies, though, are not published in textbooks or book chapters, and are instead scattered around a range of journalism, media and communication related academic journals. Since these journals are sometimes difficult to access – especially as many universities, at least in the UK, are increasingly unsubscribing to costly institutional journal memberships – these empirical endeavours warrant unravelling in detail.

A comparative analysis of UK rolling news channels and terrestrial bulletins suggested that while these share some conventions (in particular, an increasing reliance on 'live' reporting), in routine non-breaking news moments there remain key differences (Lewis et al. 2005). In reaching this conclusion, the research systematically compared the BBC's 10 o'clock half-hourly bulletin with the BBC's news channel, (then called) News 24, Sky News and the ITV News channel (no longer broadcasting) over an extended period. Contrary to Brighton and Foy (2007), live reporting (often in the form of two-way exchanges between anchor and reporter) accounted for a significant period of rolling journalism overall: namely a quarter of all air-time monitored on News 24, a fifth on Sky News, and just over a tenth on ITV News Channel. While it is to be expected the nightly bulletin would be less, the difference was perhaps less striking than anticipated: this was approximately a four-teenth of its time (a point developed later in this section, since studies show live news has continued to rise in terrestrial television journalism). But the most striking comparison overall was that television news anchors accounted for, on average, between a quarter and a third of *all* time on rolling news channels and roughly a fifteenth on the late-night bulletin. What this meant, in effect, was that anchors were spending a considerable amount of time nar-rating live, on-air, continuous news stories. This is well put by Montgomery's detailed discourse analysis of broadcast news. His examination shows that

> the role of the presenter/anchor on the dedicated news channel depends more upon
> unfolding the events through interview with correspondents, commentators or 'news-
> makers'. Their role is less scripted [than half-hourly news formats], more improvised, and
> more a question of blending together, in the real-time flow of broadcasting, the voices
> that are drawn upon to make up the news. (Montgomery 2007: 60–61)

As he points out, even if much of 24-hour news coverage is scripted, for a reasonably significant period of time – far greater when compared to more conventional half-hourly bulletins – rolling news anchors have to spontane-ously respond to events *beyond* those moments reserved for breaking news.

If news output is examined overall on both terrestrial bulletins and roll-ing news channels the comparative study further showed more analysis and context is provided in stories found on terrestrial than within 24-hour news coverage (Lewis et al. 2005). Since rolling news channels have, in theory, considerably more time than bulletins in which to elucidate stories and issues, it could be hypothesised that they also have the resources to cover news with a wider analytical context. To make this evaluation, individual news items on both formats were examined in detail. As a result, every item was quantified if it had even a very basic historical or background context or, at best, a broader 'big picture' analysis. After all, studies about news audi-ences demonstrate that wider context and analysis can increase knowledge amongst often inattentive television viewers (Lewis 2001; Philo and Berry 2004). When both formats were compared, while all the news channels had little analytical journalism – with 85 per cent of items, on average, contain-ing none – approximately half of the Ten o'clock news items contained, in some form, either context or analysis. There was no earth-shattering difference in style or tone. But whereas rolling news coverage rarely went behind the scenes of a story, the conventional bulletin was more informative, taking the time to deliver more detail and explanation.

Despite being dedicated news channels, the more superficial form of rolling journalism can be explained by the urgency they place on keeping viewers up to speed with ongoing news. For while 24-hour news channels could potentially spend time explaining the history or wider significance of a story (certainly more than a half-hour bulletin), what most rolling news channels promise is regular headline updates every 15 minutes. To maintain this promise, more sustained journalistic enquires appear structurally incongruous. Contrary to Brighton and Foy's (2007) analysis, then, beyond breaking news stories what is often delivered is a repetitious approach to journalism, recycling the day's top stories with routine – even if sometimes insignificant – updates. While terrestrial news editors have often complained about working within the brevity of half-hourly formats (Mosley 2000), the arrival of dedicated 24-hour news channels opened up, albeit in an editorially motivated fashion, the opportunity for television journalism to develop its news uninterrupted. And yet constrained by the values of immediacy they have adopted, 24-hour news channels appear unable to deliver more contextual or analytical journalism than conventional news bulletins.

Of course, news channels also operate under limited financial constraints. An ITV news channel, for example, lasted just five years (1 August 2000 to 23 December 2005) because it was unable to sustain the costs of running a competitive rolling news service. With a similar mission to bring the fastest breaking news, ITV's news channel found it difficult to compete with the BBC's huge infrastructure of reporters located around the world or Sky's technological resources such as a helicopter – or, what they call the Skycopter – delivering a bird's eye view of real-time action. When celebrating 20 years of Sky News, its head, John Ryley (2009: 19), went as far as to claim 'technology is the engine of change in how news is consumed'. Keeping up with the pace set by Sky and financing the conventions of speed and immediacy are, in this context, highly costly journalistic endeavours. But what the comparative study with the BBC's 10 o'clock news bulletin suggests is a delivery of news that is less about resources and more about approach (Lewis et al. 2005). By routinely providing more reflection than immediacy to a story, a wider context to and analysis of an issue or event were made possible. Thus, while the image of an avid rolling news viewer might connote a well-informed citizen, this comparative analysis suggests watching a half-hourly news bulletin might deliver a greater understanding of the world than undertaking a sustained period of watching 24-hour news coverage.

Subsequent longitudinal studies of 24-hour news coverage have suggested, for a wide range of reasons, that the trend towards embracing values of speed and spectacle has meant immediacy and liveness in television rolling news journalism have been exacerbated (Cushion 2010a; Cushion and Lewis 2009; Lewis and Cushion 2009; Patterson 2010). The urgency to deliver live, up-to-date news has further constrained the ability of rolling news channels to spend time unpacking an issue or event in any meaningful depth. In many ways, the strive to be live encapsulates the very immediacy and urgency rolling news channels want to continuously display. This is not an entirely new or particularly novel journalistic course of action. The significance of the live broadcast was well captured in Dayan and Katz's (1992) *Media Events*, which focuses on the historical significance of tel-evised ceremonial events spanning several decades. Since the early 1990s, however, the ease with which newsrooms can provide live and spontane-ous breaking news action has been made possible by more sophisticated advances in technology. With more breaking news reporting of disasters, wars and acts of terrors, Katz and Liebes (2007) have recently conceded that media events are being 'upstaged' by more live, disruptive incidents and greater flexibility within television schedules.

The drift towards more 'live news' has been most pronounced in the US. As Livingston and Cooper's (2001) study of CNN's rolling news coverage throughout the 1990s demonstrated, this had become a far more perva-sive and routine news practice. Likewise, in a study of CNN's international coverage, Livingston and Bennett (2003) found an increase in live cover-age with what they called event-driven news. They 'point to CNN's use of live transmission technology in Kosovo, and the Balkans more generally, during 1999' to account for the continued priority afforded to liveness on 24-hour news channels (2003: 375). Meanwhile Tuggle and Huffman's (2001) analysis of news stations more generally found live news coverage was a widespread convention. In most cases live news exceeded the time spent on more conventional taped packages, with conventions such as live introductions and tags (known in the trade as donuts and fronted package) being most commonly put in practice. They suggested, however, that there was little journalistic merit to much live reporting. And, as with Livingston and Bennett's (2003) analysis, a newsroom preoccupation with exploiting new technologies was driving much of the emphasis towards 'going live' (Tuggle and Huffman 2001).

However, while technology may enable the delivery of live news it can-not be held exclusively responsible for engineering a shift to rolling live action. For Patterson (2010), international television news agencies have played a hidden role in enabling broadcasters to 'go live' with minimal costs or equipment. Sustaining an infrastructure of cameras, crews and satellites around the world is, after all, a resource-heavy investment. Subscribing to agencies can deliver relatively cheap, live pictures on a global scale. In doing so, Patterson (2010) has argued this has encouraged a journalism that may cover the world but does little to *uncover* the reasons why events such as

protests are staged or wars are waged. He has suggested 24-hour news channels and news agencies have become more dependent on each other, which

> has necessitated a shift in resources and priorities towards the provision of every and
> any live picture to feed the rolling channels, and away from video journalism about
> otherwise poorly covered topics, which once might have contributed to more contextual-
> ized, deeper, and broader reporting by broadcasters. (2010: 111)

In other words, while live news gives the appearance of being in the thick of
the action, covering the spectacle of an event discourages the wider context
or the significance of a story to be explored. Tuggle and Huffman (2001) have
suggested these signify what they call 'black hole' live shots, devoid of meaningful substance and lacking any background information that might inform
viewers about what is happening. In another study, they surveyed a range of
US television news directors and senior reporters and found eight in ten
overall believed going 'live for the sake of live' was a regular occurrence in
US newsrooms (Tuggle and Huffman 1999). Once again, the availability of
new technologies was blamed for the over-use of reporting live 'on air'. By
delivering news live, as-it-happens, rolling news channels are thus able to give
an appearance of providing 'new' or emerging developments about a story.

In recent decades, 'breaking news' has become a widely used journalistic
phrase to characterise the convention of delivering up-to-date news. The
concept of breaking news and the priority afforded to it warrant closer attention. With most news channels promising to deliver breaking news first, the
convention is increasingly shaping the style and structure of 24-hour television journalism. In doing so, it will be suggested that some news channels
appear to believe sacrificing levels of accuracy during moments of breaking
news drama is a journalistic price worth paying.

Interrupting the news for what purpose? Exposing the myth of breaking news

On the face of it, breaking news connotes the idea that a new or significant
event or story has occurred since, in most cases, it will interrupt ongoing
news, sports and weather reports. In doing so, the image of a breaking news
story might involve a reporter 'on-location' telling viewers what is happening on the ground whilst the camera pans round to show live, rolling pictures. But a detailed analysis of Sky News and the BBC News channel in
three separate studies in 2004, 2005/6 and 2007 debunked many of the
myths associated with breaking news (Lewis and Cushion 2009).

Combining the 2004 and 2007 studies, just 16 per cent of breaking stories
involved a reporter on location. When a news story first broke, on location
reporting increased to 19 per cent. But when a breaking news story was

returned to just 12 per cent of stories featured a reporter on the ground. If this was compared to all 24-hour news coverage, reporters were more than twice as likely to be on location as with a breaking news story. In other words, breaking news did not set free television journalists nor promote more independent reporting. Far from it, since most breaking news was based in the studio, with stories simply arriving via the wires containing, at times, little substantive information. This was reflected in the limited range of sources used to inform breaking news stories. Whereas the ratio, overall, of stories to sources was 71 per cent for rolling news coverage generally, for breaking news it was significantly lower, at just one in five. While advancements in technology have arguably pushed rolling news towards covering live news, for breaking news stories their role should not be overstated. Most breaking news is neither live nor on location, with a limited range of sources used to interpret a story and a greater reliance on anchors reporting what the wires are sending into the studio.

Nevertheless, the convention of 'breaking news' has increasingly been used not only to structure 24-hour news channels' routine content but also to project the image of what a news channel should deliver. Sky News, in particular, never shies away from claiming, with on-screen graphics repeatedly stating the fact, that they are 'First With Breaking News'. Its head of Sky News, John Ryley (2006: 10), has proudly put on record that: 'Sky News customers know that we are only a heartbeat away from breaking news'. With more time and resources devoted to bringing viewers the latest update or breaking event, the character and agenda of 24-hour news channels have changed in recent years. As Table 3.1 shows, Sky more or less doubled the time it spent on breaking news between 2004 and 2007 while the BBC News channel increased its share more than fourfold. Put another way, in 2007 one in nine items was breaking news on the BBC News channel compared to just one in 30 in 2004. While less striking on the face of it, Sky News increased its proportion of 'breaking news'.

Table 3.1 Per cent of time spent on breaking news items as a proportion of news time (including sport) overall on Sky News and the BBC News channel in 2004, 2005/6 and 2007

	BBC News channel (2004)	BBC News channel (2005/6)	BBC News channel (2007)	Sky News (2004)	Sky News (2005/6)	Sky News (2007)
Percentage of stories designated breaking news	3%	11%	11.2%	4.5%	13%	11%
Percentage of news time spent on breaking stories	2.4%	8.3%	11%	7.3%	21.4%	13%

(Adapted from Cushion and Lewis 2009)

However, what this also conceals is Sky's use of the 'news alert' tag – a label that was oft-used in the 2007 coverage but not recorded as a 'breaking news' story.

Of course the growth of breaking news stories may well have coincided with periods of notably newsworthy events. There were, however, no major stories, events or issues that arose or dominated the news agenda over the monitoring periods. Moreover, a detailed breakdown of the nature of each breaking news story demonstrated a pattern in the type and nature of what was defined as 'breaking news'. If we combine the topics covered by both Sky News and the BBC News channel in the 2004 and 2007 studies, what can be observed is a shift towards 'softer' news stories (see Table 3.2).

Topics that typically fall into the softer news bracket – crime and celebrity, sport and human interest – rose from 20 per cent in 2004 to 37 per cent in 2007 as a proportion of all breaking news topics. Breaking crime news, in particular, rose significantly. Compared to the volume of 24-hour news coverage of crime generally (10 per cent), breaking news about crime generated close to three times more stories (27 per cent). In Chibnall's classic (1977) book, *Law and Order News*, personalisation, simplification and titillation are key crime news values. In breaking news terms, it is immediacy and what Chibnall labels conventionalism – where a crime narrative can be easily shaped and molded into a relevant news package – that will supersede other news values. The episodic nature of crime-related news, in this sense, lends itself to breaking 'new' updates. As a result rolling news coverage will routinely break news about court cases. With a reporter typically located outside the court, the narrative of immediacy is informed by updates either on 'ongoing' news about the trail or a verdict that is 'due any time now'. In a 24-hour news environment, then, what breaking crime stories satisfy are not only values of immediacy and

Table 3.2   Per cent of breaking news topics covered by Sky News and the BBC News channel in 2004 and 2007

Topic	2004	2007
Business/consumer news	8%	8%
Crime	14%	27%
Celebrity/sport/human interest	6%	10%
Politics	9%	8%
Accidents/disasters	6%	20%
Terrorism	27%	9%
Socio-economic issues	8%	4%
Iraq	12%	3%
Other war/conflict	8%	10%
International law/diplomacy	2%	1%
Total	100	100

(Adapted from Lewis and Cushion 2009)

conventionalism but also predictability, in that a news update is always on the horizon. Indeed part of the study systematically mapped whether breaking news stories were predictable (a ministerial announcement, say, or a Champions League football draw) or unpredictable (a natural disaster, say, or a terrorist attack). In 2004, just two in every ten breaking news items fell into the predictable category. By 2007 this had increased to more than a half of all breaking news coverage. This chimes with Livingston and Bennett's (2003) suggestion that event-driven news was increasingly shaping the schedule of 24-hour news channels.

It would be wrong, nevertheless, to suggest breaking news stories are entirely composed of soft news. News about politics, or business or consumer affairs, or international law and diplomacy issues, or more socio-economic stories, between them account for a reasonable share of breaking news traffic (see Table 3.1). However, the longitudinal trend here shows these topics either remained at the same level or decline – in some cases by as much as a half – in volume. What this suggests, overall, is that the decision to cover more breaking news stories is also a decision to increase the agenda of softer news topics – of ongoing crime stories, celebrity, sport and human interest. The shift towards breaking news, in short, represents a retreat from covering harder news stories.

But the definition of a breaking news story appears to be a more contradictory category to define. Despite the high news value that might be attributed to a breaking news story, there was little shared agreement about what constituted a breaking news story on Sky News and the BBC News Channel. The 2007 study found just one in four items over the same period was labelled as breaking news on both channels. The striking divergence in the classification of a breaking news story would appear to suggest it is less a marker of news value and more an arbitrary editorial decision. Since the competition to break news first is central to each channel's ethos, there may be an editorial reluctance to tag a story as 'breaking' if a competitor has already done so. Breaking news, in this context, can almost be seen as a branding exercise, with news channels ferociously scrabbling to add a breaking news strap *first* even if a story is not all that new or significant.

Apart from when there are the big, atypical breaking news stories – the terrorist attacks in New York, Madrid and London, say – when news audiences will significantly rise, most of the time viewers watch 24-hour news channels in short bursts. In doing so, the routine breaking news straps that often trigger coloured on-screen graphics or sound effects may simply pass ordinary viewers by. Since rolling news channels are acutely aware of this, what this suggests is that breaking news stories are marketed not for an average Joe the Plumber but for a more selective niche audience. For much industry currency is based on what the news channels' key elites keep their eye on. Take, for example, Sky News's press office website, which quotes key figures as using the news channel as a constant backdrop to their busy working routines:

> I have two televisions on in my office; one of them is permanently tuned to Sky News. I think its a marvellous product. (Lord Carter, The Minutes of Evidence taken before the Select Committee on Communications, 11 February 2009)

> You will recall that when things happen there is that period of real uncertainty where all of us, in a sense, are watching Sky TV and it would be wonderful if somehow central government really knew better than Sky TV what was going on, but it is hard. (Mr Nicholas Macpherson (Permanent Secretary of the Treasury) Departmental Report, 2005, Minutes of Evidence 16 November 2005)

> Sky News ... a remarkably good service that has managed to use its slimness to wriggle into places other news channels were far too fat for, and it's the station of choice for most print newsrooms. (A.A. Gill, the *Sunday Times*: Culture, 15 February 2004)

> Quotes taken from www.skypressoffice.co.uk/skynews/aboutus/viewsskynews.asp

Whether geared for politicians in the White House or 10 Downing Street, fellow journalists in the online world, or newspapers and magazines, never far from sight at political institutions or crowded newsrooms is the muted television set tuned into one or more news channels.

In appealing to opinion formers, a huge institutional weight is put on the shoulders of news channels to conform to a fast-breaking, rolling news service. Since its inception in 1997, the BBC News channel, in particular, has been at the heart of much political and industry criticism for not keeping up with the pace set by Sky News or not attracting as many viewers. Richard Lambert was appointed by the Labour Government in 2002 to evaluate the BBC News channel's performance. While Lambert suggested the BBC should remain distinctive in some respects, its breaking news policy was interpreted as a little tame and overly cautious at times. To quote Lambert at length:

> Sky has a strong record of being first with the news ... the BBC submission suggests that it is more concerned with accuracy than its competitors, which sometimes makes it hold back on news stories ... An absolute determination to be the first to break accurate news must be at the heart of everything the channel does. It does not matter how sophisticated its analysis may be if news seekers are tuned in somewhere else. (2002: 13–14)

The BBC, in turn, emulated Sky's emphasis on breaking news not only by increasing its use of the convention (Lewis and Cushion 2009) but also by beginning to hype up its semiotic display of breaking news, with a large red strap filling much of the screen when a story broke. Whereas breaking news may have once been reserved for those moments when high drama unfolded – for example, the Boxing Day tsunami in South East Asia, the terrorist attacks in New York, Madrid and London, or the impact of Hurricane Katrina in New Orleans – less memorable events have also filled breaking news traffic. Most notably a bottle-neck whale stuck in the River

Thames in London became the subject of a competitive breaking news event, with Sky and the BBC rushing out helicopters to carry live footage of its eventual demise (see Cushion 2010b).

However, as a consequence of buying into this commercial ethos of breaking news the BBC's values of caution and accuracy have slowly waned over the past decade. The commercial imperatives of breaking drama first has encouraged the BBC to relax its more public service spirited policy on breaking news. In 2005, for example, according to the director of BBC television news, Roger Mosey, its coverage of the terrorist attack in London was to

> get confirmed facts on air immediately but it's true we're cautious about some wire copy or internet-type rumours that we can't substantiate ourselves ... At times ... we were getting 'eyewitness accounts' saying completely contradictory things that couldn't possibly all be true ... [the BBC News channel] ... put on screen what we know is right – reports from our own correspondents, the official emergency service figures and information from members of the public that we've checked out.

If this is compared with how the then head of Sky News, Nick Pollard, interpreted how breaking news story should be handled on 24-hour news channels, there is a striking divergence.

> ... we will tell viewers what we believe is going on, we will attribute every source, claim and figure that we quote. We will also tell viewers what we don't know. I have a feeling that viewers, who are now quite attuned to 24-hour news, understand the rhythm and dynamics of an evolving story and would rather be told what we believe is the detail of an unfolding story, rather than waiting until the whole story is known. (Pollard, cited in Burrell 2005)

For many within the news industry, including Nick Pollard, the BBC's breaking news policy made them slow to report a bomb had exploded – as Sky had done within minutes – and to alert viewers to the terrorist attacks (Burrell 2005). With hindsight, Sky News had beaten its main rival, the BBC, to the finish-line, accurately establishing that a bomb had exploded and a terrorist attack was on the cards. In the aftermath, Sky received much industry praise and further enhanced its kudos for breaking big news first and fastest. But what this breaking news moment also triggered was a shift in the BBC News channel's policy. For the pressure to succumb to rolling news pressure appeared to have encouraged the BBC to relax its breaking news policy and adopt values of speed at the expense of accuracy.

The systemic impact of rolling news journalism: towards 24-hour news values and audience expectations?

Having lived in the shadow of Sky News for many years, senior figures at the BBC were highly sensitive about being seen as 'out of touch' with rolling news journalism. Sky's proclaimed victory in breaking news first when compared to the BBC's more cautious approach to the terrorist attacks in London brought this into sharper focus. The head of BBC News, Peter Horrocks, implied the age of rolling news journalism had begun to change audience expectations of what a 24-hour news service stood for: 'Waiting until there is definitive information is not necessarily the thing that serves the viewer best in that situation. Some of the research we've done in recent months shows that if viewers think we're holding information back it can actually make them more suspicious' (Horrocks, cited in Gibson 2005:1). Helen Boaden, the Director of BBC News, was a little more circumspect, drawing a distinction between the output a 24-hour news channel should provide and a conventional news bulletin:

> In the major bulletins audiences expect a very high level of accuracy and they are very unforgiving if we get things wrong ... But with 24-hour news people understand that stories unfold and change. As long as we are trying as hard as humanly possible to get it right they are happy. (Boaden, cited in Gibson 2005: 1)

If both views represent a retreat from previous breaking news policy where accurate reporting superseded the need for speed, this remains firmly at odds with the BBC's more general editorial guidelines about adhering to strict codes of accuracy. To provide a rough sense of the BBC's editorial principles, the introduction to its accuracy guidelines is worth reflecting on:

> The BBC's commitment to accuracy is a core editorial value and fundamental to our reputation. Our output must be well sourced, based on sound evidence, thoroughly tested and presented in clear, precise language. We should be honest and open about what we don't know and avoid unfounded speculation. For the BBC accuracy is more important than speed and it is often more than a question of getting the facts right. All the relevant facts and information should be weighed to get at the truth. If an issue is controversial, relevant opinion as well as facts may need to be considered.

Rolling news journalism would appear, at least in this context, not only to be fraying the edges of the BBC's editorial guidelines, but also to be making a serious dent in the rules previously established for television journalism to follow. Breaking news, in other words, is even pushing public service broadcasters like the BBC to adopt more conjecture into its reporting of fast-moving events, inviting anchors and reporters to change tack as stories unravel in real-time.

Moreover, this approach to broadcast journalism, by the BBC's own admission, would appear to diminish the chances of achieving high degrees of accuracy. Freed from journalistic constraints such as searching for robust and relevant sources, a story is instead guided by instinct and visual intrigue. The reporter, in this sense, is cast in the role of a cameo sports commentator, watching attentively but reacting excitedly to the slightest twist or turn of a story. Meanwhile, verifying one's sources is the first casualty in the need for speed, since to corroborate and cross reference a key witness or known expert would take time and distract from pursuing the live action. For what appears to be driving the relaxation of breaking news policy, according to senior BBC figures, is the belief that rolling news audiences have become accustomed to – and now almost expect – reporters to be more open and transparent with regard to rumours or speculation. Even when the evidence is thin on the ground or a news channel may simply have chosen the wrong tack, this appears to be mere collateral damage in the pursuit of unfolding breaking news drama.

While the BBC's internal research into rolling television news audiences needs to be more heavily scrutinised, what it suggests is that the generic expectations of a journalist and a news service may well be changing. The pursuit of 'truth', of course, has always been more an aspiration and less an empirical destination. But for all its limitations, the path towards 'truth' has previously been paved with the five W's: the who, what, where, when and why questions. By abandoning these standard journalistic endeavours 'truth' is now, more than ever, a less empirically-grounded concept, anchored by what journalists can *immediately* hear, see, or worse still speculate on. If news audiences expect this from journalists, the genre of television news appears to be moving into new territory. For while television news once did indeed establish 'facts', in this context journalism is about chasing breaking stories, live, on-air, with audiences invited to watch and share in the unfolding drama. In this context rolling news channels are cultivating a new type of spectator sport, delivering live, breaking pictures to viewers who are sharing these as real-time action. But with no clear-cut result or decisive conclusion, how far this satisfies the instincts of a rolling news viewer remains to be seen. The danger, in this sense, is that 24-hour news journalists are responding obligingly by finding immediate answers to complex questions. This view is echoed by an experienced former BBC and ITV journalist who has suggested television reporters are increasingly steering 'the viewer into what to think' without letting them weigh up the facts and figures to draw and reach their own conclusions (Sissons, cited in Brown and Brook 2009).

To understand the changing nature of rolling news audiences, of course, greater understanding into viewers' attitudes towards balancing the need for speed with levels of accuracy is needed. As it stands, there is a limited range of audience studies into what viewers want or how they react to breaking news drama. Using an observational method one US study found breaking news coverage did grab, at least early on, the attention of viewers (Miller 2006). For reasons that are not entirely clear, however, breaking news stories did not sustain the attention of viewers for any longer than non-breaking reports would. A large-scale survey of 18–24 year olds in the US found that breaking news first was not a decisive factor for choosing one news channel over another (Tuggle et al. 2007). In fact, while it was understood live, breaking news brought with it immediacy, many respondents appeared somewhat cynical of stories that did not warrant their breaking news status. The research, however, did show some variations in responses amongst respondents from different parts of the US.

If the impact of 24-hour news channels on viewers' attitudes and understanding of news conventions remains a little hazy, the broader influence of rolling television news journalism *within* the broadcast industry is slightly more tangible. Without the luxury of time, of course, the values and conventions of 24-hour news are not always immediately apparent in conventional news bulletins. The impact, in this sense, is more subtle, more systemic. Routine bulletins, at times, resemble the immediacy and pace of 24-hour news channels whilst not openly embracing all of their conventions. Since bulletins are unable to provide sustained periods of liveness for a lack of time, there nevertheless remains, whenever possible, a strong impulse to go live to a reporter on the ground. Whether standing outside the White House or Number 10 Downing Street, the Supreme Court or the Old Bailey, the quintessential image of a roving television news journalist is a single stalwart soul braving the snow or rain in order to bring live the latest 'vital' developments to viewers.

Since conventional bulletins are always up against the clock, punctuating a half-hour programme with breaking news stories is not an option. Unless something relatively big has happened whilst on-air, very rarely would one witness, for instance, a breaking news strap or news alert light up the screen. To generate a sense of immediacy and inject a greater degree of pace, recent studies have shown bulletins are increasingly turning to conventions of liveness, such as the two-way or what is sometimes known as a 'donut' (Tuggle and Huffman 2001; Lewis et al. 2005). These typically involve an anchor going live to a reporter on location who introduces his or her package and, once finished, provides a live update on the 'latest developments'. Even if nothing necessarily new or newsworthy is discovered, the two-way injects an immediacy that contemporary television journalism finds hard to resist. For the reporter on the ground becomes an ever-important presence, delivering live, on-the-spot views about what has just happened and, more importantly, what lies ahead. This has given rise to 'the correspondent' – who is communicating what is happening on the ground – as opposed to a 'reporter' – who is striving to figure out the facts and get behind the scenes of a story. Retiring from over 30 years in television journalism, Peter Sissons put this well when he suggested his colleagues should

> ... go back to basics. Report on the news ... The term reporter is the noblest word in the language, not this term 'correspondent'. Increasingly, reporters are being invited by reporters to give their opinion. Far too much opinion is creeping into news reporters, with pay-off lines, to steer the viewer into what to think. Let them make up their own minds on the facts. (Cited in Brown and Brook 2009)

The values of 24-hour news channels, in this respect, appear to encourage journalists to make hasty judgments and deliver quick-fit verdicts. Much attention, of course, has been paid to the rise of the television pundit in recent decades (Alterman 2000). But while pundits are often specialist experts – the political, crime or world affairs editor, say – the rise of news channels is forcing less senior journalists, from one day to the next, to impart their wisdom on areas or topics they may know little or next to nothing about.

Of course, not all 24-hour news channels will share the same values or conventions. From a global perspective 24-hour news channels come in all shapes and sizes, making grand generalisations about news channels problematic (Cushion 2010a). While dominant rolling news conventions – the strive to be live, to break news first – have emanated from the US and been imported to other parts of the world (Cushion 2010b; Thussu 2007), how far these have been embraced across different countries remains open to question (see Chapter 6). Nor would it be right to caricature day-to-day, conventional half-hourly bulletins as programmes full of tripe, conjecture, or superficial live fluff. As previously explored, comparative research conducted into the UK's news coverage of conventional news bulletins and rolling news journalism demonstrated that the former contained more contextual and analytical material than the latter. Despite, in theory, being freed from the brevity that conventional bulletins routinely contend with, 24-hour news channels are in the paradoxical position of being constrained by the value of immediacy and the rhythms of producing continual rolling drama.

And yet while television news bulletins remain relatively distinctive from much 24-hour news coverage, there are signs that the values inherent in rolling news journalism are beginning to rub off on them. Where once conventional news bulletins used to primarily consist of pre-packaged stories covering the day's events, the 'thirst to be first' has had a knock-on effect, with news values of speed and spectacle, immediacy and liveness on full display. Montgomery (2007: 66–67) has observed a 'subtle' but increasing convergence between what he calls 'open' (rolling news channels) and 'closed' (half-hourly news bulletins) texts. His detailed analysis of broadcast news is worth quoting at length:

> ... although these two kinds of news discourse – the closed and the open – are rooted in different frameworks of consumption – the relatively focused versus the relatively free-floating, intermittent sampling – the open news structures are emerging as dominant and influential tendencies, ones which have begun to recast the sharpness of the older structures. The emphasis on news from the field and on updates, on constant forward projection through time and to later moments in the programme, seems best understood as a feature of the newer structures now beginning to permeate the whole of broadcast news. (2007: 67)

Even public service broadcasters such as the BBC, as we have already witnessed, are subscribing to the view that breaking news first is, above all, a journalistic necessity in the age of 24-hour television. While the evidence available from rolling news audiences is somewhat flimsy, there appears to be an editorial acceptance that sacrificing a degree of accuracy in a fast-moving breaking news story is a journalistic price worth paying. For in the pursuit of 'immediate truth' and the desire to out-manoeuvre a rival, levels of accuracy represent collateral damage in this breaking news warfare. Time will tell how far these values will begin to shape and infect the wider culture of television journalism or the degree to which news audiences expect live, breaking action in routine bulletins, but rolling news journalism is pushing the editorial boundaries of television news. It remains to be seen whether rolling news journalism will change what audiences expect from television news more generally in the future.

The next chapter, in part, will consider this question. It charts the rise of US cable news channels and new comedy-news formats, asking how much of a wider impact they have had on television news's political coverage and audience consumption habits.

4

THE RISE OF PARTISAN NEWS CONSUMPTION: TOWARDS A POLARISATION OF TELEVISION JOURNALISM AND AUDIENCES?

Network news in retreat: a new era of political journalism?

When television was in its so-called 'golden age', American viewers had just a handful of channels to choose from. Three networks – ABC, NBC and CBS – dominated the airwaves in the 1960s, while in the UK viewers had just BBC1 or ITV. As Chapter 2 showed, in the decades since, these stations had begun to shape the kind of television news conventions and practices that many viewers today have become accustomed. In doing so, television news stations have built up a strong relationship with viewers, cultivating not only trust in their journalism but also a shared sense of national identity. Having established a close rapport with radio listeners during World War II, BBC television, for example, came to embody this most strikingly in its reporting of national ceremonial events such as the Queen's coronation. In the US – where an anchor's personality has often played a far greater role in the presentation of television news – the viewing public invested a great deal of trust in journalists such as Walter Cronkite and Dan Rather. Famously signing off each broadcast with 'That's the way it is', Cronkite, in particular, played a significant part in the rise of CBS News by repeatedly winning most trusted man in America awards. Television viewers, in short, largely believed in the journalism reported and how stories were told.

If we fast forward in time ten years into the new millennium, while there have been some changes in how UK television journalism is viewed and interpreted, it is in the US where we will find that attitudes towards the conventional news formats and anchors have changed remarkably. Of course, viewers have increasingly had a far wider range of news media at their disposal from the 1980s, from cable television channels and radio stations, newspapers and magazines, to online news sources and mobile phone applications. But if we put to one side the proliferation of news media generally, what counts as television news has become increasingly uncertain in recent years (Baym 2010; Delli Carpini and Williams 2001; Jones 2005, 2009). Entertainment and news have gradually become interwoven, redefining a once exclusively 'serious' genre of journalism. Before exploring the shifting boundaries of television news, the changing character of journalism more generally needs to be addressed.

For while the focus of this book is television journalism, its impact cannot be divorced from broader developments. Over the last two decades, the wider culture of news journalism and consumption has been transformed. If cable and rolling news stations were first to deliver an alternative to network news coverage, the advent of online and mobile technologies news accelerated the pace of change within journalism, bringing with it a new breed of political bloggers and enabling greater access to ordinary citizens who wished to air their opinions and vent their frustrations. As the Internet has evolved, tools such as Google alerts, Facebook or Twitter have made the delivery of news more niche by delivering personalised news through someone's choice or because 'friends' – or 'followers' – may have drawn attention to a story. News, in short, had become far more personal and more opinionated.

In this context, conventional US television news bulletins were losing their authority. Because while television news anchors were once the exclusive symbols of trust and credibility within the industry, over many decades viewers have begun investing more trust beyond the three major news networks alone. This was well put in a Pew Report in 2007:

> Two decades ago, the vast majority of Americans had a 'favourite' journalist or news person ... Today, only a slim majority can name the journalist they admire ... the top ten journalists named by the public are drawn from the networks, cable news channels, public television and even Comedy Central. (Pew Research Center for the People and the Press 2007)

What respondents were telling Pew – and other pollsters – was that journalism and journalists were no longer conventionally defined by the three giant network operations. As Morris (2005: 73) has noted, 'Gone are the days when the homogeneous network news programs dominated'. In previous decades television news audiences have been migrating from the big three networks to a range of new channels and emerging television genres (see Lotz 2007). This is well traced in Baym's (2010) *Cronkite to Colbert: The Evolution of Broadcast News*. In the face of intense market competition, Baym has argued that television news networks have all but abandoned their aspirations of fulfilling a Fourth Estate role to inform viewers about the world or meaningfully hold power to account. He has written that:

... a number of transformations – technological, economic, and cultural – would shatter the existing hegemony, loosening ... the network's dominance of the airwaves ... news was recrafted as infotainment, a fusion of genres engineered in the commercial pursuit of audiences now assumed to be consumers, not citizens ... this meant not just the embracing of the techniques and topics of entertainment, but also the privileging of story over actuality, of narrative over the real. (2010: 170–171)

Baym goes on to suggest 'objectivity itself was reconceptualized' by broadcast news more generally in the promise to report 'fair and balanced' journalism. In doing so, claims to accurately represent the world and convincingly tell viewers – as Cronkite once did – 'that's the way it is' at the end of each bulletin, no longer appeared credible or believable. Under pressure to compete in a multichannel and increasingly multimedia environment, television news had started to undergo an identity crisis and – as the next section explores – was to begin searching for new ways to engage audiences.

News audiences go political: which television channels are people watching and why?

By the end of the 1990s three key cable news channels – Fox News, CNN and MSNBC – had emerged and begun chipping away at the networks' stranglehold on the industry. By 2004, '38% of Americans say they regularly watch cable news channels, compared with 34% who regularly watch the nightly news on *one* of three major broadcast networks' (Pew Research Center for the People and the Press 2004; author emphasis). Between 1998 and 2008, the average median prime-time audience for all three channels had increased from roughly 1.25 million viewers to over 3.5 million viewers (Pew Project for Excellence 2009). These figures should not be overestimated in importance, however, since a total of 22 million people were watching the network news evening bulletins. According to the State of the News Media (2010), network viewing of the evening bulletins was 'five times the number of people watching the three cable news channels at any given moment' (Pew Project for Excellence in Journalism 2010).

However, since the early evening news bulletins on the three networks are scheduled at the same time (see Chapter 1), cable news viewers are increasingly capturing a greater share of the market and, more importantly, are also cultivating a new brand of television journalism and gaining politically loyal audiences in the process. As this chapter will argue, when the regulation enforcing broadcasters to be impartial in their news coverage was relaxed in 1987 a new era of political journalism was to develop. No longer obliged to balance political news or comment, this had allowed reporters to morph into commentators, and some – though not all – news outlets began to push broadcast journalism in a more politicised direction.

This is not to suggest, of course, that the Fairness Doctrine could regulate 'objective' journalism or was able to police a non-ideological culture of news production. Far from it, since even in countries with strict impartiality rules shaping broadcast news journalism remains deeply ideological (see Chapter 7). Journalism studies has long established that news can only aspire towards rather than reach something definitively defined as 'objective'. Thus, without wanting to mythologise the Doctrine's influence or recommend a return to the years when the big networks dominated television news, the chapter will argue that the abolition of the Fairness Doctrine has enhanced the ability for broadcast news to pursue a more *explicit* ideological agenda.

The rise in popularity of shock-jock radio hosts such as Rush Limbaugh, a far-right wing commentator, for example, began to draw millions of listeners during the late 1980s and 1990s and, as the new millennium dawned, an army of conservative stations was in force across America (O'Connor and Cutler 2008). In 1996 the Fox News television channel was also to arrive on the scene and, freed from the constraints of delivering impartiality, it began splicing news with opinion and pursuing an explicitly conservative and pro-Republican agenda.

It is difficult to isolate the influence the increasingly partisan nature of journalism evident on some cable network channels had made on its television viewers. Television news, of course, is not consumed in isolation and nor are viewers immune from external influences beyond those of the mass media. But surveys of cable news audiences suggest there is an emerging pattern of partisanship shaping what viewers will most regularly tune into. So, for example, according to a 2004 Pew survey Fox News viewers in 1998 'mirrored the public in terms of both partisanship and ideology'. By 2004, however, this had more than doubled, with 35 per cent of Fox viewers identifying themselves as Republicans. In 2004 CNN – a station largely viewed as liberal or moderate – had more regular Democrat (28 per cent) and independent (22 per cent) than Republican (19 per cent) viewers. While the difference is less striking, there remains more than a hint of partisanship. However, the polarisation of news audiences was not as evident across the board for either cable or network news viewers (see Table 4.1).

If there is an overall pattern of partisanship, it is that the Republican preference for Fox News is stronger than the Democratic one for CNN. Democrats, moreover, routinely view a range of channels on cable (including 21 per cent for Fox) and network news bulletins. In a survey four years later, this picture of partisanship had gained greater momentum. It showed Republicans were, in most cable and network bulletins, less likely to believe in all or most of what a news organisation said than Democrats would (see Table 4.2).

Trust, in other words, was something Republicans reserved primarily for Fox News. The demographic make-up of Fox News, in the space of over a decade, had shifted dramatically. Where once its audience had broadly reflected the political views of the American public, in recent years many would subscribe not only to a more conservative and pro-Republican view of the world, they would also appear to be suspicious of rival channels' coverage, both on cable news channels and in network bulletins.

Table 4.1 Per cent of US viewers who regularly watch news channels who were either Republican, Democrat or Independent in 2004

Channel	Republican	Democrat	Independent
Cable News			
Fox News Channel	35%	21%	22%
CNN	19%	28%	22%
MSNBC	10%	12%	12%
Network News			
NBC Nightly News	15%	18%	19%
CBS Evening News	13%	19%	17%
ABC World News	15%	20%	12%

(Source: Pew Research for the People & The Press 2004 http://people-press.org/report/215/news-audiences-increasingly-politicized)

Table 4.2 Per cent of Republican or Democrat viewers likely to believe in all or most of what a news organisation says in 2008

Channel	Republican	Democrat	Difference between Republican and Democrat
Cable News			
Fox News Channel	34%	19%	15%
CNN	22%	35%	13%
MSNBC	18%	29%	11%
NBC Nightly News	16%	31%	15%
CBS Evening News	18%	26%	8%
ABC World News	19%	28%	9%

(Source: Pew Project for Excellence in Journalism: The State of the News Media 2009 http://stateofthemedia.org/2009/overview/public-attitudes/)

Jamieson and Cappella (2008) have argued in their book, *Echo Chamber,* that right-wing media outlets, such as Rush Limbaugh's radio show, the editorial pages of the *Wall Street Journal,* and the Fox News Channel, have collectively worked together to undermine the credibility of rival news programmes and channels. Accusations of a 'liberal bias', of course, have plagued much of mainstream America's media. What Jamieson and Capella suggested was that more partisan news formats and commentators had created an 'echo chamber' whereby routine criticism of mainstream media and Democrat politics is repeated – or 'echoed' – by right-wing shows and thus legitimised by this repetition. Conversely, more conservative views or Republican policies are repeatedly favoured and a wider Reaganite ideology is promoted and defended. By establishing a rapport with audiences in an 'engaging and entertaining' way, it is argued that big personality figures like Rush Limbaugh have become important opinion formers, making audiences more likely to return for more news they can trust. All of which, Jamieson and Cappella concluded, has cultivated greater hostility not only towards Democrats but also towards the liberal establishment of the mainstream media. As a result, audiences have increasingly been drawn to conservative media, thus limiting their understanding of the world to primarily right-wing outlets. They have written:

> ... the impulse to absorb ideologically agreeable information draws conservative parti-sans to the protective shelter of the conservative media, where reassuring frames of argument decrease their susceptibility to other ideological points of view ... The regu-larly repeated refrain 'liberal media' and the menu of past sins of mainstream omission and commission are central means of ensuring what the conservatives take away from non-exposure to nonconservative sources shores up their ideology. (2008: 237–238)

In making this judgment their analysis is not entirely divorced from the wider social, economic or cultural environment in which news was con-sumed or understood. Needless to say, viewers bring their own ideological baggage and personal prejudices along with them. They are not simply duped into believing that what Fox says goes. But what these right-wing networks appear to have orchestrated, it is argued, is a shared loyalty and trust that ideologically resonates not only with how viewers understand the world but also with what they should reject.

Cable news grew up while journalism was becoming more opinionated and its continued growth – compared to the networks' sharp decline – has been driven by a more partisan pursuit of television viewers. Between 2007 and 2008 nearly a million additional viewers tuned in regularly to cable news networks. However, from 2008 to 2009 their overall growth

Table 4.3 Prime-time audiences on cable news network programmes in 2009

Time	Fox News	CNN	MSNBC
7pm	Fox Report with Shepard Smith (2,075,000m)	Lou Dobbs Tonight (1.328,000m)	Hardball with Chris Matthews (1,175,000)
8pm	O'Reilly Factor (3,771,000m)	Campbell Brown (1,328,000m)	Countdown with Olberman (2,107,000m)
9pm	Hannity & Colmes (2,756,000m)	Larry King Live (1,705,000m)	Rachel Maddow Show (1,826,000m)
10pm	On the Record with Greta Van Suseren (2,468,000m)	Anderson Cooper 360 (1,753,000m)	Olbermann replay (1,156,000m)

(Source: Pew Project for Excellence in Journalism: The State of the News Media 2010 http://stateofthemedia.org/2010/cable-tv-summary-essay/audience/)

was more moderate – 7 per cent, with 3.9 million viewers collectively – suggesting their penetration of the market may have begun to plateau (Pew Project for Excellence 2009). In order to sustain their share of the market, cable news networks have become, according to a Pew report, 'noticeably more partisan in tone in 2009, adding ideological talk show hosts to prime time and shedding dissenting viewers' (Pew Project for Excellence 2010). This reinforces a previous annual report where it was stated 'the fastest-growing shows continued to be personality-driven talk shows' (Pew Project for Excellence 2009). Table 4.3 indicates the coveted prime-time slots on cable news were not reserved for continuous news but for more opinion-led and ideologically-charged programming.

Each programme, of course, has a varying level of adversarialism in their interviewing style and different degrees of partisanship in their agendas. It would be difficult, for example, to compare the mild mannered *Larry King Live* (or even his replacement Piers Morgan) with Bill O'Reilly's aggressively charged show on Fox News (see Conway et al. 2007). To capture the prime-time market, what this shows represents is an increasingly opinionated approach to television news and a more explicit politicisation of its journalism. As Dagnes has stated:

> The primary function of prime time personality programming is that it clearly defines a network, giving it a brand and a direction. Once Fox News Channel gained a significant conservative audience with its personality-driven pundit programming, the rest of Fox News programming followed suit to create the brand we see today. (2010: 81)

Even if not as explicitly partisan as Fox News, other channels – MSNBC and CNN – have followed suit, with more opinions and personality-driven shows. The consequences of this increasing polarisation of television journalism and its audiences will be taken up at the end of this chapter. For now a broader historical context is needed to explain when and why television news was allowed to retreat from conventions of objectivity that had previously been central to television journalism's identity.

Letting the Fox off the leash: the relaxation of the Fairness Doctrine and the 'Foxification' of television news

The rule requiring broadcasters to be impartial in how they covered news and public affairs or to pursue public issues, known as the Fairness Doctrine, was abolished in 1987. In its original incarnation, the rationale behind the Fairness Doctrine was to prevent a relatively small number of media outlets from shaping the kinds of views that could be heard on controversial matters (Croteau and Hoynes 2000). But in a new, multi-channel landscape this had changed. In the words of the FCC, 'it is no longer sustainable in the vastly transformed, diverse market that exists today' to argue that government regulation was needed to achieve media pluralism or tell broadcasters what public issues to report (FCC 1987). Broadcasters were thus freed from their commitment to more serious news agendas and allowed to interpret their own sense of impartiality. Where journalists had previously constructed balance – by the inclusion of opposing voices on healthcare, say, or crime – the removal of the Fairness Doctrine no longer made this mandatory. In addition, the FCC found the Fairness Doctrine to be an affront to free speech. Since the rules within the First Amendment applied to the press – the freedom of expression – it was argued that there should be no preferential treatment of broadcasting as was in place for other countries such as the UK.

As Chapter 2 explored, the Fairness Doctrine began in 1949 – after the FCC had taken on regulatory duties of television – and survived more or less intact despite several legal challenges (Croteau and Hoynes 2000). But as the free-deregulatory spirit grew stronger in the 1980s the number of legal cases mounted. A controversial dispute into reporting whether or not a nuclear power station should be built has been widely seen as *the* legal case that broke the doctrine's back. Finally, in 1987, the FCC withdrew the Fairness Doctrine after Ronald Reagan's intervention, but stipulated 'personal attacks' and 'political editorialising' had to remain prohibited. Thirteen years later these stipulations were also withdrawn. While there was an attempt by the FCC to study the short-term impact of removing these impartiality guidelines, by the end of 2000 television journalism had finally seen off the remaining rules within the Fairness Doctrine (Craig and Smith 2001).

It is something of a myth that the abolition of the Fairness Doctrine in 1987 had immediately triggered the arrival of partisan news channels or, for that matter, talk radio. For it took Fox News close to a decade to launch its news channel and, in the case of talk radio, this had already become well established and had not fallen foul of the doctrine despite one case in the 1960s (this will be explored in a moment). What did immediately change was the sheer number of radio stations that were launched just after the Fairness Doctrine had been abolished. Even if this had a whiff of conspiracy behind it, the rise of conservative talk shows under Ronald Reagan had more to do with available bandwidth and the arrival of new technologies. As Randall (2007) has pointed out, while conservative talk radio was on the ascendancy and 'musical programming fled to higher-fidelity FM signals, AM programmers were left with schedules to fill. At the same time, improvements in satellite technology and cheaper 800-number telephone lines were making national call-in shows more feasible'. In addition radios became nationally syndicated, meaning little known talents like Rush Limbaugh moved from being local stars to nationally recognised voices.

And yet while technology had significantly enhanced the talk radio genre, its widespread appeal could not be entirely apportioned to technological advances. Having been freed from needing to counterbalance controversial debates with woolly liberal commentators, the genre breathed a collective sigh of relief. Even the small radio operations which soon flooded the market could hand jockeys a free rein to vent their grievances without fear of legal reprisal. For while the Fairness Doctrine had, over the years, been more of a deterrent than a brutal regulatory force, there had also been legal precedence, well ahead of the 1980s, to stamp out talk radio's infringement of the Fairness Doctrine. According to Heather Hendershot (2007), pockets of far right-wing talk show hosts from a new evangelicalism movement did emerge in the 1960s, such as Carl McIntire, but 'media studies scholars have ignored him altogether'. A temporarily rejuvenated Fairness Doctrine soon silenced McIntire, however, and discouraged any more vociferous voices before they could establish themselves. After losing his battle, Hendershot argued

> ... the number of stations that would broadcast the show [McIntire's] dwindled rapidly under the threat of the Fairness Doctrine enforcement. Indeed, as nervous stations dropped McIntire's show, they also increasingly lessened their support of other right-wing programs ... the ruling against McIntire nipped the sixties renaissance of right wing broadcasters in the bud, and it was only following the demise of the doctrine that broadcasters like Rush Limbaugh and Bill O'Reilly would later come into their own. (2007)

How far broadcasters right across the US feared the backlash of the Fairness Doctrine is difficult to assess. But once the doctrine was consigned to history, it would be hard to imagine the genre of talk radio not having a renewed zeal to exploit what could be said or to see what influence it could wield. For when politicians have since suggested the Fairness Doctrine should be repealed, Rush Limbaugh and other right-wing commentators have been quick to label it a 'Hush Rush' law, testifying to Rush Limbaugh's wider impact on radio and his *perceived* exploitation of the Fairness Doctrine.

The backdrop of Rush Limbaugh's rise in prominence and popularity is important to the development of Fox News and, in subsequent years, the creeping partisanship of television journalism more generally, since Fox News did for television news what Rush Limbaugh did for talk radio – namely exploit the relaxation of impartiality guidelines and push journalism in a more politicised direction. To put it more colourfully, the FCC had chosen to let Fox off the leash to run wild without regulation. In doing so Fox News has not only promoted a Republican and conservative agenda by engaging a growing army of loyal viewers, it has also demonised the Democrat Party and undermined the credibility of the mainstream media more generally (Jamieson and Cappella 2008). As Dagnes (2010: 81) has put it, 'By asserting a liberal bias in the rest of the mainstream media, Fox News has carved for itself a niche audience of conservative viewers'. Despite its coy insistence on being 'Fair and Balanced', studies were soon to find evidence of Fox News's Republican partisanship after its launch in 1996 (Ackerman 2001; DellaVinga and Kaplan 2006; *Outfoxed* 2004). During the 2000 presidential elections, for example, DellaVinga and Kaplan's (2006) study concluded that up to 8 per cent of viewers may have been persuaded to vote Republican after regularly watching Fox's coverage. And according to one inside account of the White House, journalist Bob Woodward (2004) was able to witness the head of Fox News advising Karl Rove, the Republican party's chief spin doctor.

It is worth noting that Fox's ascendancy to America's most watched news channel was to begin during its coverage of the second Gulf War in 2003. While American news media have often displayed their patriotism during wars, conflicts and terrorist attacks (Zelizer and Allan 2011), during the invasion of Iraq Fox News was to hype up its coverage and conventions to huge jingoistic effect. When France vetoed a UN sanction against the invasion, Fox News's coverage turned decidedly anti-French. Needless to say, when reports of US senators renaming their French fries at the Congress's cafeteria to 'Freedom Fries' emerged, Fox News prominently ran with the story. Likewise, when millions all around the world protested against the war in Iraq, Fox News's coverage was fairly minimal and, at times, dismissive of the protestors' motivations. This was not done subtly or discreetly. As a Fox News executive put it, 'But a lot of these protestors now are International Workers Party Members and socialists ... If you don't support the decision to go to war, once the decision has been made, you're not being patriotic' (Hill, cited in Farhi 2003: C7).

During the conflict itself Fox was unashamedly pro-war, with a US flag waving permanently on-screen next to a tagline reading 'Operation Iraqi Freedom'. Fox's correspondents, many of whom were embedded with US forces, referred to US military personnel as 'our troops'. There was, in other words, no pretence about objectively covering the war (see Cushion 2012 for more detail). According to Ryan (2006: 17), compared to other cable news and networks, 'Fox News once again took the lead in reinforcing the "us versus them" dichotomy'. Again, this is not something Fox News appear to contest. Jerry Burke, a Fox News executive producer, has said:

> I encourage the anchors to be themselves. I'm certainly not going to step in and censor an anchor on an issue ... you don't want to look at a cookie-cutter, force feeding of the same items hour after hour. I think that's part of the success of the channel, not treating our anchors like drones. They're, number one, Americans, and number two, human beings, as well as journalists. (Cited in Kutz 2005)

A Pew Project For Excellence in Journalism study showed that in Fox News's coverage of the Iraq war in 2004 73 per cent of war reporting contained opinions from anchors and journalists, whilst 29 per cent did so on MSNBC and just 2 per cent on CNN. Fox News's reporting not only shone a partial light on the war, it also left many viewers in the dark about the broader reasons for why the invasion of Iraq took place. This, of course, had important political consequences since it encouraged audiences to focus on military actions rather than the justification of the war. In doing so, surveys showed regular viewers of Fox News's explicitly pro-war coverage, when compared to audiences' knowledge of rival news channels, tended to be far more misinformed about the reasons for why the invasion of Iraq went ahead (Kull 2003). This was not down to them being inattentive or distracted television viewers. They found the more Fox News was watched, the *less* informed viewers would be about why the war was being waged.

All in all, Fox News pioneered with considerable gusto a far more partisan promotion of war coverage than television journalism had previously been accustomed. In doing so, audiences for Fox News spiked significantly during the conflict and the channel has since remained the most watched news channel. With competition rife the nature of Fox News's war coverage appeared to have a ripple effect, with competing cable channels adopting some of its conventions. In order to compete on Fox's explicitly patriotic terrain, MSNBC, for example, appeared to be sourcing more pro-war and conservative sources without any counterbalancing views being proffered (Schiffers 2003). And meanwhile, in the graphics department, as with Fox News a US flag became an on-screen presence with 'a special section called "America's Bravest", where viewers could send pictures of their loved ones serving in the armed forces in Iraq' being introduced (Schiffers 2003). By this time the 'Fox Effect' or 'Foxification' had become part of the journalistic lexicon and debates about how much impact the news channel was having began to increase. A columnist for the *Washington Post*, William Raspberry (2005), claimed:

> The in-your-face right-wing partisanship that marks Fox News Channel's news broadcasts is having two dangerous effects. The first is that the popularity of the approach – Fox is clobbering its direct competition (CNN, CNBC, MSNBC, etc.) – leads other cable broadcasters to mimic it, which in turn debases the quality of the news available to that segment of the TV audience. The second, far more dangerous, effect is that it threatens to destroy public confidence in all news.

Likewise, Andrew Heyward, President of CBS News, warned 'I certainly think all the news people are watching the success of Fox … There is a long-standing tradition in the mainstream press of middle-of-the-road journalism that is objective and fair. I would hate to see that fall victim to the Fox effect' (cited in Schiffers 2003).

What the 'Fox Effect' – or Foxification – encapsulates is the imitation of Fox News's journalistic values, conventions and partisanship for financial gain or ideological muscle. As opposed to striving for balance or objectivity, Foxification pushes journalism towards more comment, speculation and politicisation. In some respects, the term 'dumbing-down' is often invoked to characterise similar trends. But while 'Foxification' embraces much of what the 'dumbing-down' charge represents, the 'Fox Effect' more explicitly raises questions about the relationship between political coverage, ownership and regulation. For since Fox's well known right-wing owner, Rupert Murdoch, launched the Fox News channel, it has fully exploited the abolition of the Fairness Doctrine and challenged the orthodoxy that television journalism should not be ideologically driven. Foxification, in other words, demonstrates how an increasingly deregulatory television culture can shape a highly partisan and politicised public sphere.

While Fox may be the purveyor of television journalism's polemic turn, in more recent years some stations have tried to adopt a more liberal line in their journalism. By 2009, Foxification had cast its spell most potently over one channel. According to the 2010 Pew American News report, MSNBC is the 'mirror image of Fox' in so far as taking on a 'role as a left-leaning prime time channel' (Pew Project for Excellence 2010). What this suggests is that while cable news channels may appear to favour either left- over right-wing views or support Republican policies over those of the Democrats, the prevailing trends of partisanship have more do with financial gain than ideological instinct. Put another way, the proliferation of television news sources and more intense market competition appears to have encouraged news channels to adopt a partisan news agenda.

The decision to end the Fairness Doctrine, of course, was to deliver greater freedom of speech and dispel claims of a so-called 'chilling effect' preventing controversial issues from being tackled. Where once a handful of news bulletins dominated the airwaves, in an age of media choice the FCC argued a multiplicity of news outlets could sustain a diversity of viewpoints in the public sphere. But as this section has shown, what did transpire was the popularity of polemic views – first with talk radio, then with Fox News, and now more recently with MSNBC – which had a paradoxical effect: it narrowed the diversity of voices by promoting the loudest and most prejudiced approach to television journalism. This was at its most vociferous during coverage of the Iraq war where Fox's highly patriotic framing of television news saw its audience numbers spike. Abandoning any journalistic aspiration to report the Iraq war impartially, Fox News began to gain partisan appeal with its audiences increasingly being made up of Republican or conservative viewers. In doing so, it appeared to make viewers more hostile to other rival news media, which it often chastised for being overtly liberal and pro-Democrat. Fox's claim to bring 'fair and balanced' journalism was, in a sense, a mission to counterbalance what it perceived as a liberal or left-wing bias that was prevalent in much of America's mainstream media.

But the partisan nature of television journalism has not been consigned to conventional cable news programming. For while Fox News may have cornered the conservative market, the success of the strongest liberal voice and influence in television journalism has arguably been on the comedy circuit with prime-time shows such as *The Daily Show* and *The Colbert Report*. The next section explores how news and comedy programming have begun to blur the lines of political journalism on television.

Redefining political news journalism: blurring the lines between news and comedy

To much fanfare, a 2009 *Time* online poll found that Jon Stewart – a comedian presenting *The Daily Show* – was *the* most trusted newscaster, well ahead of the more conventional anchors from the three networks, Brian Williams (NBC), Charlie Gibson (ABC) and Katie Couric (CBS). While the poll was far from being a representative survey, it alerted the wider industry to how comedians such as Jon Stewart were beginning to redefine what a journalist was and which television programmes and formats audiences were increasingly putting their trust in. Not only were the cable news networks pushing television journalism into a more politicised arena, comedy programming had also started to engender widespread trust and credibility.

The Daily Show began life under Craig Kilborn in 1996, but three years later it was taken over by Jon Stewart who introduced more content and humour about politics. The show's influence was soon demonstrated, with politicians like John Kerry desperate to appear on the programme during the 2004 presidential elections. Mixing news with comedy, it gained a certain notoriety for providing a satirical twist to political journalism, thereby challenging the long-held conventions and practices that had been associated with how politics should be covered on mainstream television. Stewart's influence on political news has since impacted on the wider culture of television journalism. Appearing on an episode of *Crossfire* – a CNN programme where guests are vigorously quizzed by aggressive pundits on both the left and the right – Stewart attacked the highly partisan way the show aimed to invigorate debate. Pleading with the interviewers' to tone down their fast-paced 'partisan hackery' and adopt a friendlier, more rational and civilised approach to political discussions, Stewart humiliated both them and in the process the very premise of the programme. Concerned about damaging CNN's reputation as a neutral broadcaster, *Crossfire* – a show then spanning 23 years (1982–2005) – was brought to an end just a few months later. Whether this was entirely down to Stewart is not clear but the lasting impression was that CNN appeared to be part of the old-guard establishment which was unable to reach out to those same viewers that Stewart and other comedians were connecting with.

Because while young people were turning off network news programming, Stewart's approach to covering politics was appealing to many younger audiences. A Pew report showed close to a quarter of 18–34 year olds regularly learned about the 2004 presidential elections by watching comedy programmes (Pew Research Center for the People and Press 2004). Within the wider journalistic community, whether a comedy format should constitute a serious or legitimate source of news became a much debated topic. Feldman (2007) has explored how journalists had reacted to and reported on the impact of *The Daily Show* from 1999–2004. She found that trade journals such as *American Journalism Review, Columbia Journalism Review, The Quill,* and *Editor & Publisher* had barely mentioned Jon Stewart. By contrast, news about the programme was far more widespread in the popular press and on news networks. Feldman (2007: 421) suggested this reflected the editorial line of each genre: while trade journals saw *The Daily Show* as soft news territory the popular press and networks did not feel threatened and instead embraced it by reflecting on how 'comedy and entertainment need not be incompatible with substantive journalism'. She has also argued that 'journalists' admiration for and envy of Jon Stewart reveal a deep consideration of what it means to be a journalist and of the weaknesses perceived in aging journalistic conventions' (2007: 421). This opinion was not, of course, shared by the entire journalistic community. But at the very least, late night comedies had sparked a debate about how effectively television journalism was communicating politics to its viewers.

Within academic circles, scholars have grappled with the relative merits of mixing comedy and news, and about how far shows such as *The Daily Show* can be accepted as a legitimate form of television journalism and as a progamme that enhances democratic dialogue and deliberative debate. At a November 2006 National Communication Association conference in San Antonio the role of Jon Stewart on *The Daily Show* triggered a lively argument after a conference paper mockingly tried him for a crime against democracy. The charge – 'unbridled political cynicism' (Hart and Hartelius 2007: 263) – was rigorously opposed by members of the audience (Bennett 2007; Hariman 2007) and the proceedings were published in the journal, *Critical Studies in Media Communication. The Daily Show* was accused of 'making cynicism atmospheric, a mist that hovers over us each day' (Hart and Hartelius 2007: 264). Rather than engaging viewers in a constructive way about contemporary political discourse, according to Hart and Hartelius (2007) Stewart was too full of contempt and/or cynicism to propose alternative agents of change. Drawing on classical forms of Cynicism, they argued that 'Our basic contention is that Stewart's antics let him evade critical interrogation, thereby making him a fundamentally anti-political creature. Stewart does not stimulate a polis to have new and productive thoughts; like his ancient predecessor, he merely produces inertia' (2007: 264).

This apparently provoked much contention and a 'packed, rowdy' audience of academics rose to the defence of Stewart and his comedic contemporaries (Lule 2007: 262). Bennett (2007: 279), for example, argued that 'Stewart does not offer us cynicism for its own sake, but as a playful way to offer the kinds of insights that are not permitted in more serious news formats that slavishly cling to official accounts of news'. Hariman (2007) likewise agreed, stating *The Daily Show*'s humouristic conventions made political news more meaningful since it unpacked much of the spin and empty rhetoric espoused by the political and media classes. He stated 'Stewart's display of cynicism is valuable today because it is one of the few effective antidotes to a deeply cynical political culture' (2007: 275).

Despite Stewart's attempt to define *The Daily Show* strictly within the generic realms of comedy, scholars have compared its content with that of news network and cable programming. Fox et al.'s (2007) study suggested it remained on a par with the networks' nightly coverage of the 2004 political conventions, containing more or less the same level of substantive information. Brewer and Marquardt's (2007) content analysis showed that in 2005 almost half of *Daily Show* stories were about world affairs. Far from it being soft news, what these studies suggest is the programme addresses hard news topics that may even elude the supposedly more highbrow networks. Baym has written extensively about the comedy show's foray into television news territory (Baym 2005, 2007a, 2007b, 2010) and more widely about finding authoritative models for engaging viewers in politics (Baym 2007a). *The Daily Show*, in Baym's reckoning, offers a 'reinvention of journalism' that can 'revive a journalism of critical inquiry and advance a model of deliberative democracy' (2005: 259). His (2010) book, *From Cronkite to Colbert: The Evolution of Broadcast News*, argues that in splicing together news and comedy conventions some comedy programmes have been able to produce a high-modernist form of journalism that is reminiscent of the days when authoritative figures such as Walter Cronkite were on air. Since then viewers have gradually lost faith with how the networks have covered politics and public affairs. Stephen Colbert and Jon Stewart's emergence, in this context, had delivered 'a hybrid form of truth telling and public dialogue' by deconstructing contemporary political rhetoric and news practices in a cynical yet more meaningful way to media savvy viewers who had grown up dealing with the spin and froth of mainstream media and politicians (Baym 2010: 167).

In conveying *The Daily Show*'s humour, Jon Stewart has always maintained it provides nothing more than 'fake news'. It should not, in other words, share the same democratic weight or significance apportioned to television news journalism. When challenged about his own journalistic qualifications, Stewart has been quick to remind viewers that he works in comedy and not the television news industry. By parodying mainstream news conventions or mocking the rhetoric of party politics, *The Daily Show* perpetuates this position by appearing as an oppositional voice to the institutions being satirised. At the same time, however, Stewart has been a victim of his own success. In connecting with such a large and loyal television viewership across the US, according to Baym (2005, 2010) the programme has become more 'real news' for many viewers than that shown on many network or cable news channels.

In order to achieve this, Baym has suggested *The Daily Show* has rejected many of the conventions that have turned people away from watching network news. Thus, for example, while many television news outlets rely heavily on official accounts of the world, often uncritically accepting what is created by government spin-doctors, *The Daily Show* questions the wisdom and caricatures the practices of conventions such as the quick-fix sound bites used to inform viewers about the world. Baym (2010: 111) has highlighted that 'In an age in which few power holders are willing to speak clearly and honestly, *The Daily Show* uses humor as a license to confront political dissembling and misinformation and to demand a measure of accountability'. Much attention has been paid to Stewart's interviewing style in this respect, where serious topics are addressed but humour is often employed whilst interrogating guests about an issue. Likewise, Stewart's sidekick, Stephen Colbert, has sought to challenge – or undermine – the conventions of authority via mock interviews. Taking the position of a partisan hack typically associated with figures like Bill O'Reilly, in a segment of his *Colbert Report* show, 'Better Know a District', politicians from the House of Representatives are interviewed ostensibly to learn about what they do and what it is they stand for. While some of the questions posed do contain substantive information about political affairs, for the most part they encourage politicians to be reactionary or are designed to expose them as dull or in order to generate a cheap retort. In doing so, some scholars have suggested it makes watching politics a more humorous and pleasurable pastime, and 'illustrates the possibilities of emerging hybrid forms to offer novel and much needed ways of conceptualizing, confronting, and creating political media' (Baym 2007b: 374). For Meddaugh (2010: 386) also, the *Colbert Report* challenges 'the rational practices and normative values of traditional information industries' and 'operates as a critic of the press, as well as a unique site of media literacy education'.

And yet while there have been an increasing array of scholarly readings into comedy's new found romance with mainstream politics, evidence to support claims that they enhance media literacy or advance democratic dialogue have been less forthcoming. There have, nevertheless, been some attempts to quantitatively measure who watches comedy shows and how much impact these have had on viewers' political engagement, understanding and knowledge of mainstream politics. While the stereotypical image of a late-night comedy viewer might be distinctively apolitical, Young and Tisinger's (2006) analysis of national surveys paints a picture of a far more politically savvy consumer. They concluded that contrary to popular wisdom, young people are not watching late-night comedy as their exclusive source of news or instead of traditional news. Rather, they are watching both. In fact, watching late-night comedy is positively and significantly correlated with watching almost all forms of traditional news examined here, even when controlling for variables.

Likewise, in a poll analysis during the 2004 presidential primary season, Feldman and Young (2008) found late-night audiences routinely tuning into comedy programming were more likely to watch other network and cable news channels than viewers who did not. They also found comedy viewers' attention to election news appeared to gain momentum over the campaigns and was greater than for those audiences who did not watch it.

Large-scale surveys have shown *The Daily Show* and other political comedy shows have encouraged previously inattentive or less politically motivated viewers to engage with mainstream news media (Cao 2010; Xenos and Becker 2009). This is not something necessarily desired or consciously recognised by viewers. Baum's surveys of soft news audiences – including those for *The Daily Show* – revealed they search primarily for 'entertainment, not enlightenment' (2003a: 187). But in doing so this provides what has become known as a 'gateway effect' (Baum 2003b; Young and Tisinger 2006) whereby regular viewers appear to be encouraged to tune into other political programming. The long-term effects of gateway viewing – such as sustaining meaningful behavioural patterns including political understanding, efficacy or engagement – are not entirely clear. Even after receiving much scholarly attention, for Cao (2010: 43) this 'mixed evidence suggests that it may be too early to draw a definitive conclusion and the potential effect of *The Daily Show* and other late-night shows on the democratic system in the US'. It is necessary, in this context, to distinguish between many of the late-night shows that fill US television schedules.

Young and Tisinger (2006) also managed to shed light on a revealing insight that was unique to viewers of *The Daily Show* when they were compared to those for other late-night shows – the less politically partisan like David Letterman's and Jay Leno's – about audience consumption. They have shown:

> *The Daily Show* follows a pattern more akin to traditional political information consumption than to consumption of purely entertainment-orientated media … *The Daily Show* should be considered – in the sprit of *Monty Python* – something *completely* different: a program designed to entertain but that functions predominantly as a political program. (Young and Tisinger 2006: 128)

What this suggests is that while the programme might encourage audiences' further engagement with the news media's coverage of politics and public affairs, viewers may also be indulging in *The Daily Show*'s (largely) pro-liberal comic values as opposed to a broader appreciation of its political humour.

For if *The Daily Show* is seen to eschew political partisanship, a systematic content analysis found it attacking the Republicans more so than the Democrats over an extended period.

> Republicans in 2007 tended to bear the brunt of ridicule from Stewart and his crew. From July 1 through November 1, Stewart's humor targeted Republicans more than three times as often as Democrats. The Bush Administration alone was the focus of almost a quarter (22%) of the segments in this time period.
>
> The lineup of on-air guests was more evenly balanced by political party. But our subjective sense from viewing the segments is that Republicans faced harsher criticism during the interviews with Stewart. Whether this is because the show is simply liberal or because the Republicans control the White House is harder to pin down. (Pew Research Center for Excellence in Journalism 2008)

Depending on how one interprets it, *The Daily Show*'s either anti-Republican tendencies or pro-Democrat sympathies could be fuelling the motivation of its loyal fan base. Of course, as LaMarre et al.'s (2009) experimental study of Republican and Democrat consumption of *The Stephen Colbert Report* has demonstrated, any impact may be minimal since both groups bring their own biases to how they interpret Colbert's satire. In this context, the audience reception of politics is shaped by each viewer's individual ideological instinct as opposed to the comedian's. Morris's (2009) study suggested a greater degree of influence, however, at least for regular *Daily Show* viewers. In his analysis of the programme during the 2004 national party seasons, coverage was more critical of the Republican Party rather than the Democrats. Drawing on audience panel data of the impact this had on viewers, Morris (2009: 99) concluded that 'watchers of the Daily Show became increasingly hostile toward President Bush and Vice-President Cheney, while attitudes toward John Kerry and John Edwards remained very consistent'. The *Daily Show*'s pro-Democrat humour or comment, in other words, cultivated *increased* partisanship amongst Republican viewers.

More research, in this respect, is needed to assess whether *The Daily Show* or other political comedy programming are encouraging partisanship among American television audiences. But even if *The Daily Show* is not actively cultivating anti-Republican attitudes, a detailed report into the political typology of American news/political shows found barely any staunch conservatives regularly tuned in to watch it (Pew Research Center for the People and the Press 2011: 43). Moreover, the report found audiences more generally tended to watch programmes ideologically similar to their own views:

> Some of the broadest gulfs between typology groups in terms of media consumption can be found for specific programs. Staunch Conservatives are more than twice as likely as any other typology group to say they regularly watch or listen to Glen Beck (23%) [on

Fox News] and Rush Limbaugh (21%). At the same time, 21% of Solid Liberals...are regular viewers of The Daily Show with Jon Stewart, the highest percentages among the typology groups. (Pew Research Center for the People and the Press 2011: 44)

Consciously tuning in to television programming that reflects people's own political persuasions is known as 'partisan selective exposure' (see Stroud 2008). Since some television news stations have become more explicitly partisan in recent years, it has become easier for audiences to 'channel surf' and cherry-pick programmes more politically attuned to their interests and beliefs. But this approach to news consumption could have profound implications for how people routinely make sense of politics and public affairs. So, for example, Stroud's (2010: 569) cross sectional survey of media use during the 2004 presidential elections found 'partisan selective exposure contributes to political polarization'. While there are many possible factors that could influence polarised political attitudes, the role of political comedy shows such as *The Daily Show* was not part of the analysis.

Despite the innovative ways in which political comedy news shows have engaged audiences in the democratic process, it could be that they are polarising television news audiences along partisan grounds. This raises similar questions to Fox News's partisan coverage of politics, which has been roundly condemned by scholars for abandoning any sense of objectivity. While *The Daily Show* is clearly not a comical version of Fox – it is, after all, on the comedy network and focuses on 30 minutes of entertainment largely critiquing other news media rather than developing its own newsgathering – the difference in format should not prevent a comparison about the changing culture of news and political discourse in the US. For while many scholars and journalists (even Jon Stewart himself) might be reluctant to call *The Daily Show* a 'news' programme, whether they like it or not some viewers are interpreting it as 'news' and its presenter as a journalist (Feldman 2007; Pew Research Center for the People and the Press 2007).

The next section explores scholarly readings into new forms of political television news programming.

Making sense of comedy news: scholarly readings into 'popular' political programming

As LaMarre et al. (2009: 212) have pointed out, 'there has been a surge of political entertainment studies within mass communication' in recent years. Scholarly *readings* of how late-night political output like *The Daily Show* has enhanced democratic knowledge and engaged viewers in politics have, on balance, outweighed those suggesting it trivialises political news or promotes cynical attitudes towards politicians. Since these political comedy shows operate at a far more sophisticated level than network or cable news broadcasting, appealing to media savvy audiences in a pleasurable and entertaining format, it is perhaps easy to see why 'for many academics, Stewart is a savior, an emblem of the subversive, take-no-prisoners attitude needed to comfort the afflicted and afflict the comfortable' (Hart and Hartelius 2007: 264). It has almost become academically fashionable to argue figures like Stewart represent a more effective and engaging Fourth Estate role than much mainstream news media.

The gradual encroachment of popular culture into the political sphere, of course, has attracted a great deal of scholarly attention in recent decades (Delli Carpini and Williams 2001; Jones 2005, 2009; Street 1996, 2001, 2010; Van Zoonen 2005). For Delli Carpini and Williams (2001: 161), the rise of new media and the prominence of popular culture have made 'the very distinction between news and nonnews increasingly untenable'. Whereas much of the world of entertainment was marginalised from academic scrutiny prior to the 1990s, scholars such as John Street (2001: 79) still sought to 'look beyond the traditional corrals of news and current affairs, and to analyse the ways in which political values and the representation of politics are part our daily routines'. This was part of a wider trend where traditional values of high or low, popular or quality were being broken down by cultural relativists (Hartley 1996; Langer 1998; Sparks and Tulloch 2000). Book-length explorations of new types of political media such as television shows (Baym 2010; Jones 2005, 2009) and internet fan sites (Van Zoonen 2005; cf. Van Zoonen 2007) began speculating on how this might reshape democratic culture and citizenship. A new wave of scholars, freed from the shackles of studying serious or highbrow journalism, were arguing that 'Entertaining Politics' (Jones 2005) was making citizenship a more exciting and pleasurable experience (Van Zoonen 2005).

In doing so, it has brought popular communication into the mainstream of disciplines such as journalism studies and political communication with a range of compelling readings into what new forms of political media could democratically achieve. But while it would be difficult to argue against much of what these scholars have observed, what counts as being 'politically' significant or democratically promising has increased in recent years as media continue to proliferate. In this context, it is worth reflecting on Stephen Harrington's (2008a, 2008b) intervention that a new critical approach to the study of popular news is needed. Although Harrington is primarily arguing the case for political comedy shows such as *The Daily Show* to be taken more seriously in journalism studies, his framework for evaluating the 'quality' of news can equally be applied to how one might critique the contribution comedy news programmes make to democratic culture. To quote him at length:

> We should not simply pass something off merely because it is popular – or indeed emotional, feminine, personal, sensational, and so on … or because it does not conform to the key textual features of journalism, but gather a critique around *what information* is being used

in this way. 'For what purpose?', journalism and cultural studies academics should ask, and, perhaps, 'in whose interests?', rather than the less important – and, in fact, far more easily answered – textual question of 'how … ?'. This way we can acknowledge what popular news offers, but not be blind to the pitfalls that can often come with it. (2008a: 279)

It is, in this spirit, where the limits of shows like *The Daily Show* or *The Colbert Report* can be critiqued. While the former may 'revive a journalism of critical enquiry and advance a model of deliberative democracy' (Baym 2005: 259), in order to do so it tends to favour one political party over another and rarely attempts to balance conflicting perpectives on an issue or story. For deliberation is encouraged (with humour and informative interviews) but underlying much of *The Daily Show's* content is anti-Republican jokes and ridicule (e.g. Pew Research Center for the Project for Excellence in Journalism 2008). Far from marking a radical departure from cable news channels (e.g. MSNBC and Fox News), the effect of new political comedy programming like *The Daily Show* appears to be replicating editorial strategies to appeal to audiences ideologically. Even if many Americans (or academics) may interpret this as a welcome left-leaning counterbalance to the right-wing bias of Fox News, what it reinforces is the emerging trend of supplying political media that are ideologically consistent with the values audiences already hold. Journalism, in other words, is pushed towards *informing* (which MSNBC and Fox would claim) or *entertaining* (which *The Daily Show* and *The Colbert Report* would claim) viewers about politics and public affairs in increasingly partisan ways.

Whether informative or entertaining, what this new form of journalism retreats from are values of objectivity that have conventionally defined journalistic norms of professionalism (Schudson 1995; Tuchman 1972). While comics like Colbert mock right-wing figures by claiming 'Truthiness' – a term characterising how truth is often defined on intuitive rather than empirical grounds – as an increasingly legitimated source of 'popular news', in doing so he perpetuates the distance between journalism and 'truth'. For media scholars, this may be seen as a welcome form of media literacy. As many journalism students first learn, news is far from being a 'window on the world' and its semiotic attempts to reflect 'reality' should be readily exposed and challenged (Fiske 1987). If new forms of television news were, in this sense, promoting a polysemic view of the world that invited multiple ways of understanding an issue or event, it would be difficult to argue against the merits of those programmes where self-reflexive journalism was encouraged. But what these new forms of television news appear to be encouraging is a polarisation of audiences and, depending on what channel you are watching, the cultivation of either an explicitly Republican or Democrat 'window on the world'. There are, of course, times when liberal shows will challenge Democrats and conservatives will attack Republicans. So, for example,

Jon Stewart's *Daily Show* has been critical of President Obama's time in office despite championing his presidential campaign (Harris 2010). But rather than reflecting a retreat from partisanship, this could be viewed as Stewart expressing a wider liberal disapproval at Obama's cautious brand of conservative politics.

Coe et al.'s (2008) study of viewers' perceptions of CNN, Fox News and *The Daily Show* demonstrated how, irrespective of whether it was a conventional news programme or a political comedy show, audiences were hostile to politics they disagree with and would claim bias in its coverage. At the same time, they also appeared to be more comfortable with and trustworthy towards television news that replicated their own politics. They concluded that

> When exposed to programs thought to align with their own political perspective, viewers were more likely to find the content interesting and informative ... viewers are likely to select news programs they think will align with their partisan perspective ... the world of cable news is increasingly one in which partisanship is a driving force. (Coe et al. 2008: 216)

The convergence towards a favoured and familiar ideologically-slanted agenda, in other words, is increasingly shaping television news consumption.

It is perhaps easy to draw conclusions about media influence here. This chapter has shown how the abolition of the Fairness Doctrine enabled television news to self-regulate, thereby allowing channels like Fox to slip their leash and report journalism without enforcing norms of objectivity. At the same time, the wider proliferation of media – most notably the rise and influence of the Internet (itself a largely unregulated medium) – has helped legitimise the convergence towards politically partisan channels. The blogosphere, for example, has put more credible extremist voices into the political public sphere that are regularly used as reliable sources in television and print journalism. As with television viewing, online news users appear to be just as partisan in how they consume and respond to competing media sources. Iyengar and Hahn's experimental (2009) study of online news audiences found partisan affiliations shaped their reception and understanding of journalism. Put simply, they discovered that 'conservatives and Republicans preferred to read news reports attributed to Fox News and to avoid news from CNN and NPR. Democrats and Liberals exhibited exactly the same opposite syndrome – dividing their attention equally between CNN and NPR, but avoiding Fox News'. Of course, not all television news bulletins (ABC, NBC and CBS) have explicitly pursued a partisan agenda. However, the Pew data suggest that while audiences for the networks have declined year-on-year in previous decades the partisan channels have grown and sustained their regular viewing figures. The increasing choice of television news has, in short, pushed audiences into right- or left-leaning ideological camps.

At the same time, the broader social, economic and political forces in American society cannot be divorced from making sense of this prevailing trend of partisan television viewing. In *Big Sort: Why the Clustering of Like-Minded America Is Tearing Us Apart*, Bishop and Cushing (2008) drew on a range of social science research to demonstrate how Americans have not only become increasingly polarised in the sorts of media they consume but also in where they choose to live or who they decide to socialise with. Tracing a wide range of social trends, economic patterns and political changes since the 1960s, they have argued citizens have become segregated into largely liberal and conservative communities for a multiplicity of reasons. This relates not only to which news they seek out but also to the religion they practise, the politics they champion, the charities they volunteer for, and so on. The consequences of all this, they have suggested, are profound: 'Balkanized communities whose inhabitants find other Americans to be culturally incomprehensible; a growing intolerance for political differences that has made national consensus impossible; and politics so polarized that Congress is stymied and elections are no longer just contests over polices, but bitter choices between ways of life' (Bishop and Cushing 2008: 14). Television news, in other words, cannot be exclusively blamed for the ideological relationship viewers are increasingly forging with news programmes and channels. At the same time, however, this chapter has suggested that the relaxation of impartiality regulation may have exacerbated or, at least, reinforced a culture where ideological choices not only inform where people live (Bishop and Cushing 2008) but also which television news channels they routinely tune into.

The final section of this chapter examines the implications of an increasingly polarising news culture. Beforehand the prospect of Fox-style journalism being imported to the UK's television journalism is explored.

Keeping the Fox on a leash: towards the polarisation of news audiences in the UK?

Shifting patterns in US television journalism and consumption often foreshadow developments in other parts of the world such as the UK. In *News As Entertainment*, Thussu (2007) has argued US-style television journalism has encouraged the global rise of infotainment, where values of entertainment supersede more serious and hard news stories. But while commercial news values may have been able to bypass the more robust public service structures and regulatory frameworks that shape many broadcast ecologies (see Chapter 2), the prospect of a more politicised television culture or more polarised pattern of viewing emerging is harder to envisage. For newspapers the ideological instinct to explicitly advertise their partisanship is nothing new and, in many cases, it will routinely shape editorial agendas. Of the polling evidence conducted, there does appear to be a broad pattern where readers tend to vote for whichever political party their paper supports editorially (Greenslade 2010a). However, the editorial positions newspapers adopt are not always accepted by their readers. So, for example, in a poll of whether readers supported the Iraq war or not many did not support the position of its paper's editorial stance, such as the *Mirror* which was famously anti-war yet 49 per cent of its readers supported the invasion (Greenslade 2003). Even in the ideologically-driven world of UK newspapers, then, readers would appear to be more resistant to replicating the same degree of partisan instincts as US cable news audiences have done in recent years.

Comparing US and UK news consumption and political behaviour, of course, is so problematic in a number of respects. America has a population roughly five times the size of that in the UK, making it a far more diverse and complicated country to understand socially, politically and culturally. There are no major divisions – gun control, abortion rights, tax and spend, religion and so on (Bishop and Cushing 2008) – which will routinely split sections of US society as they would in the UK. The ideological space between the two main UK parties – Conservative and Labour – is considerably smaller than that between Republicans and Democrats. In addition, while elections are closely fought between the Republican and Democrat parties, votes in the UK are spread more thinly not only across the three main parties but also amongst smaller, mostly nationalist parties. So, for example, despite what is often framed as Obama's overwhelming 2008 presidential victory, he won by just 6.8 per cent of the vote with only 1.2 per cent of the share of the vote made up of non-Republican or Democrat supporters.

In the 2010 General Election, by contrast, the Conservative party gained 36.1 per cent of the vote while Labour and the Liberal Democrats gained 29 per cent and 23 per cent respectively. The margin in victory was broadly similar – 7.1 per cent – yet in the UK this triggered a hung parliament where a new coalition government was the result. Partisanship between the two rival parties, in other words, was – at least at the time of writing – temporarily put on hold. Whether we have witnessed an end to tribal party politics is highly questionable, but what it does suggest is that the ideological territory of mainstream politics can swing in a reasonably consensual way without a huge public backlash. Putting aside the college voting system that would prevent a hung presidency, it would, in this context, be difficult to imagine America's political elite – or, for that matter, its wider electorate – compromising on a five year bi-partisan term in office.

In evaluating whether more ideologically driven or, at least, more politically opinionated forms of television journalism might spread across the Atlantic, the disparity in the broader social and political culture of the US and the UK should not be ignored. But, most significantly, what strikingly divides the countries are the far stricter regulatory requirements UK broadcasters operate under. As previous chapters have explored, broadcast structures in the UK have tightly regulated the impartiality of television news. According to Ofcom, which regulates commercial television and radio, UK broadcasters must

> ... ensure that news, in whatever form, is reported with due accuracy and presented with due impartiality ... Impartiality itself means not favouring one side over another. 'Due' means adequate or appropriate to the subject and nature of the programme ... presenters of 'personal view' or 'authored' programmes or items, and chairs of discussion programmes may express their own views on matters of political or industrial controversy or matters relating to current public policy. However, alternative viewpoints must be adequately represented either in the programme, or in a series of programmes taken as a whole. (Ofcom 2003)

Likewise, the UK's wholly publicly-funded organisation, the BBC, regulated by the BBC Trust, has editorial guidelines that strictly state its news, current affairs and factual output 'must be treated with due impartiality, giving due weight to events, opinion and main strands of argument'. There have, of course, been moments – for the BBC in particular – when that impartiality has been questioned. As Chapter 2 explored, since the General Strike of 1926 the corporation has routinely defended its journalistic balance and independence from governments of the day. Controversially, in 2009 the BBC allowed the leader of the British National Party (an extreme right-wing group) to appear on *Question Time* – a political debate programme – on the basis the party had won sufficient votes to gain a democratic voice. While the BBC was criticised for seeking widespread publicity to boost its ratings, from another perspective they were defiantly defending their status as an impartial broadcaster.

Even if ITV does not attract the same degree of scrutiny, it too comes under attack for undermining public service values of impartiality. Industry eyebrows were raised, for example, when ITV's political editor, Tom Bradby, mounted what appeared to be a tabloid partisan attack in the *Mail on Sunday* on the Conservative Party's policy of cutting child benefit for top-rate tax payers (see Greenslade 2010c). It may be taken for granted that Fox News personalities – like Glen Beck – explicitly promote their own political agendas, such as supporting the Tea Party Movement, but in the UK this is widely seen as an attack on a journalist's political independence and the broadcaster he or she represents. And despite these moments where a broadcasters' impartiality is temporarily challenged, both commercial and public service broadcasters operate in a strict impartiality framework that would be hard to routinely flout let alone explicitly emulate to the extent where a Fox-style partisanship is pursued.

While the debate about relaxing the impartiality guidelines in the UK often revolves around a Fox-style end-product, pressure has recently been exerted on the impartiality guidelines from other perspectives. It has been suggested within the industry and in some academic circles that impartiality is a regulatory relic of old-fashioned party politics. For Tambini and Cowling (2002), contemporary politics is far more complex and multi-layered. Working within the impartiality guidelines, they have suggested it pushes journalists 'to focus on ritualized formal politics when the real story, and the real challenge for public information, is elsewhere' (2002: 84). There was, in addition, more than a hint of relaxing the impartiality guidelines in an Ofcom-commissioned report into the future of television news (Hargreaves and Thomas 2002). More recently, it has been suggested that some commercial broadcasters could be given leniency in how they interpret the 'due impartiality' guidelines (namely Channel 5, in particular).

From a different perspective, in another Ofcom report into impartiality, it was suggested that 'universal impartiality may become less enforceable in a digital environment, where regulated and unregulated services exist side by side on the same platform' (2007: 605). What this implies is that technology may well erode the distinction between television and online services – which is already slightly blurred since websites like YouTube can already operate on conventional television sets that are hooked up to broadband services. Mark Thompson, Director General of the BBC, surprised many at a seminar in December 2010 when he suggested that while BBC news should maintain its impartial editorial standards, all broadcasters should not have to conform to regulations established well before the age of the Internet and multi-channel television. He stated that:

> There was [once] a logic in allowing impartial broadcasters to have a monopoly of the broadcasting space. But in the future, maybe there should be a broad range of choices? Why shouldn't the public be able to see and hear, as well as read, a range of opinionated journalism and then make up their own mind about what they think about it? The BBC and Channel 4 have a history of clearly labelled polemical programmes. But why not entire polemical channels which have got stronger opinions? I find the argument persuasive. (Thompson, cited in Sherwin 2010)

Petley (2009: 609) has critically challenged the role played by the Internet, since far from diversifying the public sphere he has argued it swiftly resulted in a 'diminution of diversity'. As with the right-wing dominance of the UK press, Petley is of the opinion that a largely unregulated online world has manufactured a set of influential reactionary conservative bloggers.

Despite pressures to relax impartiality for sometimes well-intentioned reasons or technological advances, on balance, consecutive Media and Culture Secretaries of State have vetoed all recommendations. There have, nevertheless, been concerns that a 'Foxification' of television journalism might spread across the Atlantic without any deregulation. Murdoch is on record for wanting to export Fox-style journalism around the world, including to the UK. At a House of Lords Communications Committee, the minutes showed Murdoch would like Sky to act as a 'proper alternative to the BBC' (cited in Gibson 2007). While impartiality rules prevent full-blown 'Foxification', Murdoch seems to suggest that Fox's style and format could be emulated by Sky. For Steven Barnett (2010a), even with strict impartiality in place, there remains a potential for the owners of television news to wield considerable editorial influence. Barnett has argued that:

> While impartiality rules may be adequate protection against systematic and blatant promotion of a partisan political view, they cannot cater for stories which are excluded, demoted or selected according to a particular editorial agenda. A news channel, for example, which chooses to concentrate on stories about the 'growing problems' of crime, immigration or welfare dependency cannot be accused of breaching statutory impartiality rules. Similarly, an editorial position which starts with deep skepticism about man-made climate change can safely prioritise stories which undermine the thesis and ignore stories which support it. (Barnett 2010a: 15)

A systematic content analysis of the BBC news channel and Sky News between 2004 and 2007 confirms that while there were traces of Fox News-style journalism (primarily around breaking news coverage, as explored in Chapter 3), neither channel resembled its partisan coverage or overtly opinionated approach to journalism (Cushion and Lewis 2009). In fact, since Sky's main competitor is a popular public service news provider – the BBC – it was argued that it could be seen to restrain any moves towards 'Foxification'. For opinion polls routinely show audiences value impartiality and expect television news to remain above party politics. Viewers are aware, of course, that impartiality is a difficult aspiration to maintain within a complex or fast-changing news story. But as Julian Petley's (2009) analysis of attitudes towards impartiality amongst news audiences has shown, while viewers may be disengaged about how particular topics or issues are routinely covered by UK broadcast journalists, there is no evidence to support the case that relaxing broadcasters' obligations to report news impartially would enhance audience engagement with television news.

In understanding viewers' relationship with television news organisations, the most convincing evidence about the role impartiality plays in journalism is not necessarily about the concept itself, which can often be viewed somewhat vaguely or in abstract terms. Surveys that evaluate the levels of trust viewers hold towards different news media are often more revealing. While Chapter 6 will examine attitudes towards journalists across types of television news more generally, it is worth drawing attention to a clear pattern about how trusted television news programmes are compared to different types of newspapers. In recent years, the amount of trust people invest in television news has declined more sharply than for rival media output but it nevertheless remains strikingly more trusted than the more partisan and self-regulated world of newspapers. So, for example, a YouGov poll in 2010 (cited in Kellner 2010) found that whereas journalists on red-top newspapers and mid-market were trusted by 10 and 21 per cent of readers respectively, for broadsheet newspapers it was 41 per cent. By comparison, BBC and ITV television news journalists were trusted by 60 per cent and 48 per cent respectively.

If we compare this with the US – as this chapter has previously explored – television news tends to be viewed more suspiciously and along ideological lines. Whereas television news in 1993 was, according to Gallup's longitudinal data, trusted either 'a great deal' or 'quite a lot' by 46 per cent of the population, by 2010 just 22 per cent did so. It is, of course, hard to isolate media impact and influence and apply it casually to levels of trust in television news. But since this coincides with the aftermath of the abolition of the Fairness Doctrine, as well as the subsequent rise of ideologically-driven cable news and comedy shows, these do appear, at the very least, plausible explanations for why people's trust in television news is at an all time low in the US. For if we scratch below the surface of the Gallup figures and break trust down by party political affiliation just 16 per cent of Republicans and 18 per cent of Independents put their trust in television news compared to 31 per cent of Democrats. Once again, a pattern of news audiences being polarised is apparent.

For countries wrestling with whether or not to relax their impartiality guidelines to allow more explicit news or comedy shows, it would be difficult not to conclude that America's increasingly deregulated culture of television news has contributed to the promotion of partisanship in television programming. If the increasing choice of television news sources might have once been cause for media pluralists to celebrate this has arguably been short lived, since it does not appear to have encouraged viewers to watch a range of television programmes with different political perspectives.

This chapter, overall, has suggested that television news's increasingly deregulated infrastructure and partisan pursuit of viewers have encouraged audiences to tune into their own brand of politics. Of course, television news has always been a partial 'window on the world', distorted by a set of news values that are often inimical to delivering high degrees of accuracy or even-handed objectivity. And yet most television journalism has, nevertheless, historically sought to conform to values of impartiality, striving to balance out conflicting political viewpoints without being patently partisan or brazenly bias (Cushion 2012). In retreating from television news's conventional impulse to cover the world objectively, viewers have responded by placing less trust in what they say or what they report.

With the Fairness Doctrine abolished, the right-wing media baron, Rupert Murdoch, challenged the liberal orthodoxy that television journalism should not be ideologically driven. This became widely known as the

'Fox Effect' – or Foxification – where Fox News's journalistic values, conventions and partisanship were being emulated for financial gain or ideological muscle. Foxification, in this context, was pushing journalism towards more comment, speculation and politicisation. Cable network news channels have since employed more opinionated segments in their prime-time programming, often with adversarial presenters stamping not just their personality on a show but also their own highly partisan politics. This chapter has also shown how over the last decade or so new political comedy shows have been arriving on the scene – *The Daily Show, The Colbert Report* and their subsequent spin-offs – that have proved appealing, in particular, to younger audiences. On the face of it, they have shaken up what might be defined as television news journalism and made some journalists reflect on their own profession. Comedy news programmes, in this context, have rightly received much scholarly attention and praise for both informing and engaging viewers in politics and public affairs. This chapter argued, however, that a more critical appraisal of 'political' television programmes needed to be developed since the evidence suggests these also appear to be encouraging the political polarisation of audiences by promoting their own humorous but informative brand of partisan comedy news.

Far from diversifying the public sphere, the insurgence of opinionated or ideological television news has encouraged viewers to watch and trust sources that will reinforce their own ideological beliefs. When television news operates without strict regulation and has to compete in a highly competitive market, it is perhaps understandable why news organisations will seize on what makes journalism profitable and engaging. Since television news has broadly seen its audiences plummet in recent years, Fox News's bucking of this trend has promoted a profitable form of journalism where its partisanship has been emulated by rival news organisations that are keen to gain a share of the market audience. In doing so this demonstrates how an increasingly deregulatory television culture can quickly shape a highly partisan and politicised public sphere.

Of course, US broadcast journalism under the Fairness Doctrine was not non-ideological nor would it necessarily apply to new cable programmes that have emerged since. There should be no romantic allusions that journalism would be immediately improved if more robust regulation was introduced to police the boundaries of news about politics and public affairs. But while the period of time when the three network stations dominated news should not be nostalgically looked back on, the direction US broadcast journalism has taken since it abolished the Fairness Doctrine should not be explained without reference to deregulation. For in many advanced democracies around the world where regulation to safeguard impartiality in broadcast news has remained in place (Cushion 2012), it would be hard to imagine either Fox News or *The Daily Show* being allowed to report or joke about politics as they do in the US.

The next chapter explores deregulation and market pressures from another perspective. While the US is able to sustain a comparatively healthy and vibrant culture of regional or state television news, the range and quality of local news coverage in the UK is increasingly dependent on public service broadcasting. Without commercial investment or competition, television journalism has struggled to reflect the affairs and politics of the whole of the UK at a time when its political system has been devolved. Starved of information, the chapter discusses the implications of political devolution without a meaningful devolution of news media to inform citizens about what is happening in all parts of the UK or about the decisions being made in their democratically-elected political institutions.

5

REPORTING THE POLITICS OF DEVOLVED NATIONS: TOWARDS MORE LOCALISED TELEVISION NEWS?

Localised news, national media: sustaining journalism locally

In understanding contemporary television journalism, the focus of the book so far has been on interpreting trends in *national* news coverage. This, of course, excludes the role of local or regional television news stations, many of which attract large audiences and are valued and trusted above national television bulletins or cable news services, not least in the US, where local television news is the most widely consumed form of journalism. According to the 2010 Pew State of the News Media report on American journalism, there are approximately 800 stations operating in 200 markets (Pew Project in Excellence 2010). These are dominated by network affiliate stations (ABC, CBS, Fox and NBC) with independent stations accounting for just 1 per cent of overall local television viewership (what is estimated at 25 million network viewers compared to 290,000 respectively).

Television stations, in some parts of the US, have formed links with local newspapers and media organisations in order to deliver an integrated news service that can commercially exploit lower economies of scale. This has been partly born out of necessity since audiences have plummeted over the last decade due to more intense competition from rival news sources. Consequently, networks have sought to achieve greater returns from the sums cable channels pay to their affiliated local stations. Meanwhile, local television news has suffered from national network scheduling agendas – a 'Leno effect' – where decisions made on evening programming such as NBC's *Jay Leno Show* (which was cancelled) have adversely impacted on evening television viewing (Pew Project in Excellence 2010). All of which – with wider economic forces at play too – has put the future of the local television market in a precarious state, facing many of the challenges that confront national television news and journalism more generally. Nevertheless, while local television stations are struggling to compete in a multi-channel and multi-media world, they remain competitive news businesses and valued news sources, capturing a sizeable portion of the market and attracting national and local advertising.

In recent years the UK has paid more attention to how local television news in the US has operated, commercially sustaining itself in a competitive media market. On the face of it, comparisons with the US are somewhat hard to sustain since local American television markets are far more diffuse than the UK, with a greater population size and geography to cover and more complicated political and cultural identities across its 50 states. The most decisive point of departure, nevertheless, is the reliance the UK has on public service funding of regional news and the robust regulation in place to ensure local journalism is produced by broadcasters. But since a new Secretary of State for Culture, Olympics, Media and Sport, Jeremy Hunt, was appointed in 2010 media policy debates about regional and local news provision in the UK have centred on delivering an increasingly market-driven approach to developing television news services to major urban cites. In one recent speech Hunt used an analogy that has come to characterise local television news policy, asking why local television in Birmingham (in the UK, with a population of over one million people) could not be commercially viable since it had eight local newspapers when Birmingham (in Alabama, in the US, with a population of less than a quarter of million) had eight television services and four local newspapers. Why, in short, could UK local television news not be self-sustaining in a commercial marketplace when it had worked effectively in the US?

Hunt has since had to scale back his market-driven ambitions, choosing instead to lean on the BBC for additional start-up funds to kick start and, at least in the early years, sustain the investment needed for a more localised television news culture to develop (Sweeney 2011). But what Hunt's vision for the future of television journalism does represent is an attempt to rely less on the state to sustain its political economy, for one of his first decisions in office was to disband a previous initiative – what were known as IFNCs (Independently Funded News Consortiums) – in order to part subsidise television provision in tandem with commercial local news industries across the whole of the UK (England, Scotland, Wales and Northern Ireland). This was proposed in the context of the BBC's growing dominance of the local and regional television market over previous decades and the gradual erosion of commercial broadcasters' – most notably ITV's – commitment to supplying localised news services. Under their public service obligations, both the BBC and ITV have a commitment to supply regional television news and a long history of serving the nations and regions of the UK. As Chapter 2 highlighted, the competition between these broadcasters cultivated a healthy market environment where both channels had to adapt to maintain their journalistic credentials and ensure television news remained at the cutting edge.

In the early years of television's formation, if the BBC represented the UK's national identity via the pomp and ceremony of its coverage of parliamentary politics or its celebration of the monarchy, ITV's intervention into the television market in 1954 established an affinity with the 'ordinary folk' from across the regions and nations of the UK. Regional news and current affairs programming played a significant role in defining ITV's brand as a watchdog for local democracies and, in addition, its role as a public service broadcaster that was distinct from the BBC. According to a former ITN News Director, Richard Tait (2007: 28), television news programming had 'always been a key determinant in the award and retention of licences' for the regional franchises that made up ITV. In its original incarnation, 15 different regions covered the UK. Corporations such as Granada, Yorkshire, and Scottish Television built up large and loyal audiences and, for many years, attracted bigger viewing figures than those for the BBC's regional evening bulletins. ITV regional television news was, in short, central to its journalistic identity, stamping its public service identity on broadcasting.

ITV's regional reign came to an end, however, when the arrival of multi-channel television challenged its broadcasting model, since advertising became an increasingly precarious commodity for sustaining local network programming. ITV had to revise its political economy in the multi-media age, forcing the network to merge many of its regional corporations, including its news and current affairs infrastructure (see Chapter 2 for how the 1990 Broadcasting Act dismantled ITV's regional identity). So, for example, where once England and Wales had many organisations reflecting their diversity, by 2004 ITV was owned by one national overarching company (e.g. Carlton-Granada). Its television journalism has since been at the mercy of the market. With licences rewarded to the highest bidders, economies of scale began to largely determine how far ITV news was, in reality, 'local' or 'regional'. In a far more competitive environment to that where it began, ITV has in more recent years been more 'light-touch' regulated in the kind of public service programming they are obliged to deliver, including the level of regional news provision. In recognition of the financial constraints commercial broadcasters now operate in, in 2010 Ofcom massively reduced the costs licence holders had to pay to maintain its public service broadcasting programming, from £20 million a year to just £10,000 (Sweeney 2010). News and current affairs, against this backdrop, have been a major casualty of ITV's commercial battle to survive in a multi-channel era.

This is not to suggest ITV has simply withdrawn from the world of regional television news or that its audiences have deserted wholesale.

When it was proposed that ITV's Border and Tyne Tees regions (covering north-east England and the Scottish borders respectively) should merge, a campaign to protect the identity of each region was launched with 14,000 complaints made to Ofcom. A 15 minute opt-out bulletin – rather than entirely homogenising the regions – was the compromise that was reached. Likewise, ITV companies have tried to keep pace with the world of a post-devolution UK – since political power was devolved to Scotland, Wales and Northern Ireland in 1999 – but have also struggled to find the resources to fund each nation.

Since the BBC had, over this period, a guaranteed source of income via the licence fee, it did not face the same level of market pressure that ITV experienced. The company grew in regional stature not just because of ITV's demise but also because renewed resources were ploughed into the BBC's regional divisions. With far larger economies of scale, it was able to integrate its national and regional resources to more professionally cover local parts of the UK. This was most strikingly the case between 6pm and 7pm on BBC1, where a half-hourly national news was followed by regional opt-outs which were previewed at the top of the hour and again 15 minutes later. As Richard Tait (2007: 29–30) has observed, 'The result was a truly integrated operation between 18.00 and 19.00, with satellite newsgathering trucks for fast response, and a more coherent, contemporary approach to set designs and graphics'. In expanding the range and quality of its regional television news infrastructure, the BBC has since established itself as the UK's most important source of localised television news.

If we break down news regions by BBC and ITV, a picture soon emerges of ITV's retreat from regional and local news coverage. In 2009 ITV plc agreed with Ofcom to reduce the news regions it covered in England, Wales and the Scottish borders from 17 to nine. Table 5.1 shows how the 17 regional news hubs have been reorganised into just nine far larger news regions across the UK. Scotland, it should be noted, is not part of ITV plc since it is owned by STV (Scottish Television) and runs north and south news bulletins.

In doing so, regional territories were stretched even further, in some cases covering huge geographies such as from Land's End (at the very tip of the English peninsula) to some areas in Hereford, many hundreds of miles north-east (e.g. the South West news bulletin). There were, nonetheless, some sub-regions within these nine news divisions where approximately six 15-minute slots of more localised news might be produced (Fitzsimmons 2009). So, for example, in the south west while *West Country Tonight* is the main flagship regional news bulletin, there are quarter of an hour opt-outs for ITV's Westcountry and ITV West regions. If we compare this to the BBC, it has many more dedicated half-hourly news bulletins at a regional and sub-regional level (see Table 5.2).

Table 5.1 List of ITV's pre- and post-2009 regional news opt-outs across the UK

Pre-2009 ITV regional opt-outs	Post-2009 ITV regional opt-outs
Anglia East	Tyne, Tees and Border
Anglia West	Yorkshire
Border	Granada
Central East	Central
Central West	Anglia
Granada	London
London	Meridian
Meridian East	South West
Meridian South	Wales
Thames Valley	
Tyne Tees North	
Tyne Tees South	
Wales	
West	
Westcountry	
Yorkshire North	
Yorkshire South	

Table 5.2 List of BBC 6.30pm regional news bulletins across the UK

Region/Nation	Title of 6.30pm news bulletin
London	London News
South West	Channel Islands
East Midlands	East Midlands Today
East (Norwich)	Look East
East (Cambridge)	Look East
North West	North West Tonight
North East and Cumbria	Look North (Newcastle)
Northern Ireland	Newsline
South (Oxford)	Oxford News
South East	South East Today
Scotland	Reporting Scotland
South (Southampton)	South Today
South West (Plymouth)	Spotlight
West Midlands	Midlands Today
Wales	Wales Today
West	Points West
Yorkshire	Look North (Leeds)
Yorkshire and Lincolnshire	Look North (Hull)

Digital satellite technology, of course, has a role to play since it has allowed for more space to run simultaneous services around the country. From 2003 the BBC was able to run all its regional networks via their own channels, for the first time allowing viewers to tune in wherever they were in the country. As an enthusiastic BBC Director General, Greg Dyke, put it at the time,

'This means that a Scot living in London can get BBC One Scotland, or a native of Yorkshire, living in Cornwall could watch regional programmes from their home region' (BBC Press Office 2003).

Running counter to ITV's centralisation of its network and the BBC's regional repositioning was the UK's changing political character. For television news and journalism more generally had to evolve to meet the considerable challenge of reporting the new and sometimes complicated world of devolved politics.

Four nations, one Union: devolving politics without devolving national media ecologies

Part of the BBC's regional news expansion was not only due to structural reorganisation but also to a response to wider political developments in the UK. For several decades political devolution – where power is devolved from the central legislator in England (Westminster) to the nations (Northern Ireland, Scotland and Wales) – had been bubbling under the surface of UK politics. Under a new Labour government these plans were to come to fruition in 1997, when referendums were won to establish – marginally in the case of the referendum in Wales – new institutions in Scotland and Wales. For Northern Ireland – which had previously been devolved – intense negotiations led to a new devolution settlement. Two years later each nation had its own institutions and elections, thereby instantly changing the UK's political identity. Each institution accrued different levels of policy and fiscal responsibilities making it complicated – as Table 5.3 shows – to comprehend the constitutional lines that now divide the UK.

The powers each institution gained varied. While Scotland had control of more fiscal responsibilities than Wales and Northern Ireland (it can potentially raise tax-levels slightly), all the devolved nations had key social policy powers transferred such as health and education. Westminster, of course, remained the significant legislator in UK politics, but Scotland, Wales and Northern Ireland have since had the freedom to move in different directions in many key areas. Over time these powers have also increased, perpetuating policy differences with England. Further reviews are expected to recommend devolving more powers and responsibilities (particularly since the Scottish National Party (SNP) won full control of the Scottish Parliament in May 2011 and are set to hold a referendum on acquiring full independence). Westminster retains, however, what are called reserved powers on macro economic issues (major tax-spending), on constitutional matters like attaining full independence, on setting levels of immigration into the UK, on making defence and foreign policy decisions, and on establishing media and broadcasting policy.

Table 5.3 List of major devolved powers for Scotland, Wales and Northern Ireland

Scotland	Wales	Northern Ireland
Agriculture, forestry and fishing	Agriculture, forestry and fishing	Agriculture
Education	Education	Education
Environment	Environment	Environment
Health	Health and social welfare	Health
Housing	Housing	Enterprise
Justice, policing and court*	Local Government	Enterprise, trade and investment
Local Government	Fire and rescue service	Social services
Fire Service	Highways and transport	Justice and policing
Economic development	Economic development	
Some transport		

*Scotland has always had its own legal system (Adopted from BBC's introduction to devolved powers: http://news.bbc.co.uk/1/hi/uk_politics/election_2010/first_time_voter/8589835.htm)

Since London and Westminster has always been the central hub where political power and decision making has taken place, the nations of the UK have had to acclimatise themselves to an entirely new culture of politicking. This has prompted many questions about how well the newly acquired political institutions would interact and relate to the citizens they represent (Davies 1999; Ferguson and Hargreaves 1999; Williams 2000). Thus, for example, despite much promise that devolution would bring a new form of politics, in *Open Scotland: Journalists, Spin-Doctors and Lobbyists*, Schlesinger et al. (2001) showed how the new Scottish parliament quickly replicated the institutional practices pursued at Westminster after power was devolved. Since many political operatives and journalists had grown up in a Westminster culture, almost by occupational habit the adversarial relationship between media and politicians, they argued, appeared to be part of the devolution act. As a result, the professionalisation of spin-doctoring and a media obsession with 'spinning' was to dominate the early years of devolved Scottish politics.

From a television broadcaster's perspective, this post-devolution UK became a far more difficult beat to cover and comprehend for reporters and audiences. Within the nations, journalists no longer had to make huge train journeys from Edinburgh to London or long motorway road trips from Cardiff. For the first time reporters had politics on their doorstep and a new set of politicians – MSPs in Scotland, AMs in Wales, MLAs in Northern Ireland – to contend with alongside the Westminster MPs. Of course, within each nation – Scotland, Wales and Northern Ireland – there were different media ecologies which had evolved from the historically long and complicated relationships each has had with England (Smith 1994; Davies 1994; Williams 1997; McLaughlin

2006). These warrant a brief exploration since they show how far news about devolved politics is able to serve various audiences across the nations.

Of the devolved nations Scotland has arguably the strongest public sphere (McNair 2006), with national newspapers articulating a relatively strong sense of national identity (Smith 1994). Newspaper sales have also remained high and, since devolution, many London-produced newspapers have strategically changed their mode of address from 'British' to 'Scottish' (Rosie et al. 2006; cf. Connell 2003; Higgins 2006). Broadcasting, however, is where a 'substantial news and current affairs output' (McNair 2006: 38) can be found, with Scottish TV, Grampian TV and Borders TV as well as a range of radio stations operating commercially. BBC Scotland, meanwhile, remains the most comprehensive source for news about devolved politics with a well resourced infrastructure of television, radio and online services. London-produced newspapers remain widely read in Scotland and English media generally remain highly influential. However, some English newspapers produce Scottish editions and reframe editorial content.

BBC Wales supplies much of the television, radio and online news about the National Assembly for Wales as election studies have shown (Thomas et al. 2003, 2004a). While ITV Wales also plays an important role in covering devolution, in recent years it has changed ownership with fewer resources being ploughed into its television news provision. Since the Welsh national identity is more fragmented than is the case in Scotland, the media ecology beyond television news has been more reli-ant on England (Jones 1993). It was once estimated 85 per cent of papers bought in Wales were London-produced. While the *Daily Mirror* briefly flirted with a Welsh *Mirror* post-devolution (Thomas 2003), most of the UK newspapers read in Wales are largely devoid of devolved politics. Papers produced within Wales – *The Daily Post* and *Western Mail* – serve largely the north and south communities respectively, but overall their sales remain relatively low. Within Wales, much debate has centred on Trinity Mirror – who owns these papers and runs Media Wales online – for dimin-ishing its Welsh local journalism in favour of profit-making (Greenslade 2010b; Williams and Franklin 2007). Meanwhile the 14 independent commercial radio stations in Wales appear to prioritise soft news over their reporting of devolution (Thomas 2006).

Northern Ireland, by contrast, possesses much more diversity within its media industry, reflecting the fragmented political identities which serve nationalist and unionist communities. UK newspapers remain well-read titles, but Northern Irish readers have five daily newspapers to choose from and 73 weekly newspapers available (McLaughlin 2006). BBC Northern Ireland is again a central medium for devolved politics with an expansive array of television, radio and online services. But while there are dominant television broadcasters in Scotland and Wales, in Northern Ireland Ulster TV remains the marginal market leader, matching the BBC's coverage of devolution (McLaughlin 2006). According to a 2003 study of Northern Ireland's Assembly campaign nightly coverage of devolved politics was at a higher volume on Ulster Television's news bulletins than on BBC Northern Ireland's (Wilson and Fawcett 2004).

These snapshot pictures of each nation's media ecology do not, of course, do full justice to the character and complexity of how devolved politics is routinely dealt with in news and current affairs provision. But while each nation has differing journalism resources, it is striking how national television news in the UK has remained high for audiences in a post-devolution environment. Devolution, in other words, has not diminished the thirst for UK-wide news media across the four nations. Table 5.4 shows BBC1 news audiences for its 1pm, 6pm and 10pm news bulletins across the four nations and, importantly, as a proportion of the population.

Whereas devolution enthusiasts had predicated UK journalism would play an increasingly marginal role beyond England's boundaries, the BBC's television news audiences demonstrate that audiences made up of all four nations do continue to watch news from all and not just parts of the UK. English viewers, needless to say, constitute most of the audience for BBC1's weekday bulletins but as a proportion of the population size throughout the UK they remain fairly similar. Perhaps counter-intuitively, Scotland has the highest audience (proportionately) for the one o'clock bulletin, while audiences in Wales are more likely to tune into all three bulletins than would audiences in England. So despite the seismic shift in the UK's political power and identity since devolution, UK television news remains, in short, a significant source of television news across the devolved nations.

Table 5.4 BBC1 news audiences by nation for weekday network news programmes

ONE O'CLOCK NEWS	UK	England	Scotland	Wales	N.Ireland
Average Audience	2.8m	2.3m	280,000	140,000	75,000
Average Audience (% pop)	4.9%	4.8%	6.0%	5.1%	4.7%
SIX O'CLOCK NEWS	**UK**	**England**	**Scotland**	**Wales**	**N.Ireland**
Average Audience	4.4m	3.7m	350,000	250,000	75,000
Average Audience (% pop)	7.7%	7.8%	7.3%	9.0%	4.7%
TEN O'CLOCK NEWS	**UK**	**England**	**Scotland**	**Wales**	**N.Ireland**
Average Audience	4.9m	4.1m	370,000	250,000	125,000
Average Audience (% pop)	8.6%	8.7%	7.7%	9.0%	7.7%

Source: BARB (12 months from Oct 2007 to Sept 2008)

At the same time, while the BBC has invested a great deal in resourcing its news and current affairs across Scotland, Wales and Northern Ireland, the corporation has 'been the subject of repeated criticisms that it has failed to report properly the differences that devolution has brought to UK politics' (Williams 2009: 178). Whether in volume or in accuracy, it has been argued that the BBC – and, moreover, television news generally – has not reflected the world of devolved politics. Even before devolution, the nations beyond England had complained they were largely peripheral within news coverage. In Scotland, a campaign for a 'Scottish Six' – to replace the London-based UK national bulletin – has been underway for over a decade. Devolution, of course, has compounded the issue, not least because many of the stories in UK-wide bulletins – on health, social care, education and so on – might not be relevant to viewers outside of England. Westminster politics may, in this context, be almost inconsequential since policies might have little relevance to viewers and listeners outside the country. In 2007, the BBC established a 'Scottish' *Newsnight* (a highbrow, UK-wide news programme that is typically aired between 10.35–11.20pm). This meant for viewers in Scotland that at 11pm the programme would switch to studios in Edinburgh for its remaining 20 minutes. This was a small but significant compromise and one that many nationalists in Wales and Northern Ireland continue to campaign for.

For UK-wide news media, devolution made the broadcast media coverage of UK politics and public affairs a more difficult and cumbersome task. Even after a decade's worth of devolution, there remain moments when Scotland, Wales and Northern Ireland seem almost superfluous to what is being discussed. Thus, for example, in a BBC3 *Question Time* special for young people on 20 October 2010, at the very end of an hour-long debate – when increased university tuition fees were under discussion – it was left to an audience member to ask if the fees were inevitable – as some Conservative panellists were arguing – for future students why would Scottish students still not have to pay? Even if the UK's decision about English universities eventually forces the Scottish Government's hand into charging fees in order to remain competitive, Scotland's exclusion from this debate and from wider media debates reveals how much devolution can be airbrushed out of UK politics.

The impact of what might be termed a 'deficit of devolved information' is reflected in people's knowledge and understanding about devolved politics. A survey conducted by the Welsh Electoral Commission (2002) found respondents had a 'fairly low awareness of the composition, remit and record of the Assembly'. The characters and personalities, in some cases, were only vaguely familiar, such as the leaders of the key political parties. With much attention having been paid to the building of the

Assembly – on its completion the bill had controversially amounted to 67 million pounds – respondents were able to point out where it was located and also express their disapproval about the cost of the institution. In terms of being able to articulate the kind of political powers the National Assembly is able to legislate for, most could not meaningfully convey which policy responsibilities it had devolved from Westminster. Of course, across many advanced democracies knowledge about politics is relatively low, to the extent where, in the US, the public's ignorance of policy has been described as 'the dirty little secret of US democracy' (Blumberg, cited in Delli Carpini and Keeter 1996: 23). But while many nations have an infrastructure where viewers have access to relevant political and public affairs coverage – even if this is marginalised to late-night slots or put on obscure news channels – television news about devolved politics from a UK perspective appears in relatively short supply.

The pace at which devolution is shaping UK policy making has accelerated rather than diminished since the process began in 1999. Further legislative powers have been granted for each institution and several elections have been and gone. Big areas of devolved responsibilities – in health and social care, education and the environment, local government and housing – have also meant the four nations are pursuing increasingly different policies. So, for example, a Joseph Rowntree Foundation report into devolution's impact on low-income people and places in 2010 found disparities across the four nations relating to poverty based on decisions made by devolved administrations (McCormick and Harrop 2010). While they cannot be divorced from the macro economic decisions made in Westminster, this shows devolution is having an effect – whether positive or negative – on the life-chances of citizens from across the UK. Much of these sometimes complicated devolved policies may bypass UK television news since they require nuanced interpretations of different institutional responses and powers. It is, in this context, where a 'quiet revolution' in the UK can be observed, with a cumulative array of social policy making changing areas such as how hospitals are run or university education is paid for.

The pressure to respond to mounting criticism of the BBC's devolution coverage culminated in the BBC Trust commissioning independent media research. This resulted in the King Report being published in 2008, based on survey data about attitudes towards BBC regional and national coverage as well as a comprehensive content analysis of BBC news and current affairs output (BBC Trust 2008). The latter was conducted by a research team at the Cardiff School of Journalism, Media and Cultural Studies, led by Professor Justin Lewis and myself. The next section examines the broad thrust of the King review and how UK national television news coverage has faced up to the challenges of reporting devolved politics.

Reflecting the four nations? The King Report and television coverage of devolved politics

Asked, in the words of the BBC Trust (2008: 4), to explore claims that 'the BBC was not covering the different policies of the nations in a way that enabled audiences to understand fully what was happening in different parts of the UK', Anthony King – a politics professor and freelance journalist – carried out an independent report based on comprehensive media analysis and survey data. He drew also on his own impressionistic analysis and conversations with BBC journalists and management, politicians and audience councils to write the report. The following section, however, primarily concentrates on the more systematic analysis of television news content and audience perceptions of BBC journalism that informed the King Report (BBC Trust 2008).

Based on a representative sample of 2000 UK adults, the survey conducted by the British Market Research Bureau (BMRB) broadly explored how audiences assessed BBC news coverage. This was not exclusively classified as television news coverage. But since television remains the most consumed source of news in the UK, it would be reasonable to assume television viewing informed the majority of the responses. The survey examined four key areas – knowledge, relevance, balance and accuracy – of BBC journalism. Testing respondents' knowledge about who had responsibility in policy areas – on health, education and media regulation – the survey found 'Respondents in England are more likely to believe that the policies and news that applied to them, also applied in other nations' (BMRB 2008: 18). In all four nations, it was found that audiences 'may be vaguely aware of policies in other nations, without having extensive, detailed knowledge' (2008: 32). Nevertheless, respondents were 'keen to understand more about the political process in other UK nations' (2008: 18). While the survey also showed BBC UK national news was a valued source of information about the four nations, and that 'BBC news in general is clear and accurate' (2008: 31), respondents were less likely to agree with these sentiments the further they live from London. This was not, in other words, entirely about the devolved nations being divorced from coverage of the UK but about a London-centric bias in BBC coverage. In interpreting audience perceptions of coverage, King (BBC Trust 2008: 35) suggested that there was a widespread sense that 'the BBC, despite its formal name, is an excessively London-centred organization, with an "us-in-here" and a "you-out-there" mentality'. The perception of viewers, in short, was that UK national television news was centred largely on London and the surrounding area as opposed to reflecting all of England and the nations beyond it.

To assess how far UK national television news routinely reported about England, Scotland, Wales and Northern Ireland and whether devolved policies were correctly applied in each nation, the Cardiff School of Journalism,

Media and Cultural Studies developed an extensive coding frame in order to measure both impartiality and accuracy in television journalism (Lewis et al. 2008). Since a great deal of time was spent piloting a code frame in order to measure the coverage of the nations and the reporting of devolution, a brief methodological reflection is warranted here about how the research was devised and developed. It was based on two comprehensive content analyses, a routine period of output and a more atypical period when the 2007 devolved elections took place. Both studies examined a range of media content, but the focus in terms of this book will be on television journalism. They contained a wealth of empirical data, indeed far too much to unpack here in full (Cushion et al. 2009a; Cushion et al. 2009b; Lewis et al. 2008). What follows is the broad thrust of key findings and, in subsequent sections, a wider reflection about the role media regulators and academics can play in producing evidence-based assessments of television journalism. Since the focus of this chapter is exclusively on examining television news *content*, whatever the trends in coverage identified these cannot be assumed either to have enhanced or diminished viewers' knowledge or engagement with the nations or devolved politics.

For comparative purposes, we examined not just BBC television news – BBC 1 (the bulletins at 1pm, 6pm, and 10pm during the week and the main evening bulletins on Saturday and Sunday Evening), BBC News 24 (now called the BBC News Channel) (5–6pm weekdays, 6–7pm weekends), and BBC 2's *Newsnight* – but also commercial television output, including ITV's 6.30pm, Channel 4's 7pm and Sky News's 6pm weekdays, 6–7pm weekends news bulletins. In doing so, the study enabled coverage on a closely regulated and public funded medium (BBC) to be compared with more lightly-regulated and commercially-driven television news bulletins (ITV, Channel 4 and Sky News). A four-week long sample of news coverage was examined over an eight week period (October and November 2007), generating thousands of news items that were subsequently analysed both quantitatively and qualitatively.

In order to explore impartiality in the reporting of UK-wide news, the volume of stories about each nation was quantified in national television news. This was measured by story location (whether it related to the UK generally or a nation or region of the UK) as well as reporter location (if a journalist was reporting from a specific locale in the UK whether live or pre-packaged). Westminster was also classified since while it may be in England it could also be relevant to all four nations (depending, of course, if a story related to the policy responsibilities Westminster wields across the whole of the UK). Table 5.5 contains all the stories reported over the sample period excluding international stories and news that applied to Britain or the UK generally, while Table 5.6 reveals where reporters were routinely located in UK news items.

Table 5.5   Per cent of news items relating to one of the four nations in BBC television and commercial news coverage

Media	England	Wesminster	Northern Ireland	Scotland	Wales	Total stories by medium
BBC TV	68.9%	23.3%	2.5%	3.3%	2.0%	100%
Commercial TV	63.5%	30.5%	2.1%	2.9%	1%	100%

Table 5.6   Per cent of news items with a reporter on location in one of the four nations in BBC television and commercial news coverage

Media	England	Westminser	Northern Ireland	Scotland	Wales	Total stories by medium
BBC TV	72%	20.4%	2.4%	3.6%	1.7%	100%
Commercial TV	68.7%	26.7%	1.5%	2.3%	0.8%	100%

In both cases England and – by extension – Westminster dominated the coverage both on BBC and commercial television news. Put another way, neither stories nor reporters regularly appear in Scotland, Wales and Northern Ireland. Of course, establishing precisely how far each nation should regularly feature is problematic, since England accounts for the substantial majority of the UK population (83.3 per cent) – far higher than Scotland (8.4 per cent), Wales (4.9 per cent) and Northern Ireland (2.9 per cent) – and since Westminster holds significant political power it is bound to dominate coverage (BBC Trust 2008: 20). However, if population did drive the volume of coverage the remaining three nations would warrant considerably more attention than is currently being paid to them. In this sense, news values are difficult to apply here (see Chapter 3) since geography and relevance – key criteria that will typically move a story up the news agenda – would appear to favour England and Westminster (Brighton and Foy 2007; Galtung and Ruge, 1965; Harcup and O'Neil 2001, 2008). In addition, the relative strengths of individual stories cannot be ignored when measuring 'fair' or 'balanced' television journalism against some form of story/population quota. Needless to say, the politics of weighting coverage appropriate to the nations is difficult to assess and agree upon. What remains, nonetheless, is that viewers from Scotland, Wales and Northern Ireland who regularly tune into UK-wide television news will be overwhelmingly watching news about England and Westminster and not about their own nations, despite each of these countries holding considerable political power.

In fact, if devolved political coverage is broken down as a proportion of television news coverage overall it makes up just a miniscule (0.7 per cent for the BBC, 0.6 per cent of commercial television news) part of the agenda.

Since key areas of policy – in health and education most prominently – are now devolved, the absence of barely any social policy related to Scotland, Wales and Northern Ireland suggests television news does not adequately reflect the new world of a post-devolution UK. This is not to suggest health or education was entirely neglected in the UK's national television news. English hospitals or English schools made up most policy stories, but there were minimal references to other UK nations let alone devolved differences across institutions. When devolved politics was mentioned, this primarily related to Scotland (with a passing reference to different approaches in social care for the elderly or university tuition fees) and, to a much lesser extent, Northern Ireland. Wales had just one news story related to devolved policy – the use and potential banning of electric dog collars. Rather than devolved politics fulfilling any routine part of television's political news schedule, what this suggests is that coverage of devolved decision making appears somewhat trivial, a quirky or light-hearted distraction from the more serious world of Westminster. Significant moments in the recent history of devolved politics – the day a major constitutional act on health or education was passed or a leadership contest or party political conflict – are by and large covered. However, these tend to be an exception as opposed to the day-to-day norm.

Beyond the daily balance of reporting the four nations, the analysis also sought to explore more qualitatively the accuracy of devolved television news coverage. News, after all, may cover health, education and social care stories but is it conveyed in a way whereby audiences are able to understand their devolved relevance? Of the inaccuracies identified, there were no wild or egregious claims where devolved responsibilities were mishandled, e.g., Wales having its own Chancellor of the Exchequer. Instead, routinely misleading or confusing television journalism was found, which made assumptions about individual policies that were not necessarily, in a post-devolution context, relevant to all four nations. So, for example, in a widely reported speech on 16 November 2007, the then Prime Minster, Gordon Brown, made promises to find 'British jobs for British workers' in a bid to improve educational or training opportunities. But what escaped the attention of many television journalists was that this only related to government training programmes in England. It was an English educational initiative the Prime Minster was making capital from, with the UK government, at least rhetorically, acting in a devolved context. On ITV's 6.30pm news, for instance, 'Britain', 'the UK' and 'England' were used interchangeably, making it hard – even for an astute observer of devolved politics – to interpret whether the educational relevance went beyond England itself. Since many journalists will take their lead from Prime Ministerial speeches, it is perhaps easy to understand why such a large number interpreted the speech literally rather than metaphorically.

Meanwhile, in day-to-day television news coverage, the scale of the slippage where the impression is given that English policies apply UK-wide is even more widespread. The reporting of an Ofsted (a regulator, like Ofcom, which represents English schools only) review into poor secondary school exam results illustrates this potentially misleading area of journalism. While the coverage referred to 'England' at the beginning, most television news items did not qualify further the relevance to English schools only. The BBC's 10 o'clock news slot began, for instance, with 'an appalling indictment of the education service, that's the verdict of the Chief Inspector of Schools after a report found that one in ten secondary schools in England are inadequate and almost half are offering a no-better than satisfactory education'. Rather than specify the 'indictment of the education service *in England*', the more general 'indictment of the education service' may be interpreted as symptomatic of educational standards in the UK more widely. In this context, if viewers were not highly attentive to how a story was initially framed – and much of the research into television viewing suggests many have poor attention spans and, particularly during the news, are liable to be distracted (Delli Carpini and Keeter 1996; Lewis 1991; Morley 1980; Philo and Berry 2004) – without reminding them about its devolved relevance, what is being discussed may appear relevant to all four nations. Incidentally, when news items related to Scotland, Wales and Northern Ireland, the geographic specificity was oft-repeated. In the case of banning electronic dog collars, six explicit mentions were made to Wales. England, in other words, appears to be the default location for UK national television and once journalists cross into Wales, say, or Scotland and Northern Ireland they are prone to reminding viewers about where exactly they are.

In making sense of how England dominates the routine perspectives of television journalism, the Cardiff School of Journalism, Media and Cultural Studies review suggested there was an untapped potential to report more comparatively across the nations. A compare-and-contrast approach would, in this respect, inform viewers about the different policy approaches of each devolved institution – which was something, according to the BRMB survey, that audiences had a large appetite for – whilst remaining relevant to audiences in England. This was picked up in the King Report which agreed 'that opportunities to "compare and contrast" politics, policy and society in the four nations and the non-metropolitan regions of England are seldom seized' (BBC Trust 2008: 64).

In order to develop a more nuanced interpretation of UK political reporting post-devolution, the BBC responded to a series of recommendations about how its coverage of the nations could be improved. Having put into place new management structures and journalistic guidelines, the BBC

Trust commissioned the Cardiff School of Journalism, Media and Cultural Studies to provide a follow-up review of media coverage. The following section explores whether the BBC Trust's intervention into television journalism's reporting of the nations and devolved politics had any meaningful influence on either the BBC or commercial television news coverage.

Market deficit, public service requirement: the BBC Trust and the impact of interventionist regulation

The publication of the King Report (BBC Trust 2008) was widely reported not only in media trade journals or their associated websites but also in the UK's mainstream press and television news bulletins. A *Daily Mail* (11/06/08) headline screamed 'London-biased BBC is failing regional viewers, Corporation finds in its OWN report', while the broadsheet *Daily Telegraph* – having had the findings leaked – pre-empted the publication date by stating 'The BBC's flagship news bulletins are failing license-fee payers across the country by being too "London-centric", a hard-hitting report will claim'. The BBC's own television news adopted a critical stance with Michael Lyons – the then head of the BBC Trust – on the day the findings were published, touring media studios promising 'to step up to the challenge' of improving devolved television journalism.

In response to the King Report the BBC quickly agreed with its regulator, the BBC Trust, to address the limited and occasionally misleading television coverage of devolution that had been identified by the Cardiff School of Journalism, Media and Cultural Studies. Although the performance of commercial television coverage – which, incidentally, was more limited on a range of measures – was not drawn attention to in press or television coverage, in the same spirit they too had a chance to reflect on what the BBC Trust's commissioned report recommended generally about devolved television news coverage. While the BBC Trust's interventions led to a set of editorial changes, Ofcom – the regulator of commercial television news – did not intervene or recommend best practices for ITV, Channel 4 and 5 or Sky News.

As a response to the King Report, the BBC introduced new structural changes to its news gathering and management strategies to deal with the complexity of reporting the nations and devolved politics. Drawing on the quantitative and qualitative parts of the media analysis, four editorial changes were recommended. Firstly, to reflect the 'different levels of devolved responsibilities and different political priorities in each nation', news packages needed to be more liberally labelled. This was part of a wider aim to be more 'accurate about whether or not the facts and views conveyed in output apply to each individual nation'. Secondly – and related to this – more comparisons should be drawn between nations, 'reflecting different perspectives from the nations on particular policy developments'. This would, it was argued, more accurately depict devolution in a UK-wide news network. In doing so, journalists were to be invited to more creatively 'feature perspectives and examples from across the nations and regions when reporting major UK stories (e.g. economy or business), to reflect the fact that stories impact differently in different parts of the UK'. And to overcome the under-representation of certain nations and regions around the UK, 'appropriate weight to coverage of stories which are of major importance to audiences in the nations and regions, including the actions and policies of the devolved administrations in Scotland, Wales and Northern Ireland' should be given. In practice, this meant enhancing the news value of devolution and the nations *beyond* England.

Part of the BBC Trust's intervention into devolved television news coverage was to commission a follow-up review – again led by Justin Lewis and myself at the Cardiff School of Journalism, Media and Cultural Studies – to explore whether management structures and new editorial directives had any transformative effect on television journalism. Approximately two years later, a broadly similar coding frame was applied to the sample of television news journalism in order to empirically assess, in detail, whether editorial trends in the reporting of the nations and devolved had meaningfully changed. The full sets of comparative findings have been unpacked elsewhere (Cushion et al. 2010; Cushion et al. forthcoming) so for now a flavour of the key findings is necessary since these demonstrate how evidence-based research with a robust regulatory intervention can reshape television journalism. Commercial television news operating in a light-touch environment, by contrast, did not broadly change its coverage of the nations. If anything, commercial television news about devolution deteriorated in some areas of journalism, most notably on Sky News, the least regulated television news channel in the UK.

In attempting to redress the marginalisation of nations beyond England, the BBC recommended 'coverage of stories which are of major importance to audiences in the nations and regions' be given 'appropriate weight'. There has, in this respect, been an editorial shift in reflecting all four nations. BBC television news bulletins, between them, increased their coverage of Scotland, Wales and Northern Ireland by 6.4 per cent compared to 2.7 per cent on commercial television. If news items featuring reporters on location in the UK are isolated, Table 5.7 shows how almost every BBC bulletin increased its coverage of the nations beyond England.

On the commercial television bulletins, by contrast, numbers of journalists on location in England increased whilst journalism live or pre-packaged from Scotland, Wales and Northern Ireland decreased. ITV improved its

Table 5.7 Per cent distribution of reporter location across television bulletins in 2007 and 2009 in BBC and commercial television news coverage

	England		Scotland		Wales		Northern Ireland	
	2007	2009	2007	2009	2007	2009	2007	2009
BBC News at One	91.5%	86.0%	3.7%	4.7%	3.7%	4.7%	1.2%	4.7%
BBC News at Six	88.8%	84.5%	4.1%	6.9%	4.1%	6.0%	3.1%	2.6%
BBC News at Ten	91.5%	83.6%	4.3%	9.6%	/	2.7%	4.3%	4.1%
BBC News Channel	91.4%	84.1%	5.4%	9.3%	/	3.7%	3.2%	2.8%
ITV News at Ten	95.2%	92.2%	1.6%	3.3%	1.6%	3.3%	1.6%	1.1%
Channel 4 News	96.2%	98.7%	3.8%	/	/	1.3%	/	/
Sky News	91.7%	98.3%	3.6%	1.7%	1.2%	/	3.6%	/
BBC Combined	90.6%	84.6%	4.4%	7.6%	2.2%	4.4%	2.8%	3.4%
Non-BBC Combined	94.0%	96.5%	3.0%	1.8%	1.0%	1.4%	2.0%	0.3%

reporting in Scotland and Wales with journalists reporting back from the Celtic nations. Sky News, on the other hand, more than halved its volume of on-location reports in Scotland and had no coverage from Wales or Northern Ireland. Channel 4, likewise, had no reports from Scotland or Northern Ireland. Put into a wider context, whilst 3.5 per cent of commercial news contained reports from Scotland, Wales and Northern Ireland 15.4 per cent did so on BBC television news.

While less striking at first glance, the BBC's television news coverage of devolution rose from 0.7 per cent of its total coverage to 1.2 per cent. This may appear relatively modest but what it represented was a shift away from other newsworthy topics – crime, in particular – towards more coverage of devolved politics. This contrasted with commercial television which decreased its share of devolved politics from 0.6 per cent to 0.3 per cent. For commercial television news, the biggest increase in topics was for entertainment/celebrity news. The proportion of stories the BBC devoted to devolved politics, of course, should not be overstated – these remain a relatively small part of the overall news agenda. But having almost doubled its coverage of devolution, the BBC's commitment to reporting the nations does compare favourably to commercial television news, which halved its reporting of devolved politics.

To explore whether the BBC's enhanced volume of devolution coverage was matched by a more nuanced interpretation of policy differences across the nations, every news item was examined to ascertain if its geographic applicability had been made clear. Whereas the previous study had shown that health and education stories largely ignored the devolved differences across the nations, the follow-up study showed the BBC had more accurately ascribed a policy to its rightful nation, although in most cases this was England. Close to two thirds of the BBC's television coverage had clearly identified a policy story that was applied to England – or, at least one other nation. So, for example, BBC news items more explicitly identified their location in the opening introduction to a story. In a BBC *News at One* story, an English review into education for infants began by stating:

> Children in *England* shouldn't start formal education until the age of six. That's according to the largest review of primary education *in England* for forty years. It says there's no evidence that starting formal learning at five brings any benefits, and could even be harmful. The government called the review disappointing and out of date. (BBC *News at One*, 16 October 2009, emphasis added)

Nevertheless, devolved politics is not always easy to interpret and understand. The decision to fast-track the building of nuclear power stations might, at first glance, appear to be a Westminster decision (e.g. energy policy) but on closer inspection it is only partly devolved since planning procedures are under the control of the devolved nations. Stories about nuclear power, in other words, will have a complex mix of devolved and Westminster powers at play. The BBC *News at Six*, to an extent, did communicate where power lay even if the justification of energy policy was a little hazy.

> The government has to keep the lights on; it also wants to cut carbon emissions. And ministers say the nuclear option is needed for both. So they've streamlined the planning system to give a fast track to projects like new nuclear stations. And here they are [points to map with UK highlighted]: ten sites, each of them at or near places already used for generating nuclear power, dotted all round the coastline. The decision doesn't fully apply to Scotland, which has devolved authority. (BBC *News at Six*, 9 November 2009)

The case could be made, of course, that the corporation still has to improve upon the accuracy of its devolved reporting since the policy relevance for each nation was not always immediately apparent. In a story about a review of criminal justice, for example, both a BBC *News at Six* and a Channel 4 report did not convey that the initiative was relevant to England and Wales alone.

> The Justice Secretary, Jack Straw, has announced a review of the way the police use cautions and out-of-court fines. A BBC *Panorama* investigation to be broadcast this evening found such penalties being used to deal with some violent offences. Mr Straw

said that guidance was clear, but that the review would examine how it was applied. (BBC *News at Six*, 9 November 2009)

The way the police issue cautions and fixed-penalty notices is to be reviewed. The Justice Secretary, Jack Straw, said that the assessment would be carried out jointly with the Home Office. Up to 40,000 assaults are dealt with by a caution every year ... (*Channel 4 News*, 9 November 2009)

Neither report drew attention to the fact that the measures were not relevant to Northern Ireland or that criminal justice was an area that was devolved in Scotland with the police caution system not operating. But despite examples of where the BBC could navigate through the world of devolved politics more surely, clear enough qualitative difference emerged between commercial and public service television. For while the BBC correctly attributed two thirds of devolved coverage to the appropriate nation just over a third of commercial television news was accurate in this respect. Put another away, commercial television news viewers more often than not may have been left confused about the relevance of policy stories on a UK-wide scale.

The most striking recommendation the BBC put into practice was a more informative compare-and-contrast approach to devolution coverage. Relatively few instances of comparisons between policy approaches in England, Scotland, Wales and Northern Ireland had been identified in the first review (just eight). In the follow-up study a more constructive approach was undertaken (39), with enhanced passing and substantive references made to how social policy had been pursued across the nations within a news story. In an education story about proposals in England to move to a more play-based infant curriculum, a number of BBC bulletins made reference to other nations in order to put a wider UK context to the story.

In Wales and Northern Ireland, although children can start school from the age of four, in line with the rest of the UK, formal learning is put off until children are seven, with the emphasis, instead, on play. (BBC *News at One*, 16 October 2009)

Children do start school in the UK at a younger age than in many other countries, but the more important issue for the review is when the switch takes place from play-based learning, to a more formal, structured curriculum. In England and Scotland, the curriculum starts at five, whereas in Wales and Northern Ireland, the emphasis on learning through play continues right through, until children are seven. (BBC *News at Six*, 16 October 2009)

By comparing and contrasting the approaches of different nations, what these examples demonstrate is how the relevance to all four nations can be addressed, making it a far more illuminated devolved story to understand. On commercial television news, while Channel 4 doubled its record on passing references to devolved nations, both ITV and Sky News did not contain any substantive *or* passing comparisons. In not drawing distinctions between the nations it is very easy – in the case of the proposal by English infant schools to move to play-based learning – to confuse England with the UK. A Sky News story stated:

> Now, the Schools Minister has rejected proposals for children to start school a year later, at the age of six. The recommendation was made in the most comprehensive review of primary education for forty years, but Vernon Coaker said the plans were 'counterproductive'. (*Sky News*, 16 October 2009)

In a number of respects, this story could give the impression the review represented the whole of the UK. The use of 'Schools Minister' – when each of the devolved institutions have their own Schools Minister – for example, implies this may generally apply to all schools. 'England' and 'the UK' were used interchangeably throughout the broadcast and without making clear it was a review of English schools audiences may have found it difficult to pin down the immediate relevance.

Comparatively speaking, the BBC's coverage of devolution after the regulatory intervention has, on a range of measures, improved its volume of stories from across the nations and its accuracy in reporting devolved politics. There remain, of course, areas for improvement. It will perhaps always be argued – particularly by those watching in Scotland, Wales and Northern Ireland – that non-English UK stories should increase. It is hard to imagine, in this respect, a perceived 'equity' in coverage of the nations ever being agreed upon. But in enhancing coverage of compare-and-contrast UK political stories, the relevance of a 'devolution angle' can be invoked without excluding audiences from various parts of the UK. In doing so, this represents an informative and imaginative way by which devolution can be communicated in UK television journalism.

In the following section it will be suggested that collaborative efforts between a media regulator and media academics – on display here in a case study on the reporting of the nations and regions within the UK – could potentially be exploited further to identify those areas of journalism the market has so far failed to supply and where publicly-subsidised journalism could play a role.

Challenging 'light touch' orthodoxy: towards more evidence-driven interventionist re-regulation

As previous chapters have shown, television journalism has operated in an increasingly deregulated environment in recent decades, and commercial television news within a far less regulated genre. Of course, this is not to suggest that robust regulation does not remain in place or that public service broadcasting has been entirely eroded. Far from it, since this chapter has demonstrated the importance of both to local journalism in the UK. The EU Commission, likewise, has sought to re-regulate media markets and prevent unfettered market dominance, particularly as new media develop and new means of policing content need to be legislated on. Many EU countries, in this respect, have maintained a strong public service presence and robust regulatory frameworks (Cushion 2012).

Nevertheless, for all the re-regulatory efforts of many governments, sustained analysis of media policy debates in recent years has shown many countries are favouring a more 'light-touch' approach to the regulation of broadcasters (Freedman 2008). Where once broadcasters benefited from a paternalistic relationship with the state, today legislators will talk-up the potential of what it is that market competition can deliver. Less state intervention and more 'light-touch' regulation are seen as effective ways to achieve a more competitive and creative media market-place (Freedman 2008). The market, in this context, is seen as an answer to – rather than a symptom of – many of the challenges that face television journalism (Barker 2007). Meanwhile regulatory pressures and requirements are often viewed as a threat to journalistic freedom, flair and innovation. Heir to Murdoch's empire, James – Rupert's son – made this case vociferously in the 2009 Edinburgh International Television Festival's MacTaggart Lecture. In a UK context, he argued that:

> ... the expansion of state-sponsored journalism is a threat to the plurality and independence of news provision, which are so important for our democracy ... No amount of governance in the form of committees, regulators, trusts or advisory bodies is truly sufficient as a guarantor of independence. In fact, they curb speech. On the contrary, independence is characterised by the absence of the apparatus of supervision and dependency. (Murdoch, cited in Robinson 2009)

National and international regulators are increasingly dancing to this regulatory beat, retreating from robust interventions into the television news market. Too heavily intervening into journalism is often viewed pejoratively by governments, leading to accusations of 'distorting' the market or promoting anti-competitiveness (Barker 2007). It is in this context where commercial media organisations have been able to have their public service obligations relaxed or lifted in recent years since, in a more deregulated multi-channel environment, this effectively puts them at a competitive disadvantage. So, for example, ITV's public service requirements towards the provision of regional news have gradually been lessened as the commercial ecology of broadcasting has grown stronger, to the point where Ofcom expects little to potentially no local journalism when licences are renewed in 2014.

This chapter, overall, has revealed the striking comparisons in local journalism across differently funded and regulated television organisations. Cardiff's School of Journalism, Media and Cultural Studies follow-up review for the

BBC Trust provided an opportunity to explore how light-touch regulated commercial television news coverage compared to the BBC's more vigorously regulated television journalism. In doing so, the review can be viewed as an informative case study that demonstrated how a more robust re-regulatory intervention could constructively and collaboratively encourage journalism to diversify its news agenda and sharpen up its accuracy. It would, in this context, be difficult to see re-regulation as being a democratic obstruction to journalistic freedom or creativity. If anything the review prompted considerable internal self-reflection, leading to a more innovative approach to how devolution was reported (by encouraging a 'compare-and-contrast' pursuit of devolved politics, for example). On commercial television, however, UK network news's coverage of devolution has remained a blindspot. This has particularly been the case for Sky News, the least regulated television news channel. For while Channel 4 and ITV may also be commercially-driven, Ofcom currently see these as channels which are carrying a set of public service obligations in a way that Sky does not. The channel with the least public service obligations or expectations, in other words, has provided the *least* convincing commitment to covering the nations and devolved politics. Overall, the review demonstrated public service objectives in action fulfilling an important democratic role in striking contrast to commercial television, which has pushed this area of journalism to the sidelines.

The impact of editorial interventions into television journalism addresses, in part, Steven Barnett's (2010b: 3) appeal for academic debates about policing the media industry to focus less on the structural implications of media ownership and more on 'content regulation'. Since many of the structural problems in the media industry 'are in danger of extinction', there is, according to Barnett (2010b: 10), 'little point in clinging to structural solutions for preserving pluralism'. Barnett has made the case for a kind of *quid pro quo* between commercial broadcasters and government where structural limitations – in terms of ownership and funding – should be lightened if certain public interest programming is resourced and pursued, such as scheduling investigative journalism in peak-time slots. He has suggested a 'regulatory framework' could be fashioned whereby

> requirements [for the media industry to follow] would be framed by a normative vision of how diverse and well resourced journalism contributes to a healthy democracy ... for example, demonstrable safeguards for editorial freedom written into employment contracts; guaranteed investment in training, with schemes and costs subject to audible scrutiny; professional standard secured through formal commitment to codes of journalistic conduct; commitment to diversity of output and news agendas and, in particular, to investment in long-term investigative and accountability journalism. (Barnett 2010b: 13)

In order to achieve a commitment to diverse news agendas, it is in this spirit where greater regulatory interventions could be made on an evidence-based assessment of television journalism. The BBC Trust's review of coverage of the nations and devolved politics showed how and where academic scrutiny towards 'content regulation' and editorial interventionism could be effective. With questions of impartiality and diversity devised by journalism academics rather than broadcasters, the review drew on robust communication research to generate a set of editorial trends and recommendations. In doing so, the independently commissioned media research could clearly identify areas of market neglect and demonstrate where a public service broadcaster – and an empowered regulator – could improve the quality of journalism constructively.

The collaborative efforts between regulators and academics that produced the King Report and its follow-up study not only impacted on the volume and nature of domestic news and political coverage, they have also subsequently informed 'best practice' television journalism more generally. The BBC's College of Journalism – an organisation set up in 2005 to offer, in the corporation's own words, 'teaching on every aspect of journalism: craft skills like writing and storytelling; the technical skills required to operate in a digital, multiplatform world; social media and the web; and ethics, values and law' – has used the findings of the report to instruct journalists about how to report devolution during coverage of the General Election in 2010. While the BBC College claims to be 'a learning site for BBC journalists, by BBC journalists', the conclusions drawn by the King Report demonstrate how 'best practice' recommendations can be achieved beyond the industry and *within* the academy. Written in a journalistic style, these were largely shaped by the main thrust of the King Report's conclusions. Box 5.1 illustrates what the college called an 'Election Checklist'.

Box 5.1   BBC College of Journalism 2010 Election Checklist

Here's a useful checklist – questions to ask yourself to help you decide how to treat a story that's affected by UK devolution.

It's even more important as you try to cover a general election in a devolved UK.

Thinking about how devolution affects a UK story doesn't necessarily stop you doing anything – though you may have to do it differently. And it opens up other story areas.

(Continued)

(Continued)

- What's the issue? Is it an area in which powers are devolved?
- If yes, does my coverage make clear that it is a devolved area of policy?
- If no, should the SNP or Plaid Cymru be featuring in my coverage?
- How different are the policies across the four nations of the UK?
- Should I be mentioning these differences in more detail? (Are they interesting or significant?)
- Will they add value to my coverage of the story?
- Will they help people understand, or overload and confuse them? (Will my coverage fall short if I don't?)
- If I should be mentioning them, to what extent?
- Are any comparisons I'm proposing to make rigorous and fair?
- Have I checked whether terminology is different between the nations? (For example, Health Trusts in England and now Health Boards in Scotland and Wales – they're not the same thing.)
- I'm in London: what will my proposed coverage look/sound like in other parts of the UK?

College of Journalism: Part of the BBC Academy (http://www.bbc.co.uk/journalism/general-election/uk-nations/election-checklist.shtml)

Of course, if most democratic states suddenly started empowering regulatory bodies and encouraging public interventions into television journalism this would represent a significant reversal of trends in media policy making. As Chapter 2 showed, national legislators have, to varying degrees, deregulated the television industry in previous decades. The prevailing wisdom of media policy-making runs counter to the evidence here, since a 'light-touch' approach is still seen as the most effective means of policing the media market in an increasingly commercial environment. At the time of writing, Ofcom – already a relatively lightweight regulator – had become a major casualty of the UK government's deficit reduction plan (October 2010). It had been asked to reduce its budget by 30 per cent – far above the average cuts received in other policy areas – and had already scaled back some of its regulatory ambitions. For Damian Tambini (2010), 'the government's proposal for the reform of Ofcom is one of the gravest assaults on broadcasting freedom' in the UK. He also went on to say:

> Ofcom was set up as a strong independent body because it takes decisions that should not be taken by governments for the simple reason that media regulation should not be left to political backroom deals and 'Secretary of State approval'. It should be evidence-based and independent, achieving objectives that are clearly set out in law.

The BBC Trust, meanwhile, has been a political target for appearing to be an inefficient and ineffective watchdog. It has been roundly criticised within the industry and, more vociferously, in right-wing newspaper coverage. While many observers suspected the BBC Trust might be abolished in the government's deficit reduction plan it has managed to survive thus far and will most probably remain in existence until the next Charter renewal in 2017.

The BBC itself, however, has not escaped the current spending cuts. Most of the headlines in the aftermath of the spending review were about the BBC's licence fee being suspended for six years; its taking on the funding responsibility for the World Service (that had been previously subsidised by the Foreign Office), BBC monitoring, and the Welsh language television channel, S4C; together with helping with the costs towards extending its broadcast coverage in rural areas. In the context of a 16 per cent cut in its budget overall, what did escape many people's attention was the additional financial burden and management responsibly of funding local television news and online services. This involved a one-off payment of up to £25 million and an annual fund requiring approximately £5 million. In other words, a public subsidy would be necessary in order to sustain, at least in the short-term, local television journalism.

As the beginning of this chapter pointed out, when the Secretary of State for Culture, Olympics, Media and Sport, Jeremy Hunt, first started in his post he was an enthusiastic advocate of commercially-run local television news stations. However, these market-driven ambitions have been scaled back in subsequent speeches. In a Hunt-commissioned report on the feasibility of establishing local television news stations without public subsidy, the media banker Nicholas Shott (2010) concluded that 'Local television in sparsely populated areas is unlikely to be commercially viable ... Even in densely populated areas ... the economics of a TV business funded mainly by advertising will still be challenging'. Despite Hunt having initially ended plans to develop IFNCs in public/private partnerships, the Secretary of State for Culture, Olympics, Media and Sport has had to rely on a public service broadcaster to stimulate a market for local television journalism. To a degree, there has been some recognition that there are limits to what the market can achieve in television journalism. Without significant public subsidy, put simply, 'local' journalism is proving difficult to financially self-sustain.

Within media, cultural and communication scholarship, the impact of media deregulation has largely been viewed critically. But in doing so many critiques have struggled to demonstrate empirically how regulation can enhance media content compared to what a 'light-touch' system cannot. There is, of course, a voluminous literature on media policy and the critical role it plays in democracies (Freedman 2008; McChesney 2000, 2008), often examining in detail specific acts or areas of legislation (Harvey 2006; Livingstone et al. 2007; Wheeler 2004). In doing so, studies have been able to observe areas or instances where regulation has policed the editorial boundaries of television journalism. Yet it has been difficult to determine where re-regulatory interventions have either corrected or enhanced the nature of television journalism. If there was a case to be made not just for the existence of public service broadcasting but also for robust re-regulatory forces, the impact of the BBC Trust's editorial intervention into the reporting of devolution and the deficit left by the market demonstrates what can be achieved. For what this chapter has concluded is that more robust public service broadcast regulation may improve rather than impede the quality of journalism (Cushion et al. forthcoming). This is not to claim that all the challenges journalism faces can be rectified by relentless rules or intrusive regulation but merely to demonstrate the value of robust, rather than 'light-touch', regulation. As opposed to relying on the market to shape television journalism, carefully and strategically developed public interventions have, in short, a role to play in policing contemporary television journalism.

The next chapter examines journalism from a new perspective. While previous chapters have explored the impact of ownership and regulation in shaping journalism, the dominant trends in television news agendas and the changing composition of television audiences, Chapter 6 turns to look at journalists themselves by asking what role they play in shaping contemporary television news culture and journalistic practice.

PART III

JOURNALISTS AND SCHOLARS

6

ENTERING THE PROFESSION: WHO ARE TELEVISION JOURNALISTS?

Who are television journalists: a professional or occupational pursuit?

Much academic attention has been paid to debunking the myth that television news is a 'window on the world'. Rather than reflecting the social world, journalism studies has long argued that journalists are constrained by a set of predictable rules and conventions that shape, most of the time, what counts as being 'newsworthy' (see Chapter 3). While many journalists may routinely uncover stories of genuine 'human interest' or pursue issues of wider social significance, they may find it hard to pass the 'news-test' of editors who are eager to capture that exclusive or remain appealing to all viewers. In doing so, the role or agency of journalists themselves has often been pushed into the backdrop, almost casting them as passive participants in the daily grind of making and shaping news.

The aim of this chapter is to put television journalists under the spotlight, making sense of who they are, the sort of background they come from, what education or training they have undergone and, above all, how far they are trusted and valued both by viewers and within the news industry. The focus, in short, will be on the sociology of journalists, exploring how distinctive television journalists are when compared to rival news media.

To understand who journalists are, it is of course necessary to define the profession. This may seem, at face value, an obvious first move. But even suggesting that journalism is a profession has proved contentious enough since – primarily amongst journalists themselves – it has often been viewed as a trade, as something to be learnt on the job, rather than someone having to be trained or educated in a classroom (Cushion 2008). As Andrew Marr (2004: 3), one of the UK's most eminent television interviewers, has put it plainly in *My Trade*: 'British journalism is not a profession'. This is obvious, Marr argued, because the news media industry does not 'have an accepted career structure, necessary entry requirements or an effective system of self-policing' (2004: 3) compared to the US where journalism schools are closely tied up with the industry. This chapter will challenge this account of how journalism is structured by demonstrating that most journalists within the industry are drawn from similar social, ethnic and educational backgrounds.

For now, however, understanding what a journalist is and how journalism is defined needs to be established, since in the age of media convergence (see Chapter 1), journalists must increasingly multitask and move seamlessly between platforms at considerable speed. In this context, making sense of who journalists are in the twenty-first century can prove an elusive task and one that is difficult to achieve empirically. Confident predictions about how many journalists there are 'out there' – where they work, how they are employed, what values they hold, and how much they are paid – should be carefully scrutinised, since they will occupy multiple roles and also often be freelance either by choice or coercion. As Kovach and Rosenstiel (2001) point out, 'the definition of journalism has been exploded by technology'. For over the last decade or so 'ordinary people' have begun to publish their own form of journalism, online and instantaneously, for (at least potentially) mass audiences, and this action has in turn sparked debate about whether 'we are all journalists now' (Grant 2007). Where once privileged media access or the ownership of expensive publishing tools would give people a voice, the online blogosphere today is full of wannabe opinion makers who are bringing with them a new brand of 'citizen journalism'. Many excitable journalists and enthusiastic academics have speculated about how journalism will be revolutionised by aspiring journalists, a bottom-up grassroots movement that will be able to challenge mainstream media. However, even within the industry young journalists today are being encouraged to be as capable as possible multimedia-wise. In Dan Synge's (2010) *Survival Guide to Journalism*, readers are told the 'twenty-first-century journalist is a multitasking, laptop-wielding wordsmith with an active and inquisitive mind, a finger on the pulse and the nose for a good story' (2010: 5–6).

Meanwhile, within the industry, hostility has grown towards the blogging community since many question the wisdom of so-called 'citizen journalism' and the contribution it makes to journalism or, in grander terms, the public sphere. In October 2010 Andrew Marr caused much furore in a speech at the Cheltenham Literary Festival. He accused bloggers of 'being socially inadequate, pimpled, single, slightly seedy, bald, cauliflower-nosed young men sitting in their mother's basements and ranting' (cited in Plunkett 2010). While Marr conceded 'citizen journalism' was 'fantastic at times', he also warned us 'it is not going to replace journalism' (cited in Plunkett 2010). In defending journalism in the age of citizen-media, it has been revealing how the role and purpose of what it means to be a 'journalist' has been more forthcoming within the industry or amongst those who are teaching journalism at universities. Two of the latter, Gary Hudson and Mick Temple (2010: 74), for example, have argued that the 'blogger, the online pundit, the producer of an online community newsletter *can* call themselves journalists, but unless they are committed to writing new and accurate material they have no right to do so' (original emphasis). If not explicit, then implicit from their definition of journalism is that journalists should take seriously the requirement to inform people about the latest developments in the world objectively. Or, as two US journalists have put it more purposely, 'The news media help us define our communities, and help us create a common language and common knowledge rooted in reality' (Kovach and Rosenstiel 2001: 17).

However, if this hints at a consensual understanding of being a 'professional' journalist then the burgeoning literature on the professionalisation of journalism in recent decades would suggest otherwise. Hanitzsch et al.'s (2011) study of journalists across 18 countries – namely Australia, Austria, Brazil, Bulgaria, Chile, China, Egypt, Germany, Indonesia, Israel, Mexico, Romania, Russia, Spain, Switzerland, Turkey, Uganda and the US – demonstrates that while similarities do exist within the profession, there are still many differences in how journalism is conceptualised and practised on a global scale. They concluded that:

> Being a watchdog of the government, to a lesser extent, business elites, as well providing political information do ... belong to the functions that have universal appeal. In terms of epistemological foundations of journalism ... personal beliefs and convictions should not be allowed to influence reporting. Reliability and factualness of information as well as the strict adherence to impartiality and neutrality belong to the highly esteemed professional standards of journalism around the world ... Interventionist aspects of journalism ... are much less supported ... the active promotion of particular values, ideas, groups and social change is generally not a characteristic of Western journalistic cultures ... Similarly controversial is the role of subjectivity ... The ideal of the separation of facts and opinion does also account for substantial differences between countries ... journalists in the United States exhibit a remarkable tendency to let personal evaluation and interpretation slip into news coverage. (Hanitzsch el al. 2011: 14–15)

The study showed differences that not only went beyond western and non-western perspectives but also across developed countries such as the US where – as Chapter 4 argued – objectivity has become less championed when compared to the UK where impartiality remains central to many broadcasters' identity.

But more broadly, whether striving to be ethical, aspiring to be objective, competing to deliver news first or remaining editorially independent, comparative international surveys of journalistic identities in recent decades have made professionalisation a problematic catch-all concept amongst practising journalists (Weaver and Wilhoit 1986; Weaver et al. 2007). For while there may be a broad sense of what might constitute 'journalistic merit' or 'quality reporting', these are not necessarily values that are universally subscribed to (Cushion 2012). After all, news media will adopt news values based on the medium they work in (as we shall witness in this chapter). But what international comparative studies have also shown is how national variations can shape remarkably different self-perceptions of what it means to be a journalist. The wider cultural, economic and political environment journalists grow up in contributes, in other words, to the values journalists hold. One survey of students in Spain and the UK, for example, found 'distinct, national journalistic "cultures" have influenced students before they arrive at university' (Sanders et al. 2008). Professionalisation, in this context, would appear to have been cultivated prior to any journalist setting foot in a newsroom.

Mark Deuze (2005) has argued that journalism is less a profession and more a shifting occupational ideology, since when journalists 'give meaning to their newswork' they adopt new values that reflect the wider technological and cultural changes in society. Reviewing academic research into journalists' values and identification, Schudson and Anderson (2009: 99) concluded that 'claims to knowledge and professional power are often contradictory and incoherent'. In making sense of the professionalisation of a journalist, the occupational changes – and challenges – within a newsroom appear to be just as important as the broader changes that occur socially, economically and politically within different countries.

So far journalists have been discussed generally without assessing whether or not television journalists interpret the practice of journalism differently to practitioners working in rival print, radio and online news media. As Chapter 1 showed, the medium of television adopts distinctive values and operates at a different pace when compared to other media. Dimitrova and Stromback (2010: 488) have described television journalism as a 'format ... severely restricted by and intimately tied to technological developments, and ... has a special logic that follows from its format and its reliance on visuals as well as audio and verbal content'. John Hartley's classic (1982) study, *Understanding News*, demonstrated how television news acquired semiotic rules to address audiences with subtle visual cues and authoritative aural devices used to convey what was happening in the world. In doing so, television news's professional traits and editorial codes have evolved in ways that are unique when compared to forms of print, radio and, more recently, online news media.

Kimberly Meltzer's (2009, 2010) research has explored how journalists are viewed within the news media industry, discovering what she calls 'a hierarchy of cultural authority' within the journalistic community. Drawing on interviews with journalists from a range of US news media, Meltzer found that newspaper practitioners were held in most esteem and 'regarded as the legitimate craftsmen' (2009: 72). By contrast, some television journalists' abilities were questioned, with some interviewees believing they lacked basic journalistic skills and competencies. This was aimed primarily at news anchors who were seen as 'inauthentic' (2009: 61), since many appeared to blur 'the lines between opinion and factual reporting, and news and entertainment' (2009: 62). Within America's journalistic community the fame and status granted to television journalists far exceeds what other practitioners can achieve in the field. But the image of hugely paid glamorous television journalists distorts the status and pay of the 'average worker' in the industry. Table 6.1 provides a detailed list of salaries paid to local television news employees – the biggest employer of journalism in the US market.

Table 6.1 Comparisons of five and ten year median local television news salaries in the US with inflation

	2010	2005	5 year percentage change	2000	10 year percentage change
Inflation			+13.6%		+28.8%
All TV News			+2.9%		+17.6%
News Director	$75,000	$73,000	+2.7%	$59,000	+27.1%
Assistant News Director	$63,000	$60,000	+5.0%	$54,000	+16.7%
Managing Editor	$60,000	$55,000	+9.1%	50,000	+20.0
Executive Producer	$55,000	$50,000	+10.0	49,000	+12.2
News Anchor	$59,000	$55,500	+6.3%	45,000	+31.1
Weathercaster	$50,000	$50,000	n/c	40,000	+25.0
Sports Anchor	$40,000	$40,000	n/c	35,000	+14.3
News Reporter	$29,000	$30,000	−3.3%	24,000	+20.8
Sports Reporter	$26,500	$28,000	−5.4%	23,000	+15.2
Assignment Editor	$25,000	$32,500	+13.8%	30,000	+23.3
News Producer	$30,000	$30,000	n/c	25,000	+20.0
News Writer	$26,500	$27,000	−1.9%	30,000	−11.7
News Assistant	$25,000	$25,000	n/c	21,000	+19.0
Photographer	$28,000	$27,000	+3.7%	23,000	+21.7
Tape Editor	$27,000	$25,000	+8.0%	24,000	+12.5
Graphics Specialist	$30,000	$31,000	−3.2%	30,000	n/c
Internet Specialist	$35,000	$37,500	−6.7%	30,000	+16.7

(Adapted from the RTDNA/Hofstra University Survey authored by Bob Papper http://www.rtdna.org/media/Salary_Survey_2010.pdf)

What local television salaries show are not just the mostly modest wages many earn in the industry but how little incomes have risen in line with the economy. As Papper (2010) has pointed out, 'TV news salaries have slipped further behind inflation' over the last ten years. However, for national news anchor stars the opposite is true. For while what the average news worker earns is little discussed in the mainstream media, much attention is paid to what star television presenters earn across the networks. So, for example, an article for *TV Guide* (Battaglio 2010) – a magazine previewing the following week's television programmes – listing the wages of top television stars featured news anchors without any reference to the amounts the vast majority of people in the television journalism earned (see Table 6.2).

Table 6.2 The salaries for top-earning television news journalists in the US

Television journalist	Programme	Paid per year
Matt Lauer	Today	$16m
Katie Couric	CBS	$15m
Brian Williams	NBC	$12.5m
Diane Sawyer	ABC	$12m
Meredith Vieira	Today	$11m
Bill O'Reilly	Fox News	$10m
George Stephanopoulos	ABC	$8m
Keith Olbermann	MSNBC	$7m
Shepard Smith	Fox News	$7m
Wolf Blitzer	CNN	$3m
Christiane Amanpour	ABC	$2m
Lawrence O'Donnell	MSNBC	$2m

(Source: TV Guide – see Battaglio 2010)

At first glance, the astronomical salaries are most striking. But on closer inspection what stands out is that the 'journalists' on the list are not necessarily what we might consider as conventional news anchors/readers. Highly opinionated and partisan figures – Bill O'Reilly on Fox News – or political commentators – George Stephanopoulous – a former Democrat spin-doctor – feature prominently. Likewise, Meredith Vieira – an NBC journalist for *Today* – is also the host of *Who Wants to be a Millionaire?* It is noteworthy that this trend is not limited to the US. In the UK, Dermot Murnaghan, a former BBC and ITV news anchor, and now a Sky News presenter, has also been a quiz show host for the BBC's *Eggheads* and *Treasure Hunt*, and the news anchor Natasha Kaplinski – a former BBC, ITV, Sky, and most recently Five News journalist – has participated in the BBC celebrity show *Strictly Come Dancing*. In short, the role of a high-profile television journalist can, in contemporary times, move seamlessly from the genre of hard news and current affairs to the more trivial and light-hearted world of popular or celebrity culture.

In this context, television journalists are sometimes caricatured as 'lightweight' and superficial, with appearance and personality superseding any other journalistic qualities. This has resulted in growing numbers of what could be described as pseudo celebrity journalists. In Australia, Bainbridge and Bestwick (2010) have suggested television anchors are increasingly being seen as 'marketed newsreaders', in each case the strategic face of a network, someone who is projecting what a station stands for and represents editorially. They have pointed out that:

> The marketed newsreader is ... a significant figure in the domestic 'shifts' in news, for the public's interest in the person behind the news has not gone unnoticed by networks keen to cash in on the public's perceived curiosity regarding the newsreader's private life. In fact, networks work hard to make the public *want* to know. They market their personalities, including their newsreaders, so that they remain visible and ever-present in our daily lives. Furthermore, they cultivate newsreaders as celebrities because they recognize that it is through their 'well-knownness' and establishment of 'para-social' relationships with their audiences they can best function. In this way newsreaders occupy a most unusual position, relying on their celebrity to mediate journalism. (2010: 220–221)

In personalising television journalism, Meltzer (2010) has suggested that the image of journalists has been enhanced in general, since news anchors occupy such high profile roles in the mainstream media. At the same time, she argues, within the journalist community many believe news anchors are undermining conventional journalistic values. Whereas anchors once had more formalised modes of address, reflecting a greater sense of detachment when reporting news, today many presenters are informal and opinionated, disbanding previous conventions of appearing distant and remaining impartial.

A face for television? Gender and ethnic minority status amongst journalists

The changing role of news anchors – or readers – in recent years echoes debates about the role gender plays in journalism more generally. For while the world of news media, and in particular newspapers, has often been associated with a largely male and macho controlled industry, it has also been argued that the increasing proportion of female television journalists has changed the style and nature of journalism on the small screen. Exploring the growing presence of female news presenters and editors in the Netherlands, Van Zoonen (1993) has suggested a 'Tyranny of Intimacy' had increasingly shaped television news in the late 1980s, leading to a more personalised mode of address that was based on feminine values. Desmond and Danilewicz's

(2010) systematic content analysis of local television news in the US found the gender of a reporter would shape the type of stories produced. They showed 'women reporters reported "softer" news stories such as health and human interest while men reported politics' (2010: 827). However this information is interpreted, it does demonstrate women are having an impact on the values and day-to-day agendas of newsrooms.

At the same time the role and agency of young, attractive, female news anchors, within the industry or mainstream press, has been more flippantly caricatured as offering little more than 'eye candy'. At the 2001 Cheltenham Literary Festival, Kate Adie, for example, suggested all television news directors wanted were 'women with cute faces, cute bottoms and nothing else in between' (cited in Pelling 2001), while in the US a content analysis study of key national newspapers – the *New York Times*, *USA Today* and the *Washington Post* – examining the coverage of six high profile male and female television news anchors (Couric, Gibson, Schieffer, Vargas, Williams and Woodruff) found 'female anchors were regularly framed in terms of being a woman, whereas the male anchors were rarely framed in terms of being men' (Brewer and Macafee 2007: 13). And yet while this may be a mainstream reaction to more prominent female news anchors, it does not reveal what is happening behind the scenes or within the culture of news making. For what Van Zoonen and other scholars have suggested is that women do in fact contribute more than just a 'face for television'. They would argue that the feminisation of newsrooms has reshaped the character of television news since new values and conventions have been adopted as a result of this (Van Zoonen 1993). While Chambers et al. (2004: 122) have pointed out that evidence about women journalists must be carefully scrutinised and can be 'contradictory and ambiguous', they have argued that 'News agendas and priorities have clearly changed with the increasing number of women journalists, and men and women seem to adopt distinctly different approaches to reporting'.

If women's enhanced role in journalism has impacted on the editorial format and agenda impact of television news, this has not been matched by a parity in their pay or status. For while a survey of UK journalists found that more women (54 per cent) worked in television than men (46 per cent) (Journalism Training Forum 2002), they were not, on average, paid the same. As Weaver et al. (2007: 102–3) have pointed out in a US context, women in journalism generally tended to be less experienced, employed by smaller news media, and would hold fewer managerial positions than men. All of which, they suggested, meant women were proportionally receiving less wages. There has, nevertheless, been some progress on women gaining senior positions. As Chambers et al. (2004: 10) highlighted in *Women and Journalists*: 'Over the last twenty or twenty five years, in both the US and

UK, women have begun to achieve critical mass in certain subfields and to break through the barriers to decision-making positions'. So, for example, a 2008 survey in the US found 28.3 per cent of news directors were female – which represented an all-time high (Papper, cited in Television Digital News Association 2008). And in the UK Helen Boaden, who holds one of the most senior positions in television journalism as Head of BBC Television News, reportedly earns a salary of £327,800 a year (*Media Guardian* 2010).

However, even at the top end of the television news market male anchors are paid greater salaries across the board. A Freedom of Information Act question in the UK found that female news correspondents on the BBC's 1pm, 6pm and 10pm news bulletins were each paid a salary of £59,050 – which was £6,575 less than their male counterparts (Verkaik 2006). The same question also exposed an age disparity between genders (the average age for females was 41 while for males it was 46). Ageism, particularly within BBC television news but also evident elsewhere, has been a major issue for television journalists, one that was recently foregrounded by Moira Stewart (then aged 55), a longstanding female BBC news anchor, who quit the corporation in 2007 after being replaced as the news reader on the *Andrew Marr Show*. She joined a number of other high profile presenters – Kate Adie, Anna Ford and Angela Rippon – who had complained of being replaced by younger and more glamorous presenters. Selina Scott, a former BBC, ITV and Sky news anchor, also received an out of court settlement from Channel 5 at an employment tribunal after alleged age discrimination at the station (Taylor 2009). Male anchors, by contrast, can continue to anchor programmes well into their sixties. In a move to counter accusations of ageism, the BBC's Director General has had to intervene and ask for its news programming to 'have a broad range of presenters on air – including older women' (cited in Plunkett 2009). Women's role in television news, in short, may have increased in recent decades and had some impact on how journalism is produced, but there remain ongoing issues around their status and equality in newsrooms.

Exploring not just gender but ethnicity amongst US journalists, Ryan and Mapaye (2010) compared network news programmes in 1987 with 2007 and found a far more diverse range of network news anchors and correspondents twenty years later. Their content analysis discovered that 73 per cent of stories had been reported by men compared to 48 per cent two decades on – not quite on a par with women (40 per cent) but, the authors suggested, it was a significant closing of the gap. For ethnic minorities, just 5 per cent reported stories in 1987 whereas in 2007 this had risen to 32 per cent – a considerable increase and one reflecting the increasingly diverse nature of the US population. The authors noted that 'white correspondents still dominate network news staffs, but in certain prominent roles, minority groups appear in significantly higher numbers' (Ryan and

Mapaye 2010: 108). High-profile figures such as Martin Bashir, a former anchor for ABC and now at MSNBC, and a contributor to NBC's *Dateline*, broke down some of the barriers when he first appeared on US television news. And in the UK similar barriers were broken with the BBC's George Alagiah, Moira Stewart (before the ageism controversy), and Rageh Omaar (now at Al-Jazeera) and, above all, with ITV's longstanding anchor Sir Trevor McDonald. Even in France – where racial tensions have been rife in recent years – the first non-white news anchor was selected to front the 8pm bulletin on TF1 in 2006. President of a campaigning movement for minority representation in the French media, Amirouche Laidi, appeared shell-shocked at the move: 'This is like a bombshell for us – a black pre-senting the 8pm news on the biggest television station in France' (cited in BBC News 2006). There is evidence, in other words, of some major breakthroughs taking place with ethnic minorities gaining senior positions in television news.

As a proportion of all ethnic minority journalists, television news appears to be a more diverse world than those found in other news industries. If we compare the volume of ethnic minority journalists working in print, online or radio with television, surveys have shown far more to be employed in television news, proportionately speaking, than in the other news industries. Weaver et al.'s (2007: 14) survey in the US found minority journalists occu-pied 14.7 per cent of the workforce, compared to 9.6 per cent for daily newspapers, 8.6 per cent for radio, and 5.6 per cent for weekly newspa-pers. A more recent survey shows the level of minority presence in televi-sion newsrooms has increased over the last 20 years while in radio it has decreased (Papper 2010). But if we scratch below the surface, what the survey also revealed was that while there had been a 2.4 per cent increase in ethnic minority journalists in television news since 1990, this had not been as significant (9.4 per cent) given the number of minorities that make up the US population overall (see Table 6.3).

The same trend has been found in the UK where ethnic minorities make up far less of the population but remain under represented. In a 2002 study of UK journalists, it was estimated that 94 per cent of white people made up the workforce generally compared to 96 per cent of the journalistic profes-sion who were white. While this may seem fairly representative, the authors point out that in the UK:

> Journalists are predominantly employed in London and the South East and in other urban areas, which have a higher proportion of people from ethnic minorities. For example, London's black and ethnic minority population is currently estimated at being 24 per cent, and predicted to rise to 30 per cent by 2016; and journalists are young, and it would again be expected to find a higher proportion of ethnic minorities in younger age groups. (Journalism Training Forum 2002: 21)

Table 6.3 Ethnic minorities working in radio and television news as a proportion of the minority population in the US

	2010	2009	2008	2007	2006	2005	2000	1995	1990
Minority population in US	*35.3%	34.4%	34%	33.6%	33.2%	32.8%	28.6%	27.9%	25.9%
Minority TV workforce	20.2%	21.8%	23.6%	21.5%	22.2%	21.2%	21%	17.1%	17.8%
Minority radio workforce	5%	8.9%	11.8%	6.2%	6.4%	7.9%	10%	14.7%	10.8%

(Adapted from the RTDNA/Hofstra University Survey authored by Bob Papper http://www.rtdna.org/media/women_minorities_survey_final.pdf)

In other words, there appeared to be obstacles preventing more ethnic minorities from entering the profession. Many studies have explored how newsrooms have been diversified in recent years, attempting to 'identify both doors and barriers to the hiring and retention of journalists with color' (Weaver et al. 2007: 197). Some of these barriers related to social circumstances, financial resources and a degree-level education – these will be explored in the next section – but there were also cultural issues facing ethnic minority presence in television newsrooms. Weaver et al. (2007: 212) have suggested that the working conditions in newsrooms may need to change in order to increase the diversity of journalists in employment:

> To the extent that the past is a good guide, we presume news organizations will continue to work at hiring and retaining minority and women journalists. Our findings over time suggest that the task will continue to be a difficult one if those who manage news organizations – most often men and most often white men – do not make strong efforts to create the sort of working environments that convince minority and women journalists that this is an occupation they wish to dedicate themselves to throughout their careers.

A 2007 general report into the audio and visual industry within London by the Working Lives Research Institute at London found a practice of 'nepotism', with recruitment taking place from 'old-boys networks' and employment operating within 'limited cultural circles' (Holgate and McKay 2007: 11). All of which, it was suggested, had had the net effect of cultivating a largely white and middle-class workforce. For minorities – who are, on average, disproportionately poorer – any opportunities, the report argued, were further diminished when the media companies often expected new entrants to work without a salary when they first joined an organisation.

In marginalising journalists from minority backgrounds, it has been argued that their exclusion perpetuates how ethnicity is more generally represented in the news media. A study of television news produced by US college students examined source selection in how news stories were produced by ethnic minorities and Caucasians, and compared these to what local television news reported (Smith 2008). It concluded that:

> Much like what you find in newsrooms across America, student reporters who were from racial minorities were significantly more likely than their Caucasian counterparts to seek out and include racial and ethnic minorities as sources in their stories ... when compared with their professional peers, students in this study included significantly more diverse sources in their stories and included diverse voices earlier and more consistently throughout their stories. (Smith 2008: 189–190)

Overall, then, while television news now has a more diverse workforce than many other news media, with several senior ethnic minority journalists holding high profile positions, they remain disproportionately represented within the television industry more generally. This may impact on the making and shaping of news since the editorial selection and production of news is heavily dominated by white, middle-class television journalists.

Educating or training? Towards an increasingly middle-class graduate-led occupation

Of course, the demographic make-up of journalists cannot be understood without examining how they entered the profession and the sorts of backgrounds they are from. As was pointed out at the beginning of the chapter, defining who a journalist is can be increasingly problematic since new technologies and media convergence are reshaping the expectations of 'newswork' (Deuze 2007). For many within the industry, learning to be a journalist means acquiring a set of skills (whether achieving a high proficiency in shorthand or operating the latest digital camera) and applying these to produce television in various forms. It is, in other words, an occupation that can be learnt and perfected on the job. This was well put in a *Guardian Media Guide 2000* (for students gaining an insight into the industry) back sleeve endorsement:

> Most journalists over 30 tend to agree with Roger Scruton who said: "Media studies course content is sub-Marxist gobbledegook and courses are taught by talentless individuals who can't get jobs in the media, so they teach instead. There's nothing really to learn except by way of apprenticeship on the job". (Cited in *The Guardian Media Guide*, Peak and Fisher 2000: 320)

What this taps into is the underlying tension that exists between the media industry and academy, at least in the UK. This is not exclusively about what journalists should learn prior to starting work at a newspaper, say, or a television station, rather it concerns how the field of journalism studies – or, more broadly, media and communication studies, or the social sciences and humanities – makes sense of the practice of news (see Chapter 7). For what the industry expects to get out of training journalists is not always part of a university curriculum. University-based journalism programmes in the UK have historically struggled to gain acceptance throughout most of the last century until a full-time graduate degree was created at Cardiff University in the 1970s (Cushion 2008). It was distinctly vocational (Williams 1999), earning its accreditation from the National Council for the Training of Journalists (NCTJ) and, in future years, the Broadcast Journalism Training Council (BJTC) and the Periodicals Training Council (PTC).

Journalism courses in the US have had a much stronger relationship with the news media industry than has been the case in the UK (Cushion 2008). As Wahl-Jorgensen and Franklin (2008: 178) have pointed out, 'this late arrival of academic training in journalism [in the UK] contrasts sharply with the US experience, in which journalism that foregrounds a strong liberal arts training has been around for the better half of a century'. Joseph Pulitzer was a key figure in the US, shaping a university curriculum that would meet the needs of both industry and academy, leading to the establishment of the Columbia School of Journalism in 1912. Published in the *North American Review* in 1904, Pulitzer argued that journalism education should encompass core academic subjects such as ethics, literature, history, sociology, economics, statistics and modern languages. In assessing university courses in the US, the Accrediting Council on Education in Journalism and Mass Communications (ACEJMC) maintains criteria examining 'Scholarship: Research, Creative and Professional Activity'. In the UK, by contrast, there remains a lack of agreement between universities and industry about how an academic journalism programme can enhance a vocational qualification. According to Aldridge and Evetts (2003: 552), this has meant 'undergraduate degree courses in journalism are rapidly being set up, in the absence of any industry-wide training strategy'.

Some inroads have, in recent years, been built in the journalist–academic relationship. While it is common practice in the US for former journalists to enter the academic world (Zelizer 2004), this trend is now becoming increasingly prominent in the UK (see Chapter 7). However, this has led to some tension between academics and practitioners. Harcup (2011a, 2011b) has conducted many interviews with 'hackademics' – a term used to describe journalists who have switched to being scholars (see Errigo and Franklin 2004) – from the UK and Ireland (including television journalists but they are not isolated in his data) and has found many were put off by the research culture and expectations to produce journalism scholarship. Some respondents even appeared openly hostile to the intellectual pursuit of studying journalism. As one put it 'No amount of academic twaddle can teach a student what journalism is really about' (cited in Harcup 2011a). But aside from a vocal minority of 'hackademics', the study found two thirds of respondents had 'produced any form of publication (e.g. a book chapter) or conference paper about journalism' while over four in ten had 'submitted research into journalism to one or more peer-reviewed academic journal' (Harcup 2011a: 5). This would suggest that while obstacles remain in place for journalists to make sense of academic life (outlined further in Harcup 2011b) the gap between the two professions is closing up as opposed to moving further apart. Chapter 7 will examine the impact of former journalists morphing into academics in more depth. For now this chapter will explore journalist backgrounds and the kinds of education many will experience before they set foot in a newsroom.

The myth that journalists are drawn from all walks of life and require nothing but an inquisitive mind and a thirst for knowledge is somewhat misleading. This is certainly the impression put forward by Dan Synge's (2010) *Survival Guide to Journalism*. He has stated that:

> ... while degrees are an advantage, they do not guarantee immediate or lasting success in the profession. Indeed, journalists come from all sorts of social and educational backgrounds and many of today's newspaper editors were cutting their teeth in the newsroom while their more educated contemporaries languished in university libraries and student union bars. (2010: 17)

It may well be the case that some editors forged appreciation-style self-promotions when climbing to the top of the ladder without first undertaking a degree or journalistic training, but this is entirely at odds with how the vast majority of journalists currently enter the profession. Weaver et al. (2007: 31) have shown 89 per cent of all US journalists have a college degree, while 36 per cent took journalism as a major. This rose from 41 to 50 per cent between 1971 to 2002 if telecommunications, mass communication and communication courses are also taken into account. And if television news journalists were isolated, the share of graduates increased to 92.6 per cent. Based on their longitudinal survey of journalists in recent decades, they suggested that while there was 'no specific credential necessary to enter the field of journalism ... it was clearer than ever before that a bachelor's degree in journalism-mass communication was becoming the most common qualification among those recently hired' (Weaver et al. 2007: 35). According to the 2009 Annual Survey of Journalism and Mass Communication Graduates, approximately 50,850 US students were studying for an undergraduate degree in journalism while 4,480 students were undertaking a Master's programme across 483 higher educational institutions (Becker et al. 2010).

A UK survey of journalists showed an even more uniform picture of graduates entering the profession: 98 per cent held either an undergraduate or postgraduate degree. Fifty six per cent of those working in television indicated they had a vocational journalism qualification. Since accredited bodies such as the Broadcast Journalism Training Council (BJTEC) are increasingly used for key criteria entry-level television positions, it is highly likely that more graduate journalists will have acquired the qualification over the last decade. The survey also explored journalist backgrounds by examining parental occupation. The results demonstrated 'new entrants to the journalism profession are much more likely to have a parent from one of the highest occupational orders' (Journalism Training Forum 2002: 25). Just 3 per cent had parents from unskilled backgrounds (compared to 23 per cent of the population generally). What the survey revealed, in short, was that journalists were highly likely to be from middle-class families.

Despite the financial obstacles that many students have faced in recent years, the level of undergraduates studying journalism courses at UK institutions has risen fivefold since 1994/95 (Hanna and Sanders 2007). In an age of media convergence, there are few undergraduate degrees entitled 'Television Journalism' (though with some notable exceptions). Any analysis of television journalism is instead typically part of journalism courses generally or in optional modules as part of a media/communication/cultural studies programme. For postgraduate diplomas or Master's programmes, specific 'Television Journalism' courses are more commonly available. Most will have vocationally-based syllabuses as opposed to specifying an academic study of television news. For many aspiring journalists in the UK it is often not just a requirement that they must hold a degree but also that they gain a more specific postgraduate certificate. Since the fees for these courses can run to many thousands of pounds, this may explain why journalists tend to be disproportionately drawn from middle-class backgrounds and why potential students from poorer families are discouraged from entering the profession.

While many broadcasters will offer training bursaries, far more applicants will generally apply than there are places available and some will expect applicants to have already obtained (highly costly) qualifications (Greenslade 2009a). Moreover, many employers will ask for a modicum of work experience in broadcasting prior to being hired full-time. For students who are already working in order to subsidise their academic and vocational qualifications, taking either low paid or sometimes unpaid work experience is not financially viable. These and other cultural factors within newsrooms explored earlier in the chapter led a 2009 UK government-commissioned report, *Unleashed Aspirations*, to conclude that 'One of the most exclusive middle-class professions of the 21st century' was journalism. By excluding a significant proportion of the population from the newsroom, this arguably narrows down the 'interpretative communities' (Zelizer 1993) that journalists work in to routinely make and shape the news. It is worth pointing out that the current – or potential – impact of an increasingly middle-class work force dominating the newsroom and culture of production is a much neglected area within journalism studies.

Meanwhile the UK government's proposal in October 2010 to cut university teaching funds for subjects in the arts, humanities and social sciences and raise tuition fees to potentially £9,000 a year in England could perpetuate the trend of attracting mostly middle- to upper-class journalism students. For while there are promises to fund the brightest poorest students, this could still price out many lower- to middle-class families who might be reluctant to acquire a level of debt that would take decades to pay back on a journalist's wage. Two senior media and cultural studies academics, Nick Couldry and Angela McRobbie (2010), have argued this could potentially cause the intellectual study of subjects like journalism and communication to move towards a more practically crafted curriculum. They have pointed out that:

> Something important died on 12 October 2010: the idea of the university in England ... [the] ... proposals are likely, over time, to narrow the range of degree courses offered to students, so they become increasingly dominated by courses that are work-skills-oriented or carry high social prestige.

Of course, many journalism courses will already include specific 'work-skills-oriented' elements. But over the last 40 years universities in the UK have increasingly integrated their theory and practice programmes where the production of journalism is taught alongside the impact news media have on society. Promoting a more vocational culture within universities could thus reverse the academic ground journalism studies has made in recent years.

If the promotion of an entirely skills-based learning journalism programme is favoured within the industry, Thornham and O'Sullivan's (2003) study of students, staff and employers within media-related courses suggests otherwise. While the perception of a 'Mickey Mouse' degree was difficult to shake off, employers appeared to value some of the critical elements that were part of media courses. Likewise, students appreciated both the academic and vocational parts of degrees. The study also noted that students showed that even 'research – an academic skill traditionally seen as being developed in essay writing and expanded in the dissertation – is also seen as an important feature of production work, whether in journalism, TV production and radio' (2003: 729). Within a more specific journalism context, Baines and Kennedy (2008) have warned against universities being overly seduced by employer and student demands for an exclusively news industry-led sylla- bus. They suggested a more holistic approach to journalism education where 'the development within curricula of a theoretical, analytical consideration of journalism's role in society' could be advanced with core journalistic skills (2008: 101). In doing so, they speculated that it may be

> ... no longer sufficient to evaluate proficiency in tasks which reflect current industry practice (crafting a news story, shooting and editing video) in line with current industry norms. Instead, we must ask students to look beyond current practice; take risks with stories, audiences, established forms of journalism; experiment with familiar and unfa- miliar technologies. (2008: 102)

Journalism education, in this context, consists of more than just learning about on-the-job tasks. It also promotes a form of pedagogy where students are encouraged to be critical and self-reflexive journalists. After all, if we accept at face value the role journalists play in making and shaping democ- racy, an understanding of the institutions and structures that shape news media can only help journalists of the future be aware of the impact and influence that they – and journalism more generally – can have in society.

As the final section in this chapter now explores, opinion polls routinely show that many people are highly suspicious of the motivations of many journalists. It will be suggested that recognising which journalists are viewed so insidiously, and why, can reveal much about how the culture of news pro- duction and the type of regulation shapes the relationship audiences have with different forms of media, particularly television journalism.

Distinguishing between news sources: which journalists and journalism do audiences trust?

In all walks of life trust remains a precious commodity, something that is earned over time and rewarded with loyalty. This is especially the case with journalists since many would claim to act as critical watchdogs, exposing the 'truth' and holding the powerful to account. In order to be able to put their faith in what the news is reporting, audiences must establish what Gunter (2005: 395) has labelled a 'trust brand' with different forms of media, one that is cultivated over time and shaped by viewers' own experiences. Audiences, in this respect, may have very casual relationships with news media or retain strong emotional bonds (Monck 2008). An idiosyncratic fondness – for a charming television news anchor, say, or partisan loyalties – like Republicans favouring Fox News or Democrats embracing *The Daily Show* (see Chapter 4) – can play a role as well. At the same time, viewers may well tune in for diverse news agendas, erudite views and cutting-edge analysis. Whatever the reason, audiences, in short, will bring their own uses and gratifications to the consumption of news.

In order to sustain long-term trust and loyalty, intrinsic Fourth Estate values such as reliable and accurate accounts of the world remain critical in this respect. News, after all, is about information and analysis. And if audiences cannot trust what is reported or discussed, journalism's value in informing viewers about the world is diminished. News, of course, can be entertaining or engaging but if it is the case that at the same time cynicism or partisanship amongst news audiences is also cultivated – as was argued in Chapter 4 – this makes journalism a less effective democratic resource (Cushion 2012). Put more simply, public attitudes towards journalists and journalism do matter.

On the face of it, journalism is a much maligned occupation. When polls ask the public whether they trust journalists and journalism generally, the findings will usually *appear* clear cut: they will tend to show people are highly suspicious of and skeptical towards the motives of journalists. Writing in the *Media Guardian*, Roy Greenslade, for example, interpreted one poll where just 3 per cent of journalists were trusted by stating 'Here's a sobering, if not entirely surprising, poll finding. Journalists are among the least trusted professionals in Britain … Why, I wonder, is the public so disenchanted with journalists?' This interpretation can manifest itself in popular cultural expressions of journalism. While Hollywood movies may occasionally depict heroic investigative journalists striving to expose the latest Watergate-type scandal (McNair 2010), cinematic depictions also picture highly sinister characters who are eager to capture an exclusive at the expense of sacrificing their ethical principles. At the same time, on the small screen, popular portrayals in dramas or soap operas will tend to characterise more traditional, local journalists and, by and large, also represent dishonest and deceptive types. Thus, for example, in the long-running Australian soap opera, *Neighbours*, Paul Robinson – a true pantomime villain – bought a local newspaper, the *Erinsborough Post*, and immediately sanctioned numerous underhand tabloid tactics in order to capture more exclusives and boost sales. Likewise, occasional plot-lines involving local journalists in the popular British soap opera, *EastEnders* have, over the years, invariably involved dodgy-looking characters and questionable journalistic practices.

The stereotype of a dishonest, opportunistic and sensationalist reporter originates most prominently from the tabloid newspaper industry. In doing so this generalisation about journalism can distort how news media and in particular television journalists are viewed by audiences. Because by labelling journalists collectively – as many of the polls do – this arguably misrepresents how much trust people invest in *different* sources of news. The rest of this chapter takes a closer look at the survey data for attitudes towards journalists and argues that – when isolated from journalists *generally* – television journalists are mostly valued and viewed as reliable sources. If this is broken down further, what audiences appear to value, above all, is the kind of journalism supplied by public service broadcasters (Cushion 2009).

A BBC/Reuters (2006) poll of over 10,000 people from ten countries – Brazil, Egypt, Germany, India, Indonesia, Nigeria, Russia, South Korea, the UK and US – revealed how national television news was trusted above that of rival news media (see Table 6.4). 82 per cent overall indicated that they trusted television news, compared to national/regional newspapers (75 per cent), local newspapers (69 per cent), public radio (67 per cent) and international satellite TV (56 per cent). There were, of course,

Table 6.4 Level of trust towards different news media in the US, UK, Brazil, Egypt, Germany, India, Indonesia, Nigeria, Russia and South Korea

	Television	Newspapers	Radio	Internet
America	75% (national)	81% (local) 74% (national/regional) 52% (International)	73% (public radio)	55%
UK	86%	75% (local/national) 55% (International)	67% (public)	44%
Brazil	66% (national) 45% (international TV stations)	68% (national/regional) 64% (local) 40% (International)	/	40%
Egypt	77% (national) 77% (international)	68% (local) 65% (national/regional) 28% (international)	64%	32%
Germany	81%	80% (national/regional) 74% (local)	83%	/
India	85% (national)	85% (national/regional newspapers) 76% (local) 10% (international)	69%	1%
Indonesia	98% (national) 57% (international)	91% (national/regional) 87% (local) 54% (international)	90% (public) 85% (commercial)	42%
Nigeria	90% (national) 67% (international)	75% (national/regional)	72% (public) 71% (commercial)	41%
Russia	84% (national)	69% (regional/national) 32% (international)	29% (commercial)	22%
South Korea	76% (national) 32% (international)	64% (national/regional) 39% (local) 23% (international)	/	55%

(Source: BBC/Reuters 2006 poll)

differences across the ten countries but eight out of ten developed or developing countries, nevertheless, ranked television as the most trusted source.

To examine which type of television news sources are the most trusted, it is necessary to examine more closely the differences in national contexts. A 2010 representative public opinion poll in the US asked a series of questions that explored attitudes towards commercial television, cable and public service broadcasting (Roper Opinion Poll 2010). It found public service broadcasting (58 per cent) was ranked as being more important than commercial television (43 per cent) and cable television (40 per cent). Asked whether they trusted particular organisations a great deal, once again PBS (45 per cent) was viewed as a more trusted source than commercial television networks (17 per cent), newspaper publishing companies (11 per cent) and cable television networks (9 per cent). Indeed public service broadcasting was trusted a great deal more than even the federal government (11 per cent) or Congress (6 per cent). When questioned further, respondents were asked to rank how much they trusted individual news channels (see Table 6.5).

While MSNBC was trusted much less than its two main rival cable channels (Fox and CNN), the network channels were by and large the same. What stood out, however, was the large amount of trust bestowed on PBS – 40 per cent – and reflected in attitudes towards public television more generally. For when asked whether a channel was liberal, mostly fair or conservative, respondents' answers showed PBS was the most balanced television news service by a considerable margin (see Table 6.6).

At a time when many channels were cultivating partisan audiences (see Chapter 4), PBS stood out as the most fair news channel. Despite many conservative critics attacking the channel over the years for pursuing a left-leaning agenda (Croteau and Hoynes 1996), PBS was viewed as the most balanced broadcaster. Fox News and MSNBC, by contrast, were cable channels where trust appeared to be shaped by partisan loyalties (by Republican

Table 6.5 Per cent of US viewers that trust news channels 'a great deal'

News channel/bulletin	Percentage trusted a great deal
PBS/public television	40%
Fox News Channel	29%
CNN	27%
CBS	21%
ABC	21%
NBC	20%
MSNBC	18%

(Source: Roper Opinion Poll 2010)

Table 6.6 Per cent of US viewers who consider news channels liberal, mostly fair or conservative in news coverage, investigations and discussions of major issues

News channel	Liberal	Mostly Fair	Conservative
PBS/Public television	34%	40%	14%
NBC	44%	33%	12%
ABC	42%	32%	13%
CBS	43%	32%	11%
CNN	41%	31%	13%
Fox News	19%	25%	44%
MSNBC	44%	24%	10%

(Source: Roper Opinion Poll 2010)

and Democrat viewers respectively). As Chapter 4 highlighted, the trend towards more politically-motivated coverage is increasing in American journalism but PBS, compared to other US television news stations, appears to have maintained a 'mostly fair' reputation for its news and current affairs programming. Perhaps as a result of its public funding, it has not succumbed to market pressures to pursue a less objective form of journalism in order to attract more viewers.

In the UK a similar picture is evident. A 2010 YouGov poll (cited in Kellner 2010) showed huge disparities in how journalists were trusted across a range of news media (see Table 6.7). The survey echoed the conclusions drawn in similar studies where trust shown towards the media, broadly speaking, had been on the decline in the last decade or so (Gunter 2005; Jones 2004; Kohring and Matthes 2007; Tsfati and Cappella 2003). Of course such declining levels of trust are also apparent in many institutions and professions more generally. As a result the same YouGov poll found levels of trust shown towards local MPs, trade unions and civil servants had also declined. But leaving aside declining levels of trust towards institutions

Table 6.7 Per cent of UK viewers who trust journalists to 'tell the truth' in 2003 and 2010

Source of News	Per cent of trust in 2010	Per Cent decline since 2003
BBC News journalists	60%	−21%
ITV News journalists	49%	−33%
Journalists on 'upmarket' newspapers e.g. Times, Telegraph, Guardian	41%	−24%
Journalists on 'mid-market' newspapers e.g. Mail, Express	21%	−15%
Journalists on 'red-top' tabloid newspapers e.g. Sun, Mirror	10%	−4%

(Source: 2010 You Gov poll cited in Kellner 2010)

more generally, what the survey demonstrated was how television, above all, was far more trusted than even the more serious broadsheet newspapers. Since television in the UK is legally required to be impartial, its more balanced approach to journalism could engender far greater trust than the kind of more explicitly partisan news that can be found in mid-market or tabloid newspapers (where just 21 per cent and 10 per cent respectively placed their trust in them).

In addition, the manner in which a television service was funded also shaped how far it was trusted. A majority of respondents – 60 per cent – put their trust in the BBC's television coverage. While this had decreased in recent years (21 per cent since 2003), the trust embodied by the BBC was also reflected in other surveys. A recent poll into the most trusted media brands put the BBC (at 46 per cent) well ahead of its nearest rivals Google (at 32 per cent) and Amazon (at 27 per cent) (Morris 2010). And even during those times when the BBC has been heavily criticised by the government of the day and by rival commercial media, the public appeared to instinctively protect the values of the corporation. In 2004 for example – when the BBC was under considerable pressure during the Hutton Inquiry after some of its news outlets accused the government of 'sexing up' the case for war – the public service broadcaster remained six times more trusted than the government itself (Gunter 2005: 395). Another study that carried out interviews with BBC and Televisión Española (TVE) (a Spanish public service broadcaster) producers, journalists and audiences found that the British corporation was widely viewed as a model of impartiality by their Spanish counterparts (Retis et al., cited in Gomez 2010). And while many Spanish journalists suggested the image of TVE had been tarnished by repressive state forces when the country had been ruled by a dictatorship, they looked enviously at the BBC's history and reputation that had sustained its independence and authority while reporting without interference (Retis et al., cited in Gomez 2010) (see also Chapter 2).

This pattern of trusting public service broadcasters over commercial news providers was reflected more globally in a 2006 BBC/Reuters survey. It asked respondents to name – without being prompted by an interviewer – their most trusted news sources (Table 6.8). Since this put respondents somewhat on the spot by asking them to name various news sources the results should be treated with caution. But the instantaneous responses do give an indication of those news sources that were instinctively trusted.

Respondents from Brazil rated Rede Globo, a commercial channel, as the most trustworthy (52 per cent), while in Egypt Al Jazeera, an international news channel, was the most trusted (59 per cent), most probably because of its approach to covering Middle Eastern politics when compared to that of Western news organisations (see Chapter 3). But beyond this, public service broadcasters were repeatedly mentioned in countries such as Germany,

Table 6.8 Per cent of television news sources spontaneously mentioned as being trustworthy in the US, UK, Brazil, Egypt, Germany, India, Indonesia, Nigeria, Russia and South Korea

Country	News media
Brazil	Rede Globo (mentioned by 52%), TV Records (3%)
Egypt	Al Jazeera (mentioned by 59%), Channel 1 Egypt TV (12%), Al Ahran (6%), Al Akhbar (5%), Nile News (4%)
Germany	ARD (mentioned by 22%), ZDF (7%), n-tv/N24 (6%), RTL (4%), Suddeutsche Zeitung (3%), Der Spiegel (2%), Deutsche Welle (1%)
India	AAJ TAK (mentioned by 11%), Doordarshan television (10%), Dainik Jagran (7%), Sun TV (5%), Star News (4%), NDTV (4%), AIR (3%), Zee News (2%), Rajasthan Patrika (2%)
Indonesia	RCTI television (mentioned by 27%), SCTV (17%), Metro TV (14%), Trans TV (11%), Indosiar (8%), TPI television, Jawa Pos and Kompas (each 3%)
Nigeria	Channels TV, NTA television (both mentioned by 16%), AIT television (10%), Silver Bird TV (7%), Punch (5%), CNN (4%), and BBC World television (1%)
Russia	ORT television (mentioned by 36%), NTV (16%), RTR television (15%), Argumenti i Fakti (6%), Komsomolskaya Pravda (both 3%)
South Korea	KBS television (mentioned by 18%), the website NAVER (13%), Chosun (10%), MBC television (9%), DongA and ChoongAng (both 6%), Hankyoreh (3%), South Korea's National TV Station and YTN television (both 3%)

(Source: BBC/Reuters 2006 poll)

Russia and South Korea where public- or state-funded media appear to garner more trust than commercial sources. Meanwhile in Africa, Channels TV, a commercial station in Nigeria, was trusted just as much as the state-run NTA (both mentioned by 16 per cent). Likewise in India a public service channel, Doordarshan, was held in almost equal regard as the commercially-funded AAJ TAK (at 10 per cent and 11 per cent respectively). Within each country of course, how far each state broadcaster was able to operate autonomously requires close attention here. For in more developing areas of the world the media ecology might offer less choice while some other sources may be subject to state censorship or editorial interference. Nevertheless, what the snapshot responses revealed was that all the countries questioned trusted television over other news media, with public service broadcasters in particular being singled out when individual television channels were mentioned.

This chapter began by examining not only how the multichannel, online, digital environment has changed the nature of news content and delivery, but also how it has changed what it means to be a television journalist. In an era of convergence, journalists and journalism have become more difficult to define and interpret. For many journalists must now work in an integrated news environment, moving interchangeably between radio, television, online or mobile platforms. But while the everyday life of television journalists may be changing within the industry, the public still largely view television as being distinct from other news media. While polls may pessimistically conclude that journalists are *generally* not trusted by most people, on closer inspection television journalists were valued and largely viewed as reliable sources. The stereotype of a dishonest, opportunistic and sensationalist reporter derives, most prominently, from the tabloid newspaper industry. In understanding the television journalism profession, then, generalisations about journalism can distort how television journalists are viewed by audiences. And if we scratch below the surface a little more, audiences appear to instinctively trust public service broadcasters above many commercial news organisations.

Despite the proliferation of more market-driven news media in recent years (see Chapter 2), this chapter has suggested audiences are still able to distinguish between publically and privately funded journalism. Consumer choice has not, in other words, translated into consumer satisfaction. For while the dominance of publically funded news media may be diminishing (see Chapter 2), many people still continue to trust public service broadcasters above commercial stations. Since public service broadcasters tend to subscribe to values of balance and impartiality and are more tightly regulated (Cushion 2012) audiences appear to place more trust in what they are reporting. Commercially-run broadcasters, by contrast, are currently less regulated and there are some signs – most notably in the US (see Chapter 4) – that television journalism is retreating from values of objectivity and embracing a more partisan approach to news and analysis. This in turn suggests a shift towards a more deregulatory and market-driven news ecology would impact on how much trust viewers are willing to put in television journalism and the news media more generally.

The final chapter now turns to exploring how television journalism scholarship has made sense of the seismic changes happening in different broadcast ecologies in recent decades.

PUTTING TELEVISION NEWS CENTRE STAGE: THE PAST, PRESENT AND FUTURE SHAPE OF JOURNALISM SCHOLARSHIP

Introduction: studying 'journalism'

Situating television news scholarship within the burgeoning discipline of journalism studies should be a relatively straightforward task. After all, television is a distinct medium with its own set of news values, journalistic conventions and semiotic codes. And yet within the theory and practice of journalism studies the genre of news – whether this is online, print, radio or television – can often prove difficult to isolate and interrogate separately. This is understandable since journalism in general shares similar goals, aspirations and ideals, principles, theories and philosophies, skills, training and education and, in an era of convergence, job descriptions, technical equipment and newsrooms as journalists increasingly move from one medium to the next.

The *general* academic interpretation of journalism is reflected in the titles of recent high-profile books where 'Journalism' or 'News' has been prefixed before or after 'Critical Issues' (Allan 2005), 'Principles and Practices' (Harcup 2009), 'Balance and Bias' (Starkley 2006), 'Discourse' (Montgomery 2006), 'Culture' (Allan 2010a), 'Citizen' (Allan and Thornsen 2009), 'Convergence' (Koldozy 2006), 'A Critical History' (Conboy 2004) or 'Historical Introduction' (Conboy 2011), 'The Future of' (Anderson and Ward 2007; Franklin 2011), 'Local' (Franklin 2006), 'After September 11' (Zelizer and Allan 2011), 'The Handbook of' (Wahl-Jorgensen and Hanitzsch 2009) or 'The Elements of' (Kovach and Rosenstiel 2007). Likewise, entire conference proceedings – Taylor and Francis's 'The Future of' (2008, 2011) – journalism dictionaries (Franklin et al. 2005) and keywords (Zelizer and Allan 2011), as well as introductory and advanced textbooks have routinely used variations of 'Journalism' or 'News' (Allan 2010b; Calcutt and Hammond 2011; Harrison 2006; McNair 2009; Matthews 2011; Meikle 2009) in their titles without reference to a genre of news media. As with any other business it is understandable why academic conferences, dictionaries and books will aim to appeal to the widest range of people who are interested in journalism. But in doing so journalism's histories, traditions, ethics, research, practice and theory can often blend together.

At the same time, at the turn of this century journalism studies could celebrate its increasing disciplinary autonomy from associated fields, most notably mass communication in the US and sociology, media and cultural studies in the UK. There remains a significant overlap, of course, but if we examine the titles of relevant media, cultural and communication journals in the last century 'journalism' has become more recognised as a scholarly pursuit. Shaw et al. (2000: 61) explored the 'evolution of mass media research' in academic journals since the 1920s (see Table 7.1). With the exception of *Journalism Quarterly* (renamed *Journalism and Mass Communication* in 1995), journalism studies grew up within the broader discipline of mass communication research.

In the 1990s – when journalism studies became an increasingly popular undergraduate and postgraduate subject (see Chapter 6) – academic media departments grew in size and scope, employing more staff and bringing in professionals to teach and research the discipline. While journalism had featured in academic journals before the turn of the century, in this new millennium journalism studies has become established enough for 'Journalism' itself to be sufficient enough as a title in its own right. *Journalism: Theory, Practice and Criticism* and *Journalism Studies* were both launched in 2000 and in 2007 *Journalism Practice* also arrived on the scene. Each journal publishes six editions per year and yet the editors have stated they have to reject many more articles than they can accept (Harcup 2011b).

Within the life-span of these journals, journalism studies has become a more globalised scholarly pursuit. As Löffelholz and Weaver's (2008: 3) edited book, *Global Journalism Research*, has pointed out, 'research can no longer operate within national or cultural boundaries only'. Scholars are increasingly turning towards theories of global journalism (Berglez 2008), global journalism education (Deuze 2006) and globalisation (Cottle 2009; Reese 2010) in order to understand the theory and practice of the discipline. In doing so, the disciplinary boundaries of journalism have expanded. Large scholarly networks such as the International Communication Association (ICA) and the European Communication

Table 7.1 Mass media journals from 1920s to the1990s

By decade of founding:

1920s:
Journalism and Mass Communication

1930s:
Public Opinion Quarterly

1940:
Journalism and Mass Communication Educator

1950s:
Journal of Communication
Journal of Broadcasting and Electronic Media

1960s:
Journalism and Mass Communication Monographs
Journal of Popular Culture
Public Relations Quarterly

1970s:
Journalism History
Mass Communication & Society
Journal of Communication Inquiry
Newspaper Research Journal
Quarterly Review of Film and Video
Hastings Communications and Entertainment Law Journal
Public Relations Review
Journal of Advertising
Women's Studies in Communication
Media, Culture and Society

1980s:
International Journal of Public Opinion Research
American Journalism
Journal of Mass Media ethics
Media Studies Journal
Political Communication

1990s:
Journal of Computer-Mediated Communication (online)
Mediaculture Review (online)
American Communication Journal (online)

(Source: adapted from Shaw et al. 2000)

Research and Education Association (ECREA) have now established journalism divisions to encourage interdisciplinary post-national scholarship.

Journalism studies post 2000, in sum, has grown more globally diverse and popular. But while journalism studies has come of age, drawing on an increasing range of methods and theories from a wide range of inter-connected fields

(Cushion 2008), less attention has been paid to the differences *across* news media. There are, of course, books on the market that deal with aspects of journalism more specifically including the genre of news. Previous chapters in this book have drawn extensively on a range of scholarship internationally, from well-known academic texts to output in obscure journals, industry research reports or analysis in the media trade press. Of the more sustained scholarly enquires into television news in recent years most have explored particular themes or empirically dissected a topic in depth. In understanding a particular news aspect or event in detail, however, less attention has been shown to how the broader history of television journalism, its fast changing political economy, shifting regulatory structures and the wider forces beyond it, routinely make and shape contemporary television journalism. The aim of this book has been to explore television journalism in more depth, examining its history from radio to television, unravelling how its political economy evolved, asking how the culture of television newsrooms has been shaped by education and training, and understanding the challenges television journalism faces in a more crowded and competitive news environment.

In doing so, the intention has been not just to put television news centre stage within journalism studies but also to draw on detailed empirical studies so as to help shape and inform some of the key trends now evident in contemporary television journalism. Where once television news was central to journalism studies, this final chapter will suggest that developments in interactive and online journalism have tended to dominant debate and discourage research into 'old' media like television. It will also combine a further reading guide with a critical interrogation of past, present and future television journalism scholarship. What follows should not be seen as an exhaustive systematic review of television news studies (inevitably there will be some omissions that will irritate seasoned journalism academics), but should be considered as an overview where key studies are mapped out and broad patterns of scholarship are identified.

The chapter is split in three sections. To begin with, the formative years of television journalism scholarship will be explored and interpreted within broader debates in communication, sociology, media and cultural studies. The second section explores the rise and fall of television news studies as academic attention moved increasingly towards uncovering the new media landscape and emerging online cultures. In doing so it will argue that while it remains vital to make sense of journalism in a multimedia age, television news studies needs to make a decisive return to centre stage.

To conclude, the final section of the chapter will explore two dominant themes in the future of television news studies: firstly, how the more collaborative culture between the media industries and academic scholarship can be sustained and enhanced by examining the reception of academic studies and, secondly, how internationally comparative television news can be used empirically to inform how different media systems and regulatory practices shape different television news cultures. All of which, it will be argued, can demonstrate how the political economy of television news can help cultivate a vibrant and pluralistic news culture, informing and engaging democracies in politics and public affairs.

Television journalism scholarship: the formative years

As television sets became part of the furniture in the 1950s and 1960s, journalism on the small screen began to adjust itself to the visual demands of the medium (see Chapter 2). As scholars have historically pointed out, transferring journalistic conventions and practices from radio to television was anything but seamless (Conboy 2011; Williams 2010). At the time, of course, this was probably not widely viewed as all that cumbersome a transition. For while television news has a familiar format and semiotic style today, back then audiences had yet to develop a set of generic expectations. Books such as *Television News: Anatomy and Process* (Green 1969), *To Kill A Messenger: Television News and the Real World* (Small 1970) and *Television News* (Fang 1970) began to make sense of the emerging techniques of journalism in the tele-visual age without meaningfully connecting them to broader debates in mass communications.

Some of the earliest television news studies, nevertheless, remain the most influential. Halloran et al.'s (1970) study of the anti-Vietnam war protests' coverage was one of the first to systematically examine the UK's television news and print content. Like Gitlin's (1980) book examining media coverage of demonstrations and new political movements in the US, *The Whole World is Watching: The Making and Unmaking of the New Left*, television was seen as the central medium where news events were first constructed and then reconstructed in rival media. While the organisation of demonstrations has changed dramatically in recent decades, these 'classic' television news studies remain relevant to understanding the power television wields in defining and legitimising protests (Cottle 2006). New, more optimistic accounts of how mass media cover protests have subsequently emerged (DeLuca and Peeples 2002; see Cottle 2008 for an overview of the debates) but the second edition of Gitlin's *The Whole World is Watching*, published in 2003, demonstrates its continued significance 40 years on.

It was a Canadian scholar, Marshall McLuhan, who most famously drew attention to the inherent differences in mass media in the 1960s. In *Understanding Media* (1964) and *The Medium is the Message* (1967), McLuhan argued it was the medium as opposed to the content that shaped the reception of the mass media. He also suggested different media were distinctive in how they engaged audiences' cognitive senses. So, for example, while 'hot' media (radio and film, for example) tended to stimulate just one overriding sense in viewers, at either an aural or visual level, 'cold' media (like television) required an audience's multiple sensory participation even if less information was being processed. Examining a seminal moment in television news – the live televised presidential debates in 1960 between Richard Nixon and John F. Kennedy – McLuhan applied these concepts to how television viewers and radio listeners interpreted the relative success of each candidate. Kennedy's polished appearance and casual mode of address charmed television viewers compared to Nixon's apparent on-screen awkwardness and visible perspiration. But for radio listeners this was mere superficial fluff since they focused on what was said and appeared to favour Nixon's responses. Television, in short, was the new medium on the block and scholars began investing far more of their time and resources in coverage of future presidential debates and televised news more generally.

Not long after television became part of the agenda-setting studies first pioneered by McCombs and Shaw (1972). In their study of the 1968 presidential election campaign they found a significant correlation between the agenda for American networks' national news and public priorities. A sizeable literature has since developed about how far dominant trends in media coverage can shape what people think about the world (Benton and Fraizer 1976; Brosius and Kepplinger 1990; Dearing and Rogers 1996; McCombs and Shaw 1993). Academic debates have moved on from looking at how television news played an agenda-setting function to examining their more pernicious role where the routine framing of issues and events can influence how audiences understand the causes of and potential resolutions to economic, political and social issues. Shanto Iyengar's (1991) book, *Is Anyone Responsible? How Television Frames Political Issues*, examined where viewers would choose to apportion responsibility after watching stories about a range of areas such as health, crime and poverty. Television news, it was argued, tended to privilege episodic over thematic frames where the former would focus on issues and events and individuals in isolation compared to the latter which would explore the wider structural reasons. In doing so, policy areas like health were often interpreted by audiences as being the responsibility of individuals as opposed to being a collective problem for society that could potentially be resolved by elected political actors and decision making. When viewers do encounter more thematic frames in television coverage, Iyengar (1991) suggested the wider context encouraged them to turn to democratic structures for solutions and government intervention that would enhance the lives of ordinary people.

The study of television's impact in society was also central to cultivation analysis, which sought to explore whether sustained viewing could influence how people understood the world. Led by the US scholar George Gerbner,

cultivation analysis examined broad patterns of television content generally and found that heavy viewers tended to replicate the fictional world of
television opposed to the reality of social, economic and political 'real life'
(Gerbner 1976; Gerbner et al. 1986). Light viewers, by contrast, were less
likely to conform to television's dominant messages. Whether underestimat-
ing the amount of old people in society (since young people would dominate on-screen), overestimating the level of crime in society (since violence
was pervasive in US television) or reinforcing gender and ethnic stereotypes
(since many genres perpetuated the image of men as tough and ethnic
minorities as criminals), when other social variables were controlled (level
of education, class, age, geographic location, etc.) regular television viewing
contributed to how people interpreted everyday life. Television news, in particular, pictured a highly conservative 'window on the world' with the voices
of political elites drowning out what 'ordinary' citizens had to say.

Gerber and his colleagues never claimed that watching television would
cultivate a uniform pattern of influence that would be evident across *all*
viewers. But cultivation analysts have found it difficult to shake off the caricature in which audiences are seen as being uniformly mesmerised by what
appears on screen, thereby surrendering their critical faculties and succumb-
ing to the omnipotent power of television (Gauntlett 2005). What they
did find – and other studies have since backed this up – was that sustained
viewing *generally* encouraged viewers to adopt values promoted on television as compared to less habitual consumption. In doing so, many viewers
might still choose to reject, resist and reinterpret what they have watched
but they are more likely to do so if they are light as opposed to heavy viewers. Reflecting on close to 50 years of cultivation studies and the 125 new
cultivation studies published since 2000, Morgan and Shananan (2010: 337)
have suggested that 'the state of cultivation is remarkably healthy, and the
outlook in the future promising'. Since media ecologies have become far
more complex in a more globally interconnected, multi-media age, cultivation analysis has had to defend its methodological relevance. For Morgan and
Shananan (2010: 350) it remains just as relevant as when it began because
television 'still dominates the flows and words of information that pass by
our eyes and ears each day … while the number of channels continues to
multiply … the need to pay attention to their common messages and lessons
becomes even more urgent'.

If the early years of television news studies were caught up in quantitative
debates within communication studies about audience influence on a mass
scale, the 1970s and 1980s witnessed a more qualitative shift in journalism
scholarship. Micro contexts of television reception – where individual as
opposed to collective viewing was explored in more depth – as well as more
detailed studies on the content and production of television news grew more

prominent. Classic ethnographies by Gans (1980) and Tuchman (1978) in the US and Schlesinger (1978) in the UK represented new methodological pathways where researchers could secure backstage passes for understanding the inner workings of busy television newsrooms. In Schlesinger's inside account of BBC television's news, 'a theoretically informed observation of the social practices of cultural production' (1978: xxxii) was undertaken. The methodological approach adopted was colourfully described on the back sleeve of the book.

> Like an anthropologist studying a remote and suspicious tribe, Schlesinger sets out to answer … questions by seeking to become an accepted, or at least an unobtrusive, part of the community, listening to conferences and eating in canteens, observing the processes by which news bulletins are planned, prepared, strung together. (Schlesinger 1978: back sleeve)

Schlesinger cast new light on the processes behind the production of television news and his many insights remain enduring today. So for example in the daily regime of manufacturing journalism he describes news gathering as 'a system at work, operating with a determinate set of routines' (1978: 47). And in observing how editorial decisions were made, an elitist perspective was found where 'journalists write for other journalists, their bosses, their sources, or highly interested audiences. The "total" audience, however, remains an abstraction.' (1978: 107). Meanwhile, within BBC management internal pressures would lead to editorial decisions being made that would eschew deviating too far from the conventional journalistic wisdom. Schlesinger commented, 'Editors of the day, while apt to stress their independence of action, are also very aware of being entrusted to produce an output which is "reliable," consistent through time, and indistinguishable from that of their fellows … editorial soundness is identified by its consistency' (1978: 147–9).

Many ethnographic studies have since explored the 'daily routines, bureaucratic nature, competitive ethos, professional ideologies, source dependencies and cultural practices' (Cottle 2007: 1) of news media that were once behind closed doors. But Gans's, Tuchman's and Schlesinger's books still remain much cited not just for breaking new methodological ground but also because ethnographies of television production are not as prominent in journalism studies as content and audience reception studies (Cushion 2008). As one recent study into the pan-European rolling news channel, Euronews, claimed in its abstract: 'This article offers a *rare* ethnographic window into the workaday universe of 24-hour news broadcasting' (Baisnée and Marchetti 2006; author emphasis). While it has been claimed a 'second wave' of news ethnographies appeared at the turn of the millennium (Cottle 2000), television news has arguably not been at the centre of scholarly concerns in very recent times. Leaving aside MacGregor (1997), Cottle (1999), Born (2005)

and Matthews (2010), amongst others, explorations into television production more sustained ethnographic academic attention has been paid to online
news or the wider convergence of multi-media newsrooms (Domingo 2008;
Patterson and Domingo 2008, 2011; Steensen 2008).

In reflecting on the cultural practice of news prior to it being broadcast
or audiences tuning in, journalism studies in the late 1970s began exploring
news more qualitatively, drawing on the relevant theory and methods associated with fields such as sociology and cultural studies. This was particularly
embraced in a UK and European context where a wider 'ethnographic turn'
was sweeping through the social sciences. In this context, one of the most
well-known news studies into television viewing emerged. David Morley's
(1980) *Nationwide* research explored how viewers individually made sense
of news stories according to their socio-economic background. Complicating
Hall's (1980) Encoding/Decoding model of the reception of television,
Morley found viewers interpreted news either by dominant, negotiated or
oppositional 'readings'. The study found audience readings – or meaning-
making – was largely determined by social class since the significance of
news was actively reinterpreted by the knowledge, experience and thus the
understanding audiences *already* had.

For scholars frustrated with the quantitative tradition of what television
does to viewers and not vice versa, Morley and subsequent studies in Media
Studies more generally (Ing 1985, 1991; Morley 1986; Radway 1984) were
seized upon. The zombie-like status that many argued cultivation analysts
reduced audiences to (Gauntlett 1995) was challenged by a new generation of scholars emphasising audience agency and resistance studies, counter-hegemonic evidence of audience power rather than media manipulation
(Moores 1993). Within Media Studies in a UK and European context, the
dominant model of understanding audiences has arguably remained qualitative ever since. Large quantitative studies into television viewing are often
viewed suspiciously, with more energy being spent on finding evidence of
audience resistance than on establishing areas of media influence. According
to Lewis (2001: 87), however, 'the notion of media power and hegemony
has not collapsed under the weight of audience research within a broad
cultural studies and/or qualitative tradition'. While Lewis's (1991, 2001)
research into audiences is rare in that qualitative traditions inform quantitative approaches – encouraging scholars to ask 'What counts in cultural studies' (Lewis 1996) – television news studies have become embroiled in recent
decades in larger debates about the political relevance of what scholarship
is all about.

This was best captured in a series of television news studies by the Glasgow
Media Group (GMC). They caused much controversy in a 1976 book, *Bad
News*, which systemically examined television news and found coverage was
routinely biased, favouring the views of political and business elites and

marginalising alternative ways by which issues and events could be resolved. In a highly volatile political period when Britain was troubled by strikes and the government was struggling to manage the economy, *Bad News* argued that television news was not the impartial 'window on the world' it claimed (and was legally obliged) to be. As the first page boldly stated, 'Contrary to the claims, conventions and culture of television journalism, the news is not a neutral product ... it is a sequence of socially manufactured messages, which carry many of the culturally dominant assumptions of our society' (GMC 1976: 1). Subsequent studies – *More Bad News* (1980), *Really Bad News* (1982) and *War and Peace News* (1985) – reinforced the inherent bias in television news in further industrial disputes as well as other wider social, economic and political issues such as coverage of the Falklands war.

To no-one's great surprise the GMC *Bad News* studies were widely discredited by journalists, with the BBC in particular being forced to vehemently defend its impartiality (see Harrison 1985; Quinn 2007). According to Harrison (1985: 136), broadcasters 'widely suspected that underneath the academic trappings there lay a more overtly political enterprise'. But it was its reception within academic circles that was perhaps more surprising because many academics dismissed the GMC's methodological approach and challenged their conclusions not so much with counter-evidence but with being implicated ideologically in the research process. As a result one post-modern scholar, Shaun Best (1999), had argued that the 'Group is wrapped up in a romantic package about what life was like before the new right'. Since the GMC's critique rested on demystifying television news's claim to be an impartial broadcaster, what Best and other scholars had challenged was how an 'objective' truth could ever be measured unless 'a position of epistemological privilege?' was held (Best 1999; cf. Harrison 1985).

Despite the GMC's weighty evidence of television news's largely conservative view of the world (that was to be confirmed in many other content studies also), what concerned many scholars at the time was the struggle over meaning and audience interpretation. While dominant patterns of coverage could perhaps be found, it was argued their inherent discourses and values might not be uniformly shared. Leaving aside Philo's (1990) focus group studies demonstrating that regular TV viewers *did* appear to subscribe to dominant television news frameworks during the miners' strike in 1984/5, the academic reception of the GMC's studies had more than a faint whiff of cultural relativism to it. For if there was indeed no truth to measure against 'due impartiality' or a shared sense of 'television bias' this rendered grand claims about media influence almost meaningless. In the same spirit, it also downsized the significance of empirical research – why measure television news, after all, if hypotheses cannot be tested or coverage evaluated? – and promoted scholarly posturing and theoretical positioning where no absolute claims were necessary or even expected.

In Philo and Miller's (2001) book, *Market Killing*, they make the case that many academics in the social sciences had been seduced by abstract cultural theory and had shied away from empirically interrogating sites of power like television news. These complaints were not limited to the UK. McChesney (1996: 540) has chastised much of cultural studies in the US for pursuing 'trivial' agendas and being 'politically timid and intellectually uninteresting and unimportant'. At a time when the television industry, in particular, was being deregulated and media concentration (see Chapter 2) was being consolidated further, McChesney (1996) indicted media scholarship for neglecting the implications thrown up by government decisions and the power of large corporations in favour of championing the agency and pleasure of audience consumption.

As journalism studies headed into the new millennium, McChesney's demand for a more critical approach to television news was to gain momentum, not least with his own publication in 2000, *Rich Media, Poor Democracy: Communication Politics in Dubious Times*. This became a Media Studies bestseller and was widely read within and beyond academic circles, explaining as it did how television news, amongst other media, had deteriorated historically due to de-regulatory decision making by successive governments. Of course, questions of political economy represented nothing new or unfamiliar for media and communication studies. Numerous well-known scholars from Herbert Schiller, Edward Herman and Ben Bagdikian to Peter Golding, James Curran and Peter Garnham (and many more) had charted the rise in corporate media ownership and the implications of deregulatory practices. But where McChesney gained much academic appeal was not just in explaining historically how broadcasting had sold off its public service credentials, it was in also daring to imagine an alternative vision of the future, one that championed media reform and created a movement where citizens could affect changes in the communications industry.

The study of television news has been pushed and pulled in different disciplinary and methodological pathways over the last 30 to 40 years, part of wider scholarly concerns into production, content and reception in media, cultural and communication studies. But as the century drew to a close journalism studies had begun to forge a more clearly defined disciplinary identity and while television news was part of this it also had to compete with the exhilarating speed shown by new and exciting events in online journalism and new media.

As a result, the next section argues that television news has, in recent years, become less prominent in journalism studies. While journalism scholars are busy competing to make sense of the latest online twist or technological turn, it will be suggested that 'old' media continue to exert considerable influence over the development of 'new' media. Television news, in particular, continues to be the medium that wields the most influence, where most people will learn about and come to understand what has just happened in the world. The following section explores how 'new' media or Media Studies 2.0 has overshadowed television news within journalism studies, and media and communications more generally.

(Re)prioritising 'old' above 'new' media: why online journalism is punching above its democratic weight

Despite being a relatively young medium, television news can sometimes appear a little dated in academic debates when it is compared to the new and exciting world of online, interactive and multi-media journalism. So, for example, a book review of an edited book about 24-hour news (co-authored by myself and Justin Lewis in 2010) began by stating:

> As the internet has become not only an important news source, but a force that is rapidly merging traditional news platforms, television, print media and subjective postings, it is somewhat surprising that the traditional form of 24-hour news television is still in the focus of academic debate and – in fact – the theme of an entire volume. (Volkmer 2010)

In fairness, the reviewer was not discouraging research into rolling news journalism. Later on in the review it was argued that the 'book offers many fresh angles and may inspire debate'. Yet what remains revealing is how a scholarly concern with 24-hour news television can appear to be either 'old' (being just 30 years old if CNN marks the launch of the genre) or a 'surprising' object for study (since hundreds of channels have emerged in recent years impacting on the wider culture of journalism – see Chapter 3). No longer a new or novel medium, television news has been pushed down the academic agenda as scholars compete to break 'new' media research and be first to theorise the latest online developments.

From this perspective, the race to publish the latest technological twist or online theoretical turn echoes the debates about the impact of rolling news on journalism more generally (Chapter 3). For while contemporary news values increasingly prioritise the most recent events, squeezing out issues of wider historical merit or longer-lasting social significance, journalism scholarship appears to be somewhat mesmerised by the latest technological trend or digital drama. This is not to deny nor neglect the significant impact which online, multi-media or digital news delivery has had on journalism. Nor is it to criticise journalism scholars, many of whom have broken new theoretical ground and empirically exposed technologically determinist arguments about the democratic promise of the Internet and new media in general (e.g. Allan 2006; Curran 2009a). But it is necessary to point out that despite the radical shift online news has triggered in the production, content and consumption of journalism, 'old' media like television news continue to wield considerable influence on news culture and remain, by some margin, the medium most people will trust, and turn to, to make sense of the world (see Chapter 6).

Even at election times – a key democratic moment when the role of news media is put under the spotlight – television news continues to be the foil to new media enthusiasts predicting the campaign will be determined by a strong Internet campaign. The 2008 American elections may have revolutionised online campaigning by Obama's savvy use of social media but it was television (77 per cent) – not the Internet (26 per cent) – that remained the primary source of information for the vast majority of voters (Pew Internet and American Life Project 2009; for a further critique see Miller 2010: 14–15).

More recently in the UK, the 2010 General Election was to prove a sobering moment for new media enthusiasts. With broadband penetration at its highest point and the use of social media on the rise, many began predicting that the first real Internet election was on the cards. Broadcasters feared for their own relevance, appointing dedicated reporters to meticulously check the web for the latest Twitter trends, Facebook groups, YouTube clips and blog postings. Whatever appeared in these virtual worlds – the topics that were most debated, the quirky and irreverent themes that could be unearthed – began to inform ongoing news and wider election matters. Routinely filling air time and column inches with breaking online and social media gossip, no broadcaster – and, for that matter, no newspaper – wanted to miss out on what was happening in cyberspace. It was not long into the election campaign, however, when many began conceding they had seriously underestimated the role of existing 'old' media.

For rather than social media proving the dominant player in shaping election debates, or at least offering a meaningful alternative agenda to existing media, it was the first ever televised leaders' election debates that were to capture the public's imagination. For periods of the campaign, it was almost the exclusive election-related story not only on television (Deacon et al. 2011) but also on other media including Twitter, Facebook and YouTube (Newman 2010). While the agreement of the three main political parties to sign up for the deal was greeted with a certain amount of trumpeting, its direct impact on the electorate and its wider influence on the news agenda had taken many by surprise. The first of the three debates averaged 9.4 million viewers, which amounted to over a third of the television audience. But it was its knock-on effect that was perhaps more dramatic. A systematic review of the campaign coverage showed the televised debates had made up a significant volume of election news on broadcast, print and online news media (Deacon et al. 2011). While social media may have opened up new means for citizens to participate at election time, most notably for young people (Newman 2010), it was television that had overwhelmingly stolen the show, connecting more widely and sparking more public interest in the campaign than any of its counterparts. Rather than judging the significance of news media on merit, what appears to be driving journalism scholarship is a fascination with all things 'new' or entering into speculation about the kind of online future that might emerge.

In understanding the latest technological trend or speculating about what the future holds, the *current* and *continued* influence of television news is being pushed to the margins of journalism scholarship. For as this book has demonstrated, television news continues to exert considerable influence on journalism while the many democratic promises, revolutionary claims and grand counter-hegemonic narratives associated with the rise of new media have failed to materialise (Curran 2009). In Fenton's (2009) *New Media, Old News* a wealth of evidence is drawn on from different perspectives about how the Internet has far from radically reshaped journalism production, content or reception. The news values, conventions and practices shaped by 'old' media over many decades have, it is argued, largely been transferred to online or digital platforms. The 'latest "new" world of "new" media', Fenton concluded (2009: 14–15), 'has not yet destabilized the ascendancy of dominant news brands'. A quick glance at the most popular websites (Table 7.2) in the US demonstrates how 'old' media have quickly reconstituted much of 'new' online journalism (US State of the Media 2010).

Many of these websites are well-established news organisations and – apart from a local news aggregator news site – have been in operation for over ten years. Far from being 'new' these 'old' media habits die hard since many sites undoubtedly draw in their online audiences from watching television news (CNN, Fox, ABC, NBC and CBS) or from reading well-known newspapers.

The role of social media, in this context, should not be glossed over here since there are pockets of resistance increasingly available beyond the traditional gatekeepers of news media that serve national and international audiences. Hyper local sites or blogs, for example, are being increasingly used for both niche audiences and larger communities and these are operating without the commercial constraints imposed by the bigger media organisations (Ofcom 2010b). Likewise, Twitter or Facebook, amongst others, can temporarily dislodge dominant media agenda setters or set alight stories that can flow transnationally and promote alternative news cycles. But even if much of the promise – or optimism – associated with the future of online journalism or social media is accepted and shared, it would be difficult to argue that online journalism has anything like the impact television news has currently or will have in the imminent future. If journalism studies as a discipline is motivated by dominant sites of power in the communication industries today,

Table 7.2 Top 20 news websites in the US

1	Yahoo News
2	MSNBC Digital Network
3	AOL News
4	CNN.com
5	NYTimes.com
6	Google News
7	Fox News
8	ABCNEWS
9	washingtonpost.com
10	USATODAY.com
11	TheHuffingtonPost.com
12	LA Times
13	Daily News Online Edition
14	CBS Local Stations Group
15	Examiner.com
16	NBC Local Media
17	time.com
18	Fox O&O TV Stations
19	CBS News
20	BBC News

(Source: Pew Project for Excellence in Journalism: The State of the News Media 2010 http://stateofthemedia. org/2010/online-summary-essay/nielsen-analysis/)

understanding the changing nature of television news should continue to be central to contemporary research and scholarship.

And yet many academic books, peer-reviewed journals and conference proceedings appear to have put the online world above television in journalism scholarship. 'Digital', 'multimedia' and 'online' book-length publications have flooded the academic market in recent years. *News Online* (Meikle and Redden 2010), *Web Journalism* (Tunney and Monaghan 2010), *New Media, Old News* (Fenton 20009b), *Digital War Reporting* (Mattheson and Allan 2009), *Making Online News* (Patterson and Domingo 2008), *Excellence in Online News* (Craig 2011), *Internet Newspapers* (Li 2009), *Gatewatching: Collaborative Online News Production* (Bruns 2005), *Online News Gathering* (Quinn and Lamble 2008), *Online News* (Allan 2006) and *Online Journalism Ethics* (Friend and Singer 2007) are just some of the many scholarly endeavours published.

Academic journals, likewise, prioritise new media above television news. Within peer-reviewed journals in recent years studies have tended to draw on online samples to make sense of journalism theory and practice. To gain some insight into how journalism scholarship is shaped by online concerns, main articles appearing in three dedicated journalism journals – *Journalism Practice, Journalism Studies* and *Journalism: Theory, Practice and Criticism* – were systematically examined from 2007–2010.[1] In the majority of articles it was difficult to assess whether a specific media was being examined since a great deal of these explored journalism or news generally. Nevertheless, in articles about television news or online/new media a dominant trend across journalism scholarship was present. *Every journal published more articles about online journalism than television news.* Articles with some online/new media focus (62 per cent) outweighed scholarly concerns with television news (38 per cent), although several articles explored both. In one journal, for every television news article two and a half on online/new media journalism were published. The same analysis was applied to a 2009 Taylor and Francis 'Future of Journalism' conference at Cardiff University. For every paper concerned with television news, there were five more about new media or online journalism.

These dominant trends in journalism scholarship should not be over-emphasised and require five caveats. First, the figures do not represent all journalism scholarship since just three journals and one conference were examined in a far wider academic environment where journalism was researched and theorised across the humanities and social science disciplines. Second, for academics struggling to balance teaching, administrative and research commitments, online news is far less time-consuming than researching broadcast coverage. Obtaining television news retrospectively can be complicated and costly when compared to the convenience and immediacy of the Internet. Methodologically speaking also, the unit of analysis – a web story – is less difficult to attach an operational definition to than the amorphous flow of television news. Third, in isolating television and online news papers this does not mean journalism should be examined in isolation. In an age of convergence, where journalisms intersect in how they are produced, consumed and understood, any analysis of news should be done holistically. Fourth, while the figures above are being used to demonstrate how scholars have embraced the study of new media, most of the articles were not celebratory accounts of online news. Indeed this was far from the case, since many scholars questioned the technological determinism that was sometimes apparent in new media studies and empirically challenged many of the claims put forward by new media enthusiasts. Fifth, and finally, since academic journals and conferences like to be at the cutting edge of scholarship, it is understandable why these 'new' theories, practices and technologies are encouraged by editors and publishers. But they do this

---

[1] While articles might have engaged with particular types of news media, the figures here relate to the information that was provided in the abstract and key words. The findings should be interpreted as indicative trends rather than scientifically robust evaluations of how far each news media informs articles appearing in the three dedicated journalism journals.

at the expense of undervaluing the *present* and *continued* influence of television news and journalism. Notwithstanding the many methodological obstacles, commercial considerations and structural limitations associated with the production of academic work, the research culture which is currently being shaped means online/new media scholarship is punching well above its democratic weight.

What is being argued here – that there is a disproportionate focus on new media relative to the continued power of television news in academic scholarship – has been voiced more ferociously beyond journalism studies. For scholars have raised concerns about how far new digital, online, multimedia technologies are shaping the theory and practice of media, culture and communication disciplines. This was partly reflected in a reaction to Media Studies 2.0 put forward by scholars such as David Gauntlett and William Merrim. For Gauntlett (2009: 147), 'Media Studies lecturers need to catch up with their students in the digital world', while Perrim (2010) has suggested many 'students are outstripping their lecturers in their knowledge and navigation of the digital economy'. Both have argued the Internet has not just fundamentally changed the media landscape, it has also shifted how audiences, content and production should be understood and conceptualised in Media Studies. The implication here being that lecturers had fallen behind their students and conceptually ignored new sites of media power or, more importantly, audience resistance. For *audiences*, in Media Studies 2.0, are seen as empowered and pro-active consumers, able to *produce* and manage their own *content*, and freed from the influence of 'super-powerful media industries invading the minds of a relatively passive population' (Gauntlett 2007). This in turn has generated a frenzy of debate within media studies forums (see MeCCSA[1]) and has led to special journal editions being devoted to the relative merits of 1, 2 and even Media Studies 3.0 (see *Interactions* 2009; *Television and New Media* 2009). With more than a hint of sarcasm, Toby Miller (2009: 6) has argued that:

> Media Studies 2.0 claims that the public is clever and able and that it makes its own meanings, outwitting institutions of the state, academia, and capitalisms that seek to measure and control it ... A deregulated, individualised media world allegedly makes consumers into producers, frees the disabled from confinement, encourages new subjectivities, rewards intellect and competitiveness, links people across cultures, and allows billions of flowers to bloom in a postpolitical cornucopia.

If television journalism scholarship were to embrace a Media Studies 2.0 model it would run the risk of ignoring many of the themes explored in this

---

[1] See MeCCSA discussion archives in 2007 at http://www.meccsa.org.uk

book. For media ownership and regulation, dominant media institutions and mass audiences, media influence and impact are areas of media scholarship that could be interpreted as 'old' Media Studies 1.0 debates in a 'new' Media Studies 2.0 age.

Academics celebrating audience resistance to dominant sites of power can also be used by media corporations to justify the concentration of media power. As Philo and Miller (2001: 77) have pointed out, News Corporation executives have exploited the notion of the 'sovereign viewer' to argue that audiences are able to actively subvert or critically resist whatever media messages they encounter. Rupert Murdoch made the case for further concentrating his media power in a 2010 speech celebrating Margaret Thatcher's achievements. He argued that

> I am something of a parvenu, but we should welcome the iconoclastic and the unconventional. And we shouldn't curb their enthusiasm or energy. That is what competition is all about. Yet when the upstart is too successful, somehow the old interests surface, and restrictions on growth are proposed or imposed. This is an issue for my company. More important, it's an issue for our broader society. (Cited in Deans 2010b)

Underlying Murdoch's speech was the desire to own more media, control more journalism, and expand his already massive empire of media interests. While discourses of choice, freedom and creativity were repeated within his speech, what journalism studies scholarship has exposed in recent years is how an increasingly deregulated, centralised media culture achieves quite the opposite (e.g. McChesney 2000; Curran et al. 2009). If anything, concentrated media power diminishes pluralism and narrows the kind of journalism that is pursued (see Chapter 4 and Chapter 5). But according to Media Studies 2.0 theory, 'critical resistance to big media institutions, such as Rupert Murdoch's News International' is a Media Studies 1.0 neurosis (Gauntlett 2007). In a 'post-broadcast era' (Marrin 2010) 'old' media – like television news – appear to be a thing of the past and no longer the dominant sites of power.

Defending Media Studies 2.0, Gauntlett (2011; original emphasis) has argued it was once 'both fun and important to show how those big media barons are evil. And sure, they still are, and are probably getting worse. But if Media Studies can *only* talk about that, and patronising ideas of "media literacy" and the boring fruitless notion of genre … what's the point?' While Gauntlett has rightly raised new questions in Media Studies including 'the rise of everyday creativity online', it could be argued (and this chapter has done so in part) that scholarly concerns are *more* likely to revolve around new online developments and audience agency than dominant sites of power and influence such as studying television news. Media Studies 2.0, in this context, could be misleading. For while the role of new media in contemporary theory and practice may be central to the Media Studies 2.0 approach, what this *does not say* about media power and control is dangerous not just for the discipline of journalism and media studies but also for the relevance their scholarship has to broader questions about democracy and citizenship.

To illustrate this point, a Murdoch-related example of public indifference towards an old-fashioned Media Studies 1.0 debate warrants a brief mention. A representative ICM poll in December 2010 asked UK respondents if they opposed or supported Murdoch's attempt to buy the rest of the BSkyB (Robinson 2010). Interpreting the poll, a *Media Guardian* headline screamed 'only 1 in 20 back Murdoch takeover' (Robinson 2010). More revealing but given less attention was that just 41 per cent indicated they had no strong view and 11 per cent said they didn't know. Put another way, over half did not appear to be alarmed by – or, more likely, were well informed or knowledgeable about – the threat which News Corporation's bid posed to media pluralism. Far from moving on from studying Murdoch's continued influence, it could be argued media and journalism studies should pay *more* attention to this in their curriculum in schools and universities. So, for example, when students study Media Studies on some exam boards at A or AS level in the UK – typically between the ages of 16–18 – news will be an *optional* and not a compulsory part of the course.[2] Media scholarship, likewise, could play a greater role in informing public debate and raising media literacy levels.

While the general drift towards online journalism scholarship was critiqued in this section, the quality of *all* new media theory, practice and research was not. For most of new media journalism scholarship has not embraced Media Studies 2.0 nor has it abandoned a critical engagement with questions about ownership, regulation and media influence. But to remain relevant as a discipline and locate dominant sites of power in the communication industries today, understanding the changing nature of television news should continue to be central to contemporary research and scholarship.

New directions in television news studies: the future of journalism studies

Despite the proliferation of online news/journalism research, practice and theory, television news has not vanished within journalism, communication and media studies. As the bibliography in this book testifies to, television news scholarship remains part of the agenda but not to the same degree or at least the same prominence prior to the arrival of new online media. Nonetheless, debates in the field have moved on since the formative years of television scholarship with more sophisticated theory, methods and research. As part

---

[2] I am grateful to Matthew Hook for explaining to me what is typically taught on A and AS Media Studies courses in the UK.

of a rapidly expanding discipline with new journals arriving in an increasingly global research environment (Löffelholz and Weaver 2008), scholars have engaged empirically, theoretically and professionally with the production, content and reception of television news in new and exciting ways.

While journalism studies has matured discipline-wise, it remains *interdisciplinary* and has expanded in size and scope globally. This makes mapping key debates and charting the dominant narratives in television news studies an increasingly complicated endeavour. When asked to interpret where journalism scholarship is heading, prominent scholars in the field have drawn on a wide range of theories, methods and approaches to interpret how the discipline should be understood and the sorts of challenges it faces (see *Journalism: Theory, Practice and Criticism*, vol. 10(3)). But as James Curran (2009: 312) has pointed out, while 'millenarian prophecy and charismatic leadership doubtless have a place in journalism education ... empirical research' remains central to understanding where the future of journalism lies. The intention of this book has been to develop an evidenced-based understanding of the past and present trends in television news studies with one eye cast on the direction journalism is heading.

To conclude the book, two broader developments in journalism and television news research – foreshadowed in previous chapters – warrant unpacking in more detail. First, where once much of journalism scholarship was dismissed by the news industry, today there is evidence of greater collaboration in teaching and research. Critiques of television news, nevertheless, can still be greeted with suspicion and resistance from the news industry. To enhance the reception of television news studies, it will be suggested that accusing journalists of 'bias' could be more effectively put as identifying the dominant narratives where journalism can misrepresent or exclude (e.g. Street 2010).

Second, as journalism studies has become more global in scope, internationally comparative studies of television news production, content and reception have emerged. In doing so, scholars have been able to demonstrate empirically how the ecology of television news helps shape what type of journalism is pursued across different countries and what kind of knowledge this brings to democracies that are heavily reliant on the medium. It will be argued that these studies represent a decisive way of comparing market-driven and public service television journalism, or the impact of light-touch or robust forms of television news regulation.

Towards a more industry-friendly research agenda: making sense of dominant narratives in television journalism

In recent years, media and communication departments have recruited from within the industry for teachers on journalism courses (see Chapter 6).

'Hackademics' – journalists applying their trade in academia – have grown more prominent beyond the US. While practical–academic divides are still evident in media departments, Harcup's (2011a, 2011b) survey of 'Hackademics' in the UK suggested that they are beginning to adapt to the research environment and publish scholarly material. In doing so, journalism practice and theory have been pushed closer together, part of a wider trend that has brought the academy closer to the media industry since the *Bad News* studies were published. There remain, of course, moments when media scholars are subject to the same hostility experienced in the 1980s. Proposing a tax plan for the richest 10 per cent in the UK to avoid the widespread cuts in public services, Professor of Sociology at Glasgow University Greg Philo's September 2010 appearance on the BBC television show, *The Daily Politics*, was reminiscent of the reception that greeted the *Bad News* studies (c.f. Harrison 1985; Quinn 2007). 'Are you living in cloud cuckoo land?' or 'a professor of sociology, not economics' were just two of many remarks that instantly discredited an alternative plan to what the mainstream political parties were proposing.

However, the GMG's television news scholarship has, in more recent years, been more constructively welcomed by the news media industry. *Bad News From Israel* (Philo and Berry 2004), in particular, generated a widespread discussion about how television news objectively covered the Israeli–Palestine conflict. The GMG invited senior UK journalists from the BBC, Channel 4 and Channel 5, as well as other key figures within the industry to sit on focus groups where audiences would watch television coverage and ask questions about how they interpreted events. The exchanges between journalists and audiences demonstrated the assumptions television news made about what viewers knew and the need for more context in routine television reporting of the wider origins of the conflict. In other words, they made journalists face up to the impact television journalism can have on audiences.

As opposed to individual television stations being accused of 'media bias' or journalists accusing the GMG of being looney left-wing academics, the industry appeared to be more open to debates about how impartiality could be achieved. Two years later the BBC Governors (what is now the BBC Trust) commissioned Loughborough University to explore television coverage and while they found no 'systematic or deliberate bias' there were 'shortcomings' in 'coverage, analysis, context and perspective' (BBC Governors 2006: 6). The BBC Trust has since published other reports on impartiality in journalism more generally – *From Seesaw to Wagon Wheel* (2007) – and commissioned research into the accuracy and impartiality of the four nations and devolution (Chapter 4; Cushion et al. 2010; Lewis et al. 2008). There is, in other words, more critical self-reflection about impartiality – and the issues facing journalism more generally – that has been informed by many of the methods, theories and practices of journalism studies developed decades before. This was observed by Brain McNair (2009: xiii) in the preface to a fifth edition of *News and Journalism*: 'luxuriously resourced organisations such as the BBC and Ofcom ... contain data of the type once delivered by academics engaged in isolation and slow work'. While this should not replace academic research, it does represent a move towards more empirically-led evaluations of journalism and could produce more collaborative studies by academics and the news industry (see Chapter 5).

Debates that have been central in television journalism – when accusations of 'bias' are raised or 'impartiality' is questioned – have become subject to more scrutiny in the media and communication studies in the previous two decades (Gunter 1997; Starkey 2006). The notion of achieving 'impartiality' or maintaining 'objectivity' in journalism was once dismissed as being a mere delusion since anything televised, when put simply, is a construction rather than an accurate reflection of 'the truth'. All 'news', in other words, is fiction. Hence scholars like Jean Baudrillard have argued 'The Gulf War did not take place' because television news coverage, in particular, was more like a fantasy film than an accurate account of what happened on the ground. Or, less extremely, we have Douglas Kellner (1995: 198), who viewed the 1991 Gulf War as a 'cultural-political event as much as a military one', in that the US Government was able to manipulate television pictures due to an adeptly run PR campaign. Bias, in this context, was avoided since both accounts were not measuring *what should* be reported against what was. This approach, however, has its limits. To assess the accuracy of journalism, what is included remains just as important as what *is not*. For if alternative, competing, counter-claims are not compared to the media content that is produced then this invites a form of relativism where *all* portrayals are given equal weight and validity. At some point journalists have to make a judgement about which points of view warrant inclusion – or exclusion – from a story. In doing so, how far they remained impartial can be unravelled by astute audiences or media scholars interpreting how a news story *could* have been reported had X or Y been included.

Strictly applied, impartiality invites a degree of relativism since there is no absolute 'truth' it can be compared to. Using this assessment, journalism will always be 'bias' or 'prejudice' for it cannot ever live up to the 'window on the world' it once set itself up to be. However, this should not invalidate the journalistic aspiration of impartiality. John Street (2010: 47–48) has offered an alternative way of assessing journalism, arguing that news 'coverage needs to be read not just in terms of "bias", but as "narratives", as stories about the world which call into play some actors (and marginalize others), which suppose some motivations and ignore others, and so on'. While 'bias' encompasses many of these elements, it has arguably become a politically-loaded term, the expression of a deliberate distortion or intentional deception. It has also led to sophisticated media critiques being too easily dismissed for implying the media are part of a grander conspiracy to prevent the 'truth' from 'outing'. So, for example, despite developing a complex political economy argument based on five filters that shape how US journalism is produced to sustain the interests of political and business elites, Herman and Chomsky's (1988) *Manufacturing Consent* – more than 20 years since it was published – is today often caricatured as advancing an argument about how news media collectively orchestrate a right-wing bias (see Mullen 2010 for a critique of its academic reception).

The concept of narrative, instead, alludes to the construction of a story – like any other media text – and appears less conspiratorial than accusations of premeditated 'bias'. It can be used to demonstrate how dominant patterns of reporting can emerge in how issues or events are understood and covered without insinuating that journalists will deliberately conceal or obscure something from the public. As many television news studies have argued in recent years, it is well-established news conventions and practices – not deceiving or suspect journalists – that can perpetuate dominant *narratives* of exclusion or misrepresentation. This was argued in previous chapters where television journalism has increasingly embraced speed and immediacy in its news values (see Chapter 3); that opinion and partisanship has become an accepted journalistic norm in US cable television networks (see Chapter 4); that UK national journalism was excluding the nations and regions within the UK (see Chapter 5); or that journalists have become a largely graduate profession because of the kind of training or education that is required by the industry (Chapter 6).

Towards a more internationally comparative research agenda: making sense of how broadcast ecologies shape television journalism

In understanding changing television ecologies, questions about the impact of media ownership and deregulatory trends have been shaped by more internationally comparative research in recent years. At the turn of the century, Curran and Park (2000: 2) edited a book asking for Media Studies to be 'De-Westernized'. This was a 'reaction against', in their words, 'the self-absorption and parochialism of much Western Media theory'. Four years later Hallin and Manchini published *Comparing Media Systems*. It developed three models that encapsulated how media systems across the US, Canada and much of Western Europe operated. A Liberal model defined by a 'relative dominance of market mechanisms and of commercial media' (2004: 11) was used to characterise the US, UK and Ireland; a Democratic Corporatist model was adopted for Northern Europe since commercial media coexisted with 'social and political groups, and by a relatively active but legally limited role of the state' (2004: 11); and finally, a Polarised Pluralist model reflected Southern Europe because media systems were largely shaped by party politics, with the state playing a more active role than wider commercial forces. Both Curran and Park's (2000) book and Hallin and Manchini's work were early lengthy endeavours that looked at internationally comparable political and media systems *generally*. What they argued, overall, was not just that political traditions would shape what news is produced but also that different media systems would produce distinctive forms of journalism.

In more recent years, an increasing range of studies has compared *television news internationally*, exploring why journalism is shaped differently according to the wider broadcast ecology in which it is produced (for example, see Aalberg et al. 2010; Kolmer and Semetko 2010; Curran et al. 2009; Curran et al. 2010; Cushion 2012; Iyengar et al. 2010). James Curran and his colleagues studied the US, UK, Denmark and Finland and compared television news coverage and levels of public knowledge in each country (Curran et al. 2009). Their knowledge-based surveys found that in those nations where the infrastructure of public service television was stronger – most notably in the Scandinavian countries – the public's understanding of public affairs was higher than in those countries that were more reliant on commercial broadcasting, such as the US. The content analysis studies of television news in each country found public service television channels provided more hard news than nations with more market-driven journalism. While acknowledging that broader social, economic and political variables played a role in the acquisition of public knowledge, such as levels of education and poverty, interest in or engagement with politics, Curran et al. (2009) concluded that the information environment of viewers was a significant factor in explaining why public understanding of key issues diverged from one country to the next.

Another study led by Toril Aalberg expanded on this research by exploring the changing volume of television news across six countries – the US, UK, Belgium, the Netherlands, Norway and Sweden – over a 30 year period (Aalberg et al. 2010). During prime time, their detailed schedule analysis found that, in 1987, 1997 and 2007, all commercial channels had considerably less coverage of news and current affairs than public service television. Over the time period, all commercial channels had *decreased* their proportion of news and current affairs, apart from Sweden and Belgium, where this had marginally increased. All public service television, by contrast, had *increased* its provision of news and current affairs with the exception of Sweden. Aalberg et al. (2010: 268) argued that sustained public service peak-time hours of television news has meant that viewers remained in touch with hard news subjects like politics even if they were not so interested in these topics. For internationally comparative studies of television news have shown hard news topics are more rountinely part of news agendas in countries with a greater infrastructure of public service broadcasting (Curran et al. 2009; Cushion 2012; Cushion and Lewis 2009).

Kolmer and Semetko (2010) examined the proportion of foreign news – widely interpreted as 'hard' news subject matter – on German television and compared this to the most watched television news services in several European countries, South African television, and transnational Arabic satellite channels. Once again, where public service television was present foreign coverage remained high (45 per cent of the agenda in Germany, 39 per cent in the UK) compared to commercially-driven environments (23 per cent in the US). The role played by public service television historically appears also to have rubbed off on commercial broadcasters. Kolmer and Semetko (2010: 712) have suggested the long-held traditions of public service television 'may even have initially raised the bar for private channels in Germany which continue to devote a comparatively large share of the programs to foreign news, even though the channels are not subsidized nor bound by the same rules'. Likewise, in the UK, the presence of a highly respected public service broadcaster and an overarching regulatory framework – concerned primarily with policing impartiality rather than putting quotas on international coverage – has encouraged commercial channels to maintain a hard news agenda including foreign news (Cushion and Lewis 2009).

For what many internationally comparative television news studies have also drawn attention to is the different regulatory structures that influence which television journalism is produced and how this is done (Cushion 2012). Hallin and Manchin's three (2004) models of media systems suggest there is an increasing convergence towards the Liberal model where trends of commercialisation and deregulation are most prevalent. Within a European context, the influx of multi-channel commercial channels in the 1980s and 1990s has liberalised the television market and redefined the identity and funding mechanisms of public service channels (see Chapter 2).

Yet at the same time, many countries have stuck resolutely to strict regulatory commitments on news and current affairs and have prevented unfettered market power or independence from the state (Aalberg et al. 2010; Cushion 2012). This has contributed to maintaining journalistic standards, such as prime-time news programming or ensuring broadcasters remain impartial. According to Williams (2005: 61), 'where no obligations have been placed on public or private broadcasters to broadcast particular kinds of programmes or meet quota arrangements for domestic production, public service has withered'. The impact of deregulation can also be seen to depoliticise citizens, stripping them of information that is necessary for sustaining well-informed democracies. Curran et al's (2009: 22) comparative study of knowledge across four countries relative to how deregulated and commercialised its television ecology was led them to conclude that 'media provision of public information does matter, and continued deregulation of the broadcast media is likely, on balance, to lead to lower levels of public knowledge'.

In a US context, where deregulation has been on the march for many decades (see Chapter 2), the free market approach to media policy making has meant journalism has not been subjected to the same level of scrutiny in maintaining accuracy or impartiality. As Chapter 4 argued, the relaxation of the Fairness Doctrine – the legal requirement to be impartial in broadcasting – contributed to shaping what is a now a highly partisan and politicised public sphere in the US. Kull's representative (2003) survey comparing levels of knowledge about the 2003 Iraq war across viewers of American television news demonstrated that misconceptions about why the military conflict was being waged emanated from the *least* regulated channels. Many viewers of commercial channels, and those frequenting Fox News in particular, falsely believed that Iraq supported Al-Qaeda; that Iraq played a role in the terrorist attacks of 9/11; and that world opinion, despite many countries being bitterly opposed to the conflict, was largely supportive of the war. By contrast, regular viewers of PBS news were considerably less likely to hold any of these misconceptions than commercial television audiences would do. Since most Americans relied on commercial and not public television as their primary source of information, Kull's (2003) study empirically reinforced the title of Danny Schecheter's provocative (1997) book, *The More You Watch The Less You Know*. For the *more* commercial viewers paid attention to television news, the *more likely* they were to be misinformed about the reasons why America had gone to war. To put it another way, commercial television news confused rather than enlightened Americans on the reasoning for going to war, this being the antithesis of what journalism has philosophically stood for over many centuries (Keane 1991; Thompson 1991).

Since the BBC's digital channels and its online presence have become more globally accessible in recent years, Bicket and Wall (2009) have suggested the corporation has now become a key transnational public broadcaster in the US. Without the infrastructure, financial resources or political will to credibly fund an American public broadcaster (see Chapter 2), they have argued 'the role of the BBC has begun to resemble that of a domestic US alternative news source' (2009: 378). Needless to say, the American networks and increasingly the cable news channels are where viewers will overwhelmingly tune into. But despite many decades of commercial dominance, there is a demand for television news to be supplied by well-funded, independently operated, robustly regulated public service journalism. By contrast, in countries that are free to practise journalism without state interference, and where a healthy infrastructure of public service television is present, a significant number of viewers do not appear to be hunting down foreign news alternatives.

As journalism studies continues to be internationalised, what comparative television news studies encourage is how information environments can be structured, funded and regulated in ways that will maintain diverse news agendas, suitable prime-time scheduling slots and sufficient levels of audience trust. There remain, of course, distinctive cross-national variations in the public service and commercial television models. And also within countries, where many commercial and public service broadcasters have happily co-existed, and competition between the two approaches has enhanced – not diminished – the quality of journalism (see Chapter 2). But what international comparisons do bring is more choice and further evidence of how television news journalism can be imagined and put into practice. In doing so, empirical light can be shed on the consequences shifting broadcasting ecologies can have on television journalism and its ability to inform viewers about what is happening in the world.

BIBLIOGRAPHY

Aalberg, Toril, Aelst, Peter van and Curran, James (2010) 'Media systems and the political information environment: a cross-national comparison', *International Journal of Press/Politics*, 15(3): 255–271.

Ackerman, Seth (2001) 'The most biased name in news: Fox News Channel's extraordinary right wing tilt', *FAIR: Fairness and Accuracy in Reporting*, July/August, available at www.fair.org/index.php?page=1067 (accessed 21 October 2010).

Aldridge, Mary and Evetts, Judith (2003) 'Rethinking the concept of professionalism: the case of journalism', *British Journal of Sociology*, 54(4): 547–564.

Allan, Stuart (2010a) *News Culture* (3rd edition). Maidenhead: Open University Press.

Allan, Stuart (ed.) (2010b) *The Routledge Companion to News and Journalism*. New York: Routledge.

Allan, Stuart (2006) *Online News: Journalism and the Internet*. Maidenhead: Open University Press.

Allan, Stuart (ed.) (2005) *Journalism: Critical Issues*. Maidenhead: Open University Press.

Allan, Stuart (1999) *News Culture*. Maidenhead: Open University Press.

Allan, Stuart and Thornsen, Einar (eds) (2009) *Citizen Journalism: Global Perspectives*. New York: Peter Lang.

Alterman, Eric (2000) *Sound and Fury: The Making of the Punditocracy* (2nd edition). New York: Viking.

Anderson, Peter and Ward, Geoff (2007) *The Future of Journalism in the Advanced Democracies*. Aldershot: Ashgate.

Ang, Ien (1991) *Desperately Seeking the Audience*. London and New York: Routledge.

Ang, Ien (1985) *Watching Dallas: Soap Opera and the Melodramatic Imagination*. London: Methuen.

Aufderheide, Patricia (2000) *Communications Policy and the Public Interest: The Telecommunications Act of 1996*. New York: Guildford.

Avery, Robert K. (2007) 'The Public Broadcasting Act of 1967: looking ahead by looking back', *Critical Studies in Mass Communication*, 24(4): 358–364.

Ayish, Muhammad I. (2010) 'Morality vs. politics in the public sphere: how the Al-Jazeera satellite channel humanized a bloody political conflict in Gaza'. In Stephen Cushion and Justin Lewis (eds), *The Rise of 24-Hour News Television: Global Perspectives*. New York: Peter Lang.

Bainbridge, Jason and Bestwick, Jane (2010) '"And here's the news": analysing the evolution of the marketed newsreader', *Media, Culture and Society*, 32(2): 205–223.

Baines, David and Kennedy, Ciara (2008) 'An education for independence: should entrepreneurial skills be an essential part of the journalist's toolbox?', *Journalism Practice*, 4(1): 97–113.

Baisnée, Oliver and Marchetti, Dominique (2006) 'The economy of just-in-time television newscasting: journalistic production and professional excellence at Euronews', *Ethnography*, 7(1): 99–123.

Barker, Edwin C. (2007) *Media Concentration and Democracy: Why Ownership Matters.* New York: Cambridge University Press.

BARB (2008) 'BBC1 audiences by nation for weekday network programmes'. London: Broadcasters' Audience Research Board.

Barkin, Steve M. (2003) *American Television News: The Media Marketplace and the Public Interest.* New York: M.E. Sharpe.

Barnett, Steven (2010a) 'Dangermen: over to you Mr Cable', *British Journalism Review*, 21(4): 13–18.

Barnett, Steven (2010b) 'What's wrong with media monopolies? A lesson from history and a new approach to media ownership policy'. London: LSE Electronic Working Papers.

Barnett, Steven, Seymour, Emily and Gaber, Ivor (2000) *From Callaghan to Kosovo: Changing Trends in British Television News.* London: University of Westminster.

Battaglio, Stephen (2010) 'Who are TV's top earners?', *TV Guide*, 10 August. Available at www.tvguide.com/News/Top-TV-Earners-1021717.aspx (accessed 16 November 2010).

Baudrillard, Jean (1995) *The Gulf War Did Not Take Place.* Bloomington, IN: Indiana University Press.

Baum, Matthew A. (2003a) 'Soft news and political knowledge: evidence of absence of absence of evidence?', *Political Communication*, 20(2): 173–190.

Baum, Matthew A. (2003b) *Soft News Goes to War: Public Opinion and American Foreign Policy in the New Media Age.* Princeton: Princeton University Press.

Baym, Geoffery (2010) *From Cronkite to Colbert: The Evolution of Broadcast News.* London: Paradigm.

Baym, Geoffery (2007a) 'Crafting new communicative models in the televisual sphere: political interviews on *The Daily Show*', *Communication Review*, 22: 259–276.

Baym, Geoffery (2007b) 'Representation and the politics of play: Stephen Colbert's Better Know a District', *Political Communication,* 24: 359–376.

Baym, Geoffery (2005) '*The Daily Show*: discursive integration and the reinvention of political communication', *Political Communication*, 22: 259–276.

BBC Governors (2006) 'Report of the Independent Panel for the BBC Governors on impartiality of BBC coverage of Israeli–Palestinian conflict'. Available at www.bbcgovernors archive.co.uk/docs/reviews/panel_report_final.pdf (accessed 18 January 2011).

BBC News (2006) 'Black TV newsman is French first', BBC News online, 8 March, available at http://news.bbc.co.uk/1/hi/entertainment/4786376.stm (accessed 18 November 2010).

BBC News (2001) 'BBC news move "halts decline"', BBC News online, 15 October, available at http://news.bbc.co.uk/1/hi/entertainment/1600622.stm (accessed 17 January 2011).

BBC Press Office (2003) 'BBC goes in the clear on digital satellite', BBC Press Office, available at www.bbc.co.uk/pressoffice/pressreleases/stories/2003/03_march/12/digital_sat.shtml (accessed 5 November 2010).

BBC/Reuters/Media Center (2006) 'Trust in the Media: Media More Trusted Than Governments — Poll', available at www.globescan.com/news_archives/bbcreut.html (accessed 1 December 2010).

BBC Trust (2009) *Service Review: Younger Audiences: BBC Three, Radio 1 and 1Xtra*, June. London: BBC Trust.

BBC Trust (2008) *The BBC Trust Impartiality Report: BBC Network News and Current Affairs Coverage of The UK Four Nations.* London: BBC Trust.

BBC Trust (2007) *From Seesaw to Wagon Wheel: Impartiality in the 21st Century.* London: BBC Trust. Available at www.bbc.co.uk/bbctrust/assets/files/pdf/review_ report_research/impartiality_21century/report.pdf (accessed 18 January 2011).

Becker, Lee, Vlad, Tudor, Desnoes, Paris and Olin, Devora (2010) '2009 Annual Survey of Journalism & Mass Communication Graduates' for Grady College of Journalism and Mass Communication. Athens, GA: University of Georgia.

Bell, Martin (2009) cited in Harcup, Tony (2009) *Journalism: Principles and Practice* (2nd edition). London: Sage.

Bennett, Lance W. (2007) 'Relief in hard times: a defence of Jon Stewart's comedy in an age of cynicism', Critical Forum, *Critical Studies in Media Communication*, 24(3): 278–283.

Bennett, Lance W. (2004) 'Global media and politics: transnational communication regimes and civic cultures', *Annual Review of Political Science*, 7: 125–148.

Benton, Marc and Fraizer, Jean P. (1976) 'The agenda setting function of the mass media at three levels of information holding', *Communication Research*, 3(3): 261–274.

Berglez, Peter (2008) 'What is global journalism?', *Journalism Studies*, 9(6): 845–858.

Best, Shaun (1999) 'Reading ideology: an evaluation of the Glasgow Media Group', available at http://shaunbest.tripod.com/id8.html (accessed 18 January 2011).

Bicket, Douglas and Wall, Melissa (2009) 'BBC News in the United States: a 'super alternative' news medium emerges' in *Media, Culture and Society*, Vol.31(3): 365–384.

Bird, Elizabeth (2010) 'Introduction: The Anthropology of News and Journalism: Why Now?' In Elizabeth Bird (ed.), *The Anthropology of News and Journalism: Global Perspectives.* Bloomington, IN: Indiana University Press.

Bishop, Bill and Cushing, Robert G. (2008) *The Big Sort: Why the Clustering of Like-Minded Americans Is Tearing Us Apart.* Boston, MA: Houghton Mifflin.

Black, Ian (2008) 'Al-Jazeera sees off satellite rivals', *Media Guardian*, 31 December, available at www.guardian.co.uk/world/2008/dec/31/israelandthepalestinians-middleeast1?INTCMP=SRCH (accessed 10 January 2011).

BMRB (2008) 'BBC Trust – Nations' Impartiality review', available at www.bbc.co.uk/ bbctrust/assets/files/pdf/review_report_research/impartiality/appendix_b_bmrb_ research.pdf (accessed 21 January 2011).

Born, Georgia (2005) *Uncertain Vision: Birt, Dyke and the Reinvention of the BBC.* London: Secker and Warburg.

Boyd-Barrett, Claudia and Boyd-Barrett, Oliver (2010) '24/7 news as counter hegemonic soft power in Latin America'. In Stephen Cushion and Justin Lewis (eds), *The Rise of 24-Hour Television: Global Perspectives.* New York: Peter Lang.

Brewer, Paul R. and Macafee, Timothy (2007) 'Anchors away: media framing of broadcast television network evening news anchors', *International Journal of Press/ Politics*, 12(4): 3–19.

Brewer, Paul R. and Marquardt, Emily (2007) 'Mock news and democracy: analysing *The Daily Show*', *Atlantic Journal of Communication*, 15(4): 249–267.

Briggs, Matthew (2009) *Television, Audiences and Everyday Life.* Buckingham: Open University Press.

Brighton, Paul and Foy, Dennis (2007) *News Values.* London: Sage.

Broadcasting Committee (1923) Report (Cmnd 1951), Sykes Committee.

Brooker, Charlie (2009) 'Michael Jackson's death hit Glastonbury hard – and the news channels harder', *Guardian*, 29 June, available at www.guardian.co. ukcommentisfree/2009/jun/29/michael-jackson-glastonbury-charlie-brooker (accessed 24 September 2010).

Brooker, Charlie (2008) 'Is Obama elitist? Is his poor bowling a turn-off? This is the nit-picking idiocy of 24-hour news TV', *Guardian*, 28 April, available at www. guardian.co.uk/commentisfree/2008/apr/28/television.barackobama (accessed 24 September 2010).

Brosius, Hans-Bernd and Kepplinger, Hans Mathias (1990) 'The agenda-setting function of television news: static and dynamic views', *Communication Research*, 17(2): 183–211.

Brown, Maggie (2011) 'ITV considered replacing half of evening news with gameshow', *Media Guardian*, 18 January, available at www.guardian.co.uk/media/2011/jan/18/itv-early-evening-news (accessed 23 January 2011).

Brown, Maggie and Brook, Stephen (2009) 'BBC news has become a "factory", says Peter Sissons' *Guardian*, 1 October, available at www.guardian.co.uk/media/2009/oct/01/peter-sissons-bbc-news (accessed 28 July 2010).

Brubaker, Jennifer (2011) 'Internet and television are not substitutes for seeking political information', *Communication Research Reports*, 27(4): 298–309.

Bruns, Axel (2005) *Gatekeeping: Collaborative Online News Production*. New York: Peter Lang.

Burrell, Ian (2005) 'The interview–Nick Pollard: the man who put Sky on top of terrorism in London gave Sky its finest hour', *Independent*, 1 August.

Calcutt, Andrew and Hammond, Philip (2011) *Journalism Studies: A Critical Introduction*. London: Routledge.

Caldwell, John T. (1995) *Televisuality: Style, Crisis, and Authority in American Television*. New York: Rutgers University Press.

Calhoun, Craig (ed.) (1992) *Habermas and the Public Sphere*. London: MIT Press.

Cao, Xiaoxia (2010) 'Hearing it from Jon Stewart: the impact of *The Daily Show* on public attentiveness to politics', *International Journal of Public Opinion Research*, 22(1): 26–46.

CBC News (2010) 'Chilean mine rescue watched by millions online', *CBC News*, 14 October 14, available at www.cbc.ca/technology/story/2010/10/14/tech-chile-miner-video-stream.html (accessed 10 January 2010).

Chalaby, Jean K. (2009) *Transnational Television in Europe: Reconfiguring Global Communications Networks*. London: I.B. Tauris.

Chamberlin, Bill F. (1978) 'The FCC and the first principle of the fairness doctrine: a history of neglect and distortion', *Federal Communications Law Journal*, 31(3): 361–411.

Chambers, Deborah, Steiner, Linda and Fleming, Carole (2004) *Women and Journalism*. London: Routledge.

Chibnall, Steve (1977) *An Analysis of Crime Reporting in the British Press*. London: Tavistock.

Coe, Kevin, Tewksbury, David, Bradley J., Bond, Kristin L., Drogos, Robert W., Porter, Ashley Yahn and Zhang, Yuanyuan (2008) 'Hostile news: partisan use and perceptions of cable news programming', *Journal of Communication*, 58: 201–219.

Cohen, Jeffery (2010) *Going Local: Presidential Leadership in the Post-Broadcast Age*. Cambridge: Cambridge University Press.

Cole, Peter and Harcup, Tony (2010) *Newspaper Journalism*. London: Sage.

Collins, Richard (1998) *From Satellite to Single Market: New Communication Technology and European Public Service Television*. London: Routlege.

Conboy, Martin (2011) *Journalism in Britain: A Historical Introduction*. London: Sage.

Conboy, Martin (2004) *Journalism: A Critical History*. London: Sage.

Connell, Liam (2003) 'The Scottishness of the Scottish Press: 1918–39', *Media, Culture and Society*, 25(2): 187–207.

Conway, Mike (2009) *The Origins of Television News in America: The Visualizers of CBS in the 1940s*. New York: Peter Lang.

Conway, Mike (2007) 'A guest in our living room: the television newscaster before the rise of the dominant anchor', *Journal of Broadcasting and Electronic Media*, 51(3): 457–478.

Conway, Mike, Grabe, Maria E. and Grieves, Kevin (2007) 'Villains, victims, and the virtuous in Bill O'Reilly's "No-Spin Zone"', *Journalism Studies*, 8(2): 197–223.

Cooper, Mark (2004) 'Hyper-commercialism and the Media: The Threat to Journalism and Democratic Discourse'. In David Skinner, James R. Compton and Michael Gasher (eds), *Converging Media, Diverging Politics: A Political Economy of News Media in the United States and Canada*. Lanham, MD: Lexington.

Corner, John (2010) 'British Media and Regulatory Change: The Antinomies of Policy'. In Jostein Gripsrud and Lennart Weibull (eds), *Media, Markets and Public Spheres: European Media at the Crossroads*. Bristol: Intellect.

Cottle, Simon (2009) 'Journalism Studies: coming of (global) age?', *Journalism: Theory, Practice & Criticism*, 10(3): 309–311.

Cottle, Simon (2008) 'Reporting demonstrations: the changing media politics of dissent', *Media, Culture & Society*, 30(6): 853–872.

Cottle, Simon (2007) 'Ethnography and journalism: new(s) departures in the field,' *Sociology Compass*, 1(1): 1–16.

Cottle, Simon (2006) *Mediatized Conflict: Developments in Media and Conflict Studies*. Maidenhead: Open University Press.

Cottle, Simon (2000) 'New(s) times: towards a "second wave" of news ethnography', *Communications: The European Journal of Communication Research*, 25(1): 19–41.

Cottle, Simon (1999) 'From BBC Newsroom to BBC Newscentre: on changing technology and journalist practices', *Convergence: The Journal of Research into New Media Technologies,* 5(3): 22–43.

Cottle, Simon and Rai, Mugdha (2010) 'Global News Revisted: Mapping the Contempoary Landscape of Satellite Television News'. In Stephen Cushion and Justin Lewis (eds), *The Rise of 24-Hour News Television: Global Perspectives*. New York: Peter Lang.

Cottle, Simon and Rai, Mugdha (2008) 'Global 24/7 news providers: emissaries of global dominance or global public sphere?', *Global Media and Communication*, 4(2): 157–181.

Couldry, Nick and McRobbie, Angela (2010) 'The death of the university, English style' in *Culture Machine*, Interzone, available at www.culturemachine.net/index.php/cm/article/view/417/429 (accessed 19 November 2010).

Craig, David (2011) *Excellence in Online News*. London: Sage.

Craig, Robert J. and Smith, B.R. (2001) 'The political editorializing rules, the courts, and election year 2000', *Communications and the Law*, 23: 1–18.

Crisell, Andrew (1997) *An Introductory History of British Broadcasting*. London: Routledge.

Crook, Tim (1998) *International Radio Journalism: History, Theory and Practice*. London: Routledge.

Croteau, David and Hoynes, Williams (2000) *Media/Society: Industries, Images, and Audiences*. Thousand Oaks, CA: Pine Forge.

Croteau, David, Hoynes, William and Carragee, Kevin M. (1996) 'The political diversity of public television: polysemy, the public sphere, and the Conservative critique of PBS', *Journalism & Mass Communication Monographs*, No. 157.

Curran, James (2009a) 'Technology Foretold'. In Natalie Fenton (ed.), *New Media, Old News*. London: Sage.

Curran, James (2009b) 'Prophecy and Journalism Studies', *Journalism: Theory, Practice and Criticism*, 10(3): 212–214.

Curran, James and Park, Myung-Jin (2000) *De-Westernizing Media Studies*. London: Routledge.

Curran, James and Seaton, Jean (2010) *Navigating the Rocks: Power Without Responsibility: The Press, Broadcasting and New Media in Britain* (7th edition). London: Routledge.

Curran, James, Iyengar, Shanto, Lund, Anker Brink and Salovaara-Moring, Inka (2009) 'Media system, public knowledge and democracy: a comparative study', *European Journal of Communication*, 24(1): 5–26.

Curran, James, Salovaara-Moring, Inaka, Cohen, Sharon and Iyengar, Shanto (2010) 'Crime, foreigners and hard news: a cross-national comparison of reporting and public perception', *Journalism: Theory, Practice and Criticism*, 11(1): 1–17.

Cushion, Stephen (2012) *The Democratic Value of News: Why Public Service Media Matters*. Basingstoke: Palgrave.

Cushion, Stephen (2010a) 'Rolling service, market logic: the race to be "Britain's most watched news channel"'. In Stephen Cushion and Justin Lewis (eds), *The Rise of 24-Hour News Television: Global Perspectives*. New York: Peter Lang.

Cushion, Stephen (2010b) 'Three Phases of 24-Hour News Television'. In Stephen Cushion and Justin Lewis (eds), *The Rise of 24-Hour News Television*. New York: Peter Lang.

Cushion, Stephen (2009) 'From Tabloid Hack to Broadcast Journalist: which news sources are the most trusted?' in *Journalism Practice*, 3(4): 472–481.

Cushion, Stephen (2008) 'Truly international? A content analysis of *Journalism: Theory, Practice and Criticism* and *Journalism Studies*', *Journalism Practice*, 2(2): 280–293.

Cushion, Stephen (2007) '"On the beat" not in the classroom: where and how is journalism studied?', *Journalism Practice*, 1(3): 421–434.

Cushion, Stephen and Lewis, Justin (2010) *The Rise of 24 Hour News Television*. New York: Peter Lang.

Cushion, Stephen and Lewis, Justin (2009) 'Towards a "Foxification" of 24 hour news channels in Britain? An analysis of market driven and publicly funded news coverage', *Journalism: Theory, Practice and Criticism*, 10(2): 131–153.

Cushion, Stephen, Lewis, Justin and Groves, Chris (2009a) 'Reflecting the four nations? An analysis of reporting devolution on UK network news media', *Journalism Studies*, 10(5): 1–17.

Cushion, Stephen, Lewis, Justin and Groves, Chris (2009b) 'Prioritizing hand-shaking over policy-making: a study of how the 2007 devolved elections was reported on BBC UK network coverage', *Cyfrwng: Media Wales Journal*, 6.

Cushion, Stephen, Lewis, Justin and Ramsay, Gordon (forthcoming) 'A comparison of public and private driven television news'.

Cushion, Stephen, Lewis, Justin and Ramsay, Gordon (2010) *Four Nations Impartiality Review Follow-up: An Analysis of Reporting Devolution*. London: BBC Trust Publication.

Dagnes, Alison (2010) *Politics on Demand: The Effects of 24-Hour News on American Politics*. Santa Barbara, CA: Praegar.

Dahlgren, Peter (1995) *Television and the Public Sphere: Citizenship, Democracy and the Media*. London: Sage.

Dannagal, Young G. and Tisinger, Russell M. (2006) 'Dispelling late-night myths: news consumption among late-night comedy viewers and the predictors of exposure to various late-night shows', *Press/Politics*, 11(3): 113–134.

Davies, Geraint Talfan (1999) *Not By Bread Alone: Information, Media and the National Assembly*. Cardiff: Wales Media Forum.

Davies, John (1994) *Broadcasting and the BBC in Wales*. Cardiff: University of Wales Press.

Dayan, Daniel and Katz, Elihu (1992) *Media Events: The Live Broadcasting of History*. Cambridge, MA: Harvard University Press.

de Burgh, Hugo (2005) 'Introduction: Journalism and the new Cultural Paradigm'. In Hugo de Burgh (ed.), *Making Journalists: Diverse Models, Global Issues*. London: Routledge.

Deacon, David, Downey, John, Stayner, James and Wring, Dominic (2011) 'The Media Campaign: Mainstream Media Reporting of the 2010 General Election'. Paper presented at the 2011 MeCCSA Conference, 12–14 January, Salford Quays, The Lowry.

Deans, Jason (2010a) 'Christmas television viewing at 10-year high despite "unimaginative" schedule', *Media Guardian*, available at www.guardian.co.uk/media/2010/dec/26/christmas-tv-ratings-decade-high (accessed 10 January 2011).

Deans, Jason (2010b) 'Rupert Murdoch hits back at opponents of News Corp bid for BSkyB', *Media Guardian*, available at www.guardian.co.uk/media/2010/oct/22/rupert-murdoch-news-corp-bskyb (accessed 18 January 2011).

Dearing, James W. and Rogers, Everett M. (1996) *Agenda Setting*. London: Sage.

Debrett, Mary (2010) *Reinventing Public Service Television for the Digital Future*. Bristol: Intellect.

DellaVinga, Stefano and Kaplan, Ethan (2006) 'The Fox News effect: media bias and voting', available at http://elsa.berkeley.edu/~sdellavi/wp/foxvote06-03-30.pdf (accessed 21 October 2010).

Delli Carpini X, Michael and Keeter, Scott (1996) *What Americans Know about Politics and Why it Matters*. Stamford, CT: Yale University Press.

Delli Carpini X, Michael and Williams, Bruce A. (2001) 'Let Us Infotain You: Politics in the New Media Environment'. In Lance W. Bennett and Robert Entman (eds), *Mediated Politics: Communication in the Future of Democracy*. Cambridge: Cambridge University Press.

Deloitte's TMT (2010) 'Latest global trends on consumer media preferences and behaviours', cited in *Biz Community*, 7 October, available at www.bizcommunity.com/article/196/424/52904.html (accessed 10 January 2010).

DeLuca, Kevin M. and Peeples, Jennifer (2002) 'From public sphere to public screen: democracy, activism, and the "violence" of Seattle', *Critical Studies in Media Communication*, 19(2): 125–151.

Desmond, Roger and Danilewicz, Anna (2010) 'Women are on, but not in, the news: gender roles in local television news', *Sex Roles*, 62: 822–829.

Deuze, Mark (2007) *Media Work*. Cambridge: Polity.

Deuze, Mark (2006) 'Global journalism education: a conceptual approach', *Journalism Studies*, 7(1): 19–34.

Deuze, Mark (2005) 'What is journalism? Professional identity and ideology of journalists reconsidered', *Journalism: Theory, Practice and Criticism*, 6(4): 442–464.

Dimitrova, Daniela V. and Stromback, Jesper (2010) 'Exploring semi-structural differences in television news between the United States and Sweden', *International Journal Gazette*, 72(6): 487–502.

Domingo, David (2008) 'Interactivity in the daily routines of online newsrooms: dealing with an uncomfortable myth', *Journal of Computer-Mediated Communication*, 13(3): 680–704.

Douglas, Susan J. (1987) *Inventing American Broadcasting, 1899–1922*. Baltimore, MD: Johns Hopkins University Press.

Dwyer, Tim (2010) *Media Convergence*. Maidenhead: Open University Press.

Ellis, John (2000) *Seeing Things: Television in the Age of Uncertainty*. London: I.B. Tauris.

El-Nawawy, Mohammed (2003) *Al-Jazeera: The Story of the Network that is Rattling Governments and Redefining Modern Journalism*. Boulder, CO: Westview.

Errigo, Jackie and Franklin, Bob (2004) 'Surviving in the hackacademy', *British Journalism Review*, 15(2): 43–48.

Fahim, Kareem (2011) 'State TV in Egypt offers murky window into power shift', *New York Times*, 31 January, available at www.nytimes.com/2011/02/01/world/middleeast/01statetv.html?_r=1 (accessed 1 February 2011).

Fang, Irving E. (1970) *Television News*. New York: Hasting House.

Farhi, Paul (2003) 'The gung-ho morning gang: Cable's "Fox & Friends" prides itself on patriotic patter', *Washington Post*: C1, C7.

Feldman, Lauren (2007) 'The news about comedy: young audiences, The Daily Show, and evolving notions of journalism', *Journalism: Theory, Practice and Criticism*, 8(4): 406–427.

Feldman, Lauren and Young, Dannagal Goldthwaite (2008) 'Late-night comedy as a gateway to traditional news: an analysis of time trends in news attention among late-night comedy viewers during the 2004 presidential primaries', *Political Communication*, 25(4): 401–422.

Fenton, Natalie (2009a) 'Drowning or Waving? New Media, Journalism and Democracy'. In Natalie Fenton (ed.), *New Media, Old News: Journalism and Democracy in the Digital Age*. London: Sage.

Fenton, Natalie (ed.) (2009b) *New Media, Old News: Journalism and Democracy in the Digital Age*. London: Sage.

Ferguson, Galit and Hargreaves, Ian (1999) 'Wales in the News: Monitoring of Network News July & September 1999'. A Wales Media Forum working paper.

Fiske, John (1987) *Television Culture*. London: Routledge.

Fitzsimmons, Caitlin (2009) 'Seventeen regions into nine: how the updated ITV local news services will run', *Media Guardian*, 17 February, available at www.guardian.co.uk/media/organgrinder/2009/feb/16/seventeen-regions-into-nine-itv-news (accessed 5 November 2010).

Fox, Julia R., Kolobem, Glory and Sahin, Volkan (2007) 'No joke: a comparison in The Daily Show with Jon Stewart and broadcast network television coverage of the 2004 presidential election campaign', *Journal of Broadcasting and Electronic Media*, 51(2): 213–227.

Franklin, Bob (ed.) (2011) *The Future of Journalism*. London: Routledge.

Franklin, Bob (ed.) (2006) *Local Journalism and Local Media; Making the Local News*. London: Routledge.

Franklin, Bob (1997) *Newszak And News Media*. London: Arnold.

Franklin, Bob, Hamer, Martin, Hanna, Mark, Kinsey, Marie and Richardson, John (2005) *Key Concepts in Journalism Studies*. London: Sage.

Freedman, Des (2010) 'From the "long tail" to the "bottle neck": the economics of internet media'. Paper presented at the MeCCSA conference, London School of Economics, 6–8 January.

Freedman, Des (2008) *The Politics of Media Policy*. Cambridge: Polity.

Friend, Cecilia and Singer, Jane (2007) *Online Journalism Ethics*. New York: M.E. Sharpe.

Galtung, Johan and Ruge, Mari M. (1965) 'The structure of foreign news', *Journal of International Peace Research*, 1: 64–90.

Gans, Herbert (1979) *Deciding What's News*. New York: Pantheon.

Garcia-Blanco, Inaki and Cushion, Stephen (2010) 'A partial Europe without citizens or EU-level political institutions: how far can Euronews constitute a European public sphere?', *Journalism Studies*, 11(3): 393–411.

Gauntlett, David (2011) 'New introduction: Media Studies 2.0', available at www.theory.org.uk/mediastudies2.htm (accessed 25 January 2011).

Gauntlett, David (2009) 'Media Studies 2.0: a response', *Interactions: Studies in Communication and Culture*, 1(1): 147–157.

Gauntlett, David (2007) 'Media Studies 2.0', available at www.theory.org.uk/mediastudies2.htm (accessed 8 December 2010).

Gauntlett, David (2005) *Moving Experiences* (2nd edition). *Media Effects and Beyond*. New Barnet: John Libbey.

Gerbner, George and Gross, Larry (1976) 'Living with television: the violence profile', *Journal of Communication*, 26(2): 172–199.

Gerbner, George, Gross, Larry, Morgan, Michael and Signorielli, Nancy (1986) 'Living with Television: The Dynamics of the Cultivation Process'. In Jennings Bryant and Dolf Zillmann (eds), *Perspectives on Media Effects*. Hillsdale, NJ: Erlbaum.

Gibson, Owen (2007) 'Murdoch wants Sky News to be more like rightwing Fox', *Media Guardian*, 24 November, available at www.guardian.co.uk/media/2007/nov/24/bskyb.television (accessed 21 October 2010).

Gibson, Owen (2005) 'Rolling with the punches: with the shakeup at BBC News, the relaunch at Sky and the dark clouds hanging over the future of the ITV News Channel', *Media Guardian*, 14 November, p. 1.

Gilboa, E. (2005) 'The CNN effect: the search for a communication theory of international relations', *Political Communication*, 22(1): 27–44.

Gilens, Martin and Hertzman, Craig (2000) 'Corporate ownership and news bias: newspaper coverage of the 1996 Telecommunications Act', *Journal of Politics*, 62(2): 369–386.

Gitlin, Todd (2003) *The Whole World Wide is Watching: The Making and Unmaking of the New Left* (2nd edition). Berkeley, CA: University of California Press.

Gitlin, Todd (1980) *The Whole World is Watching: The Making and Unmaking of the New Left*. Berkeley, CA: University of California Press.

Glasgow Media Group (1985) *War & Peace News*. Maidenhead: Open University Press.

Glasgow Media Group (1982) *Really Bad News*. London: Writers and Readers Co-operative.

Glasgow Media Group (1980) *More Bad News*. London: Routledge.

Glasgow Media Group (1976) *Bad News*. London: Routledge.

Glynn, Kevin (2000) *Tabloid Culture: Trash Taste, Popular Power, and the Transformation of American Television*. Durham, DC: Duke University Press.

Gomez, Rosario G. (2010) 'UK's BBC better trusted than Spain's national broadcaster, says study', *El Pais*, 22 November, available at www.elpais.com/articulo/Pantallas/UK/s/BBC/better/trusted/than/Spain/s/national/broadcaster/says/study/elpepurtv/20101122elpepirtv_1/Ten (accessed 2 December 2010).

Goodman, Geoffrey (2000) 'Time for quality to show courage', *British Journalism Review*, 11(2): 3–6.

Grant, Scott (2007) *We're All Journalists Now: The Transformation of the Press and Reshaping of the Law in the Internet Age*. New York: Free.

Green, Maury (1969) *Television News: Anatomy and Process*. Belmont, CA: Wadsworth.

Greenslade, Roy (2010a) 'Election 2010: What influence do newspapers have over voters?', *Media Guardian*, 3 May, available at www.guardian.co.uk/media/2010/may/03/election-2010-newspapers-influence-over-voters (accessed 8 October 2010).

Greenslade, Roy (2010b) 'Trinity Mirror debate: Williams defends his research in an open letter', *Media Guardian*, 22 July, available at www.guardian.co.uk/media/greenslade/2010/jul/22/local-newspapers-cardiffuniversity (accessed 21 January 2011).

Greenslade, Roy (2010c) 'Why is the ITV News political editor allowed to write a partisan column?', *Media Guardian*, 11 October, available at www.guardian.co.uk/media/greenslade/2010/oct/11/itv-mailonsunday (accessed 24 January 2011).

Greenslade, Roy (2009a) 'Recruiting working class journalists: what, if anything, can be done?', *Media Guardian*, available at www.guardian.co.uk/media/greenslade/2009/jul/23/cityuniversity-downturn (accessed 2 December 2010).

Greenslade, Roy (2009b) 'Only 3% of public trust journalists', *Media Guardian,* available at www.guardian.co.uk/media/greenslade/2009/mar/31/1 (accessed 2 December 2010).

Greenslade, Roy (2003) 'Media: Follow my leader? The *Mirror* is passionately opposed to the war in Iraq – yet half its readers are in favour', *Media Guardian*, 31 March, p. 4.

Grey, Jonathan, Jones, Jeffery and Thompson, Ethan (2010) *Satire TV: Politics and Comedy in the Post-Network Era*. New York: New York University Press.

Gripsrud, Jostein (2010) 'Fifty Years of European Television: An Essay'. In Jostein Gripsrud and Lennart Weibull (eds), *Media, Markets and Public Spheres: European Media at the Crossroads*. Bristol: Intellect.

Gripsrud, Jostein and Weibull, Lennart (2010) *Media, Markets and Public Spheres: European Media at the Crossroads*. Bristol: Intellect.

Gunter, Barrie (2005) 'Trust in the news on television', *Aslib Proceedings: New Information Perspectives,* 57(5): 384–397.

Gunter, Barrie (1997) *Measuring Bias on TV*. Luton: University of Luton Press.

Habermas, Jurgen (1989/1962) *Structural Transformation of the Public Sphere*. Cambridge: Polity.

Hall, Stuart (1980) 'Encoding/decoding', *Culture, Media, Language: Working Papers in Cultural Studies, 1972–79*. London: Hutchinson. pp. 128–138.

Hallin, Daniel C. (1994) *We Keep America On Top of the World*. New York: Routledge.

Hallin, Daniel C. and Mancini, Paolo (2004) *Comparing Media Systems: Three Models of Media and Politics*. New York: Cambridge University Press.

Halloran, James D., Eliott, Philip and Murdock, Graham (1970) *Demonstrations and Communication*. Harmondsworth: Penguin.

Hampton, Mark (2008) 'New Journalism, Nineteenth-Century'. In Wolfgang Donsbach (ed.), *The International Encyclopedia of Communication*. Oxford: Blackwell. Available at Blackwell Reference Online, www.communicationencyclopedia.com/subscriber/tocnode?id=g9781405131995_chunk_g978140513199519_ss12-1 (accessed 23 January 2011).

Hanitzsch, Thomas et al. (2011) 'Mapping journalism cultures across nations: a comparative study of 18 countries', *Journalism Studies* (first published 15 November 2010).

Hanna, Mark and Sanders, Karen (2007) 'British journalism undergraduate education: who are the students and what do they want?', *Journalism Practice*, 1(3): 404–420.

Harcup, Tony (2011a) 'Hackademics at the chalkface: to what extent have journalism teachers become journalism researchers?', *Journalism Practice*, I (first published 24 August 2010).

Harcup, Tony (2011b) 'Research and reflection: supporting journalism educators in becoming scholars', *Journalism Practice*, I (first published 4 September 2010).

Harcup, Tony (2009) *Journalism: Principles and Practice* (2nd edition). London: Sage.

Harcup, Tony and Deirdre, O'Neil (2001) 'What is news? Galtung and Ruge revisited', *Journalism Studies*, 2 (2): 261–280.

Harding, Luke (2010) 'Russian invasion scare sweeps Georgia after TV hoax', *Guardian*, 14 March, available at www.guardian.co.uk/world/2010/mar/14/russia-georgia-fake-invasion-report (accessed 17 January 2011).

Hargreaves, Ian (2003) *Journalism: Truth or Dare?* Oxford: Oxford University Press.

Hargreaves, Ian and Thomas, James (2002) *New News, Old News*. London: Independent Television Commission/British Standards Commission Research Publication.

Hariman, Robert (2007) 'In defense of Jon Stewart', Critical Forum, *Critical Studies in Media Communication*, 4(3): 273–277.

Harrington, Stephen (2008a) 'Popular news in the twenty-first century: time for a new critical approach?', *Journalism: Theory, Practice and Criticism*, 9(3): 266–284.

Harrington, Stephen (2008b) 'Future-proofing journalism: youthful tastes and the challenge for the academy', *Continuum: Journal of Media & Cultural Studies*, 22(3): 395–407.

Harris, Paul (2010) 'Jon Stewart, TV scourge of America's right, turns his satire against Barack Obama', *Observer*, 3 October, available at www.guardian.co.uk/media/2010/oct/03/jon-stewart-barack-obama (accessed 7 February 2011).

Harrison, Jackie (2006) *News*. London: Routledge.

Harrison, Jackie (2000) *Terrestrial TV News in Britain: The Culture of Production*. Manchester: Manchester University Press.

Harrison, Martin (1985) *TV News, Whose Bias?* London: Policy.

Hart, Roderick P. (1994) *Seducing America: How Television Charms the Modern Voter*. New York: Oxford University Press.

Hart, Roderick P. and Hartelius, Johanna E. (2007) 'The political sins of Jon Stewart', Critical Forum, *Critical Studies in Media Communication*, 24(3): 278–283.

Hartley, John (1996) *Popular Reality: Journalism, Modernity, Popular Culture*. London: Arnold.

Hartley, John (1982) *Understanding News*. London: Routledge.

Harvey, Sylvia (2006) 'Ofcom's first year and neoliberalism's blind spot: attacking the culture of production', *Screen*, 47(1): 91–105.

Hayes, Jeffery (2010) 'Facts and figures: television programs in China', April, available at http://factsanddetails.com/china.php?itemid=235&catid=7&subcatid=43 (accessed 17 January 2011).

Hazlett, Thomas W. (1997) 'Prices and outputs under cable TV reregulation', *Journal of Regulatory Economics*, 12(2): 173–195.

Hendershot, Heather (2007) 'God's angriest man: Carol McIntire, Cold War fundamentalism, and right-wing broadcasting', *American Quarterly*, 59(2): 373–396.

Herman, Edward S. and Chomsky, Noam (1988) *Manufacturing Consent: The Political Economy of the Mass Media*. New York: Pantheon.

Higgins, Michael (2006) 'Substantiating a political public sphere in the Scottish press: a comparative analysis', *Journalism: Theory, Practice & Criticism*, 7(1): 25–44.

Hilmes, Michele and Loviglio, Jason (eds) (2001) *Radio Reader: Essays in the Cultural History of Radio*. New York: Routledge.

Holgate, Jane and McKay, Sonia (2007) *Institutional Barriers to Recruitment and Employment in the Audio Visual Industries: The Effect on Black and Ethnic Minority Workers*. London: Working Lives Research Institute.

Holmes, Tim (2011) *Magazine Journalism*. London: Sage.

Hoynes, William (2003) 'Branding public service: the "New PBS" and the privatization of public television', *Television and New Media*, 4(2): 117–130.

Hoynes, William (1994) *Public Television for Sale: Media, the Market, and the Public Sphere*. Boulder, CO: Westview.

Hudson, Gary and Temple, Mick (2010) 'We Are Not All Journalists Now'. In Sean Tunney and Garret Monaghan (eds), *Web Journalism: A New Form of Citizenship?* Brighton: Sussex Academic Press.

Humphreys, Peter (1996) *Mass Media and Media Policy in Western Europe*. Manchester: Manchester University Press.

Huntzicker, William E. (2002) 'Television News'. In D. Sloan and L.M. Parcell (eds), *American Journalism: History, Principles and Practices*. Jefferson, NC: McFarland & Co.

ICT (2010) 'The World in 2010: ICT Facts and Figures'. International Telecommunications Union Report, available at www.comminit.com/en/node/326806/307 (accessed 10 January 2011).

IFJ (2006) *The Changing Nature of Work: A Global Survey and Case Study of Atypical Work in the Media Industry*. Research Report into International Federation of Journalists.

Iosifidis, Petros (2010) *Reinventing Public Service Communication: European Broadcasters and Beyond*. London: Palgrave Macmillan.

Interactions: Studies in Communication and Culture, 1(1): Special edition on Media Studies 2.0.

Iyengar, Shanto (1991) *Is Anyone Responsible? How Television Frames Political Issues*. Chicago, IL: University of Chicago Press.

Iyengar, Shanto and Hahn, Kyu S. (2009) 'Red media, blue media: evidence of ideological selectivity in media use', *Journal of Communication*, 59(1): 19–39.

Iyengar, Shanto, Curran, James, Lund, Anker, Salovaara-Moring, Inka, Hahn, Kyu and Cohen, Sharon (2010) 'Cross-national versus individual differences', Political Information: A Media System Perspective, *Journal of Elections, Public Opinion and Parties*, 20(2): 291–309.

Jamieson, Alastair (2010) 'BBC must end "dumbed down" gardening shows says new RHS chief', *Daily Mail*, 4 July, available at www.telegraph.co.uk/culture/tvandradio/7871022/BBC-must-end-dumbed-down-gardening-shows-says-new-RHS-chief.html (accessed 27 July 2010).

Jamieson, Kathleen, H. and Capella, Joseph N. (2008) *Echo Chamber: Rush Limbaugh and the Conservative Media Establishment*. Oxford: Oxford University Press.

Jenkins, Henry (2006) *Convergence Culture: Where Old and New Media Collide*. New York: Routledge.

Jenkins, Simon (2007) 'The British media does not do responsibility. It does stories', *Guardian*, 18 July, available at www.guardian.co.uk/commentisfree/2007/may/18/comment.pressandpublishing (accessed 24 September 2010).

Jones, Aled (1993) *Press, Politics and Society: A History of Journalism in Wales*. Cardiff: Cardiff University Press.

Jones, David (2004) 'Why Americans don't trust the media: a preliminary analysis', *Harvard International Journal of Press/Politics*, 9(2): 60–75.

Jones, Jeffery (2009) *Entertaining Politics: Satiric Television and Political Engagement*. Lanham, MD: Rowman & Littlefield.

Jones, Jeffery (2005) *Entertaining Politics: New Political Television and Civic Culture*. Lanham, MD: Rowman & Littlefield.

Journalism: Theory, Practice and Criticism (2009) Vol. 10(3): Special 10th anniversary edition – 'The Future of Journalism'.

Journalism Training Forum (2002) 'Journalists at work: their views on training, recruitment and conditions'. An independent survey by the Journalism Training Forum. London: NTO/Skillset.

Juntunen, Laura (2010) 'Explaining the Need for Speed: Speed and Competition as Challenges to Journalism Ethics'. In Stephen Cushion and Justin Lewis (eds), *The Rise of 24-Hour News Television: Global Perspectives*. New York: Peter Lang.

Jury, Louise (2002) 'John Simpson joins attack on BBC's dumbed-down *Six O'Clock News*', *Media Independent*, 29 March, available at www.independent.co.uk/news/media/john-simpson-joins-attack-on-bbcs-dumbeddown-six-oclock-news-655791.html (accessed 17 January 2011).

Katz, Elihu and Liebes, Tamar (2007) '"No more peace!": how disaster, terror and war have upstaged media events', *International Journal of Communication*, 1: 157–166.

Keane, John (1991) *The Media and Democracy*. Cambridge: Polity.

Kellner, Douglas (1995) 'Reading the Gulf War: Production, Text, Reception'. In Douglas Kellner (ed.), *Media Culture: Cultural Studies, Identity, and Politics between the Modern and the Postmodern*. New York: Routledge.

Kellner, Peter (2010) 'Number cruncher: a matter of trust', *Prospect*, 2 September, Issue 175, available at www.prospectmagazine.co.uk/2010/09/peter-kellner-yougov-trust-journalists/ (accessed 2 December 2010).

Kerwin, Anne Marie (2010) 'Ten trends that are shaping global media consumption–Ad Age has the stats from the TV penetration rate in Kenya to the number of World Cup watchers and more', available at http://adage.com/article/global-news/10-trends-shaping-global-media-consumption/147470/ (accessed 11 March 2011).

Kohring, Matthias and Matthes, Jörg (2007) 'Trust in news media development and validation of a multidimensional scale', *Communication Research*, 34(2): 231–252.

Kolmer, Christian and Semetko, Holli A. (2010) 'International television news: Germany compared', *Journalism Studies*, 5(1): 700–717.

Kolodzy, Janet (2006) *Convergence Journalism: Writing and Reporting across the News Media*. Lanham, MD: Rowman & Littlefield.

Kovach, Bill and Rosenstiel, Tom (2007) *Elements of Journalism: What Newspeople Should Know and the Public Should Expect* (2nd edition). New York: Crown.

Kovach, Bill and Rosenstiel, Tom (2001) *Elements of Journalism: What Newspeople Should Know and the Public Should Expect*. New York: Crown.

Kuhn, Raymond (2010) 'France 24: Too little, Too Late, Too French'. In Stephen Cushion and Justin Lewis (eds), *The Rise of 24-Hour News Television: Global Perspectives*. New York: Peter Lang.

Kull, Stephen (2003) *Misconceptions, the Media and the Iraq War*. Programme on International Policy Attitudes (PIPA) Research Report.

Kutz, Howard (2005) 'On *Fox News*, no shortage of opinion, study finds', *Washington Post*, 14 March, C01, available at www.washingtonpost.com/wp-dyn/articles/A32631-2005Mar13.html (accessed 21 October 2010).

Lakshmi, Rama (2007) 'The long reach of India's TV news: local stories reign in booming market', *Washington Post*, 12 September, available at www.washingtonpost.com/wpdyn/content/article/2007/09/11/AR2007091102293.html (accessed 10 January 2011).

LaMarre, Heather L., Landreville, Kristen D. and Beam, Michael A. (2009) 'The irony of satire: political ideology and the motivation to see what you want to see in the Colbert Report', *International Journal of Press/Politics*, 14(2): 212–231.

Lambert, Richard (2002) *Independent Review of BBC News 24*. London: Department of Culture, Media and Sport.

Langer, John (1998) *Tabloid Television: Popular Journalism and the 'Other News'.* London: Routledge.

Lawson, Mark (2010a) 'North Korea through western eyes: a glimpse of North Korea's TV bulletins provides valuable lessons about them – and us', *Guardian*, 30 September, available at www.guardian.co.uk/tv-and-radio/2010/sep/30/north-korea-mark-lawson (accessed 24 January 2011).

Lawson, Mark (2010b) 'TV Matters: Raoul Moat and live television news coverage', *Guardian*, 15 July, avilable at www.guardian.co.uk/tv-and-radio/2010/jul15/raoul-moat-live-television-news (accessed 24 September 2010).

Lehman-Wilzig, Sam N. and Seletzky, Michal (2010) 'Hard news, soft news, "general" news: the necessity and utility of an intermediate classification', *Journalism: Theory, Practice and Criticism*, 11(1): 37–56.

Lewis, Justin (2001) *Constructing Public Opinion: How Political Elites do What They Like and Why We Seem to Go Along With It.* New York: Columbia University Press.

Lewis, Justin (1996) 'What counts in cultural studies', *Media, Culture and Society*, 19(1): 83–98.

Lewis, Justin (1991) *The Ideological Octopus: An Exploration of Television and its Audience.* New York: Routledge.

Lewis, Justin and Cushion, Stephen (2009) 'The thirst to be first: an analysis of breaking news stories and their impact on the quality of 24 hour news coverage in the UK', *Journalism Practice*, 3(3): 304–318.

Lewis, Justin, Cushion, Stephen and Thomas, James (2005) 'Immediacy, convenience or engagement? An analysis of 24-hour news channels in the UK', *Journalism Studies*, 6(4): 461–477.

Lewis, Justin, Cushion, Stephen, Groves, Chris, Bennett, Lucy, Reardon, Sally, Wilkins, Emma and Williams, Rebecca (2008) *Four Nations Impartiality Review: An Analysis of Reporting Devolution.* London: BBC Trust.

Lewis, Justin, Williams, Andrew and Franklin, Bob (2008) 'Compromised Fourth Estate? UK news journalism, public relations and news sources', *Journalism Studies*, 9(1): 1–20.

Li, Xigen (2009) *Internet Newspapers: The Making of a Mainstream Medium.* Hillsdale, NJ: Erlbaum.

Livingston, Steven (1997) *Clarifying the CNN Effect: An Examination of Media Effects According to Type of Military Intervention* (Research Paper R-18). Cambridge, MA: John F. Kennedy School of Government, Harvard University.

Livingston, Steven and Bennett, W. Lance (2003) 'Gatekeeping, inexing and live-event news: is technology altering the construction of news?', *Political Communication*, 20(4): 363–380.

Livingstone, Sonia and Cooper, Kurtis (2001) 'The changing nature of CNN "live events" coverage and the consequences for international affairs'. Paper presented at the International Studies Association, Chicago.

Livingstone, Sonia, Lunt, Peter and Miller, Laura (2007) 'Citizens and consumers: discursive debates during and after the Communications Act 2003', *Media, Culture and Society*, 29(4): 613–638.

Löffelholz, Martin and Weaver, David (eds) (2008) *Global Journalism Research.* New York and London: Blackwell.

Lotz, Amanda D. (2007) *The Television Will Be Revolutionized.* New York: New York University Press

Lule, Jack (2007) 'The wages of cynicism: Jon Stewart tried for heresy at NCA San Antonio Convention', *Critical Studies in Media Communication*, 24(3): 262.

MacGregor, B. (1997) *Live, Direct and Biased: Making Television News in the Satellite Age.* London: Arnold.

MacMillan, Douglas (2010) 'Twitter targets 1 billion users, challenging Facebook for ads', *Bloomberg*, 12 October, available at www.bloomberg.com/news/2010-10-12/twitter-aiming-to-get-1-billion-users-matching-rival-facebook-s-target.html (accessed 10 January 2011).

Magnier, Mark (2009) 'Indian news channels criticized for Mumbai coverage', *Los Angeles Times*, 9 January, available at http://articles.latimes.com/2009/jan/18/world/fg-mumbai-tv18?pg=2 (accessed 24 September 2010).

Mariott, Stephanie (2007) *Live Television: Time, Space and the Broadcast Event*. London: Sage.

Marr, Andrew (2004) *My Trade: A Short History*. Basingstoke: Palgrave Macmillan.

Mason, Olivia (2010) 'Television is going social', YouGov, 24 August, available at http://today.yougov.co.uk/consumer/television-going-social (accessed 17 January 2011).

Matheson, Donald and Allan, Stuart (2009) *Digital War Reporting*. Cambridge: Polity.

Matthews, Julian (2011) *Introduction to Journalism Studies*. London: Sage.

Matthews, Julian (2010) *Producing Serious News for Citizen Children: A Study of the BBC's Children's Programme, Newsround*. New York: Edwin Mellen Place.

McChesney, Robert (2008) *The Political Economy of Media: Enduring Issues, Emerging Dilemmas*. New York: Monthly Review Press.

McChesney, Robert (2004) *The Problem of the Media: U.S. Communication Politics in the Twenty-First Century*. New York: Monthly Review Press.

McChesney, Robert (2000) *Rich Media, Poor Democracy: Communication Politics in Dubious Times*. Urbana and Chicago: University of Illinois Press.

McChesney, Robert (1996) 'Communication for the hell of it: the triviality of U.S. broadcasting history', *Journal of Broadcasting and Electronic Media*, 40(4): 540–552.

McChesney, Robert (1993) *Telecommunications, Mass Media and Democracy: The Battle for the Control of U.S. Broadcasting, 1928–1935*. New York: Oxford University Press.

McCombs, Maxwell E. and Shaw, Donald (1993) 'The evolution of agenda-setting research: twenty-five years in the marketplace of ideas', *Journal of Communication*, 43(2): 58–67.

McCombs, Maxwell E. and Shaw, Donald (1972) 'The agenda setting function of the mass media', *Public Opinion Quarterly*, 36(2): 176–187.

McCormick, Jim and Harrop, Anne (2010) *Devolution's Impact on Low-income People and Places*. London: Joseph Rowntree Foundation.

McKay, Hugh and Ivey, Darren (2004) *Modern Media in the Home: An Ethnographic Study*. New Barnet: John Libbey.

McLaughlin, Greg (2006) 'Profits, Politics and Paramilitaries: The Local News Media in Northern Ireland'. In Bob Franklin (ed.), *Local Journalism and Local Media*. London: Routledge.

McLuhan, Marshall (1967) *The Medium is the Message*. New York: Bantam.

McLuhan, Marshall (1964) *Understanding Media*. New York: Mentor.

McNair, Brian (2010) *Journalism in Film: Heroes and Villains at the Movies*. Edinburgh: Edinburgh University Press.

McNair, Brian (2009) *News and Journalism in the UK* (5th edition). London: Routlege.

McNair, Brian (2006) 'News from a Small Country: The Media in Scotland'. In Bob Franklin (ed.), *Local Journalism and Local Media*. London: Routledge.

McNair, Brian (2003) 'What a difference a decade makes', *British Journalism Review*, 14(1): 42–48.

Meddaugh, Priscilla Marie (2010) 'Bakhtin, Colbert: and the center of discourse: is there no "truthiness" in humor', *Critical Studies in Media Communication*, 27(4): 376–390.

Media Guardian (2010) '21. Helen Boaden BBC Director of News, Helen Boaden inches up the Media 100 after a successful election – despite budget cuts', *Media Guardian*, 19 July, available at www.guardian.co.uk/media/2010/jul/19/helen-boaden-mediaguardian-100-2010 (accessed 25 January 2011).

Mehta, Nalin (2010) 'India Live: Satellites, Politics, and India's TV News Revolution'. In Stephen Cushion and Justin Lewis (eds), *The Rise of 24-Hour News Television: Global Perspectives*. New York: Peter Lang.

Meilke, Graham (2008) *Interpreting News*. Basingstoke: Palgrave Macmillan.

Meikle, Graham and Redden, Guy (eds) (2010) *News Online: Transformations and Continuities*. Basingstoke: Palgrave Macmillan.

Meltzer, Kimberly (2010) *TV News Anchors and Journalistic Tradition: How Journalists Adapt to Technology*. New York: Peter Lang.

Meltzer, Kimberly (2009) 'The hierarchy of journalistic cultural authority', *Journalism Practice*, 3 (1): 59–74.

Miles, H. (2005) *Al Jazeera: How Arab TV News Challenged the World*. London: Abacus.

Miller, Andrea (2006) 'Watching viewers watch TV: processing live, breaking and emotional news in a naturalistic setting', *Journalism and Mass Communication Quarterly*, 83(3): 511–19.

Miller, Toby (2010) *Television: The Basics*. London: Routledge.

Miller, Toby (2009) 'Media Studies 3.0', *Television and New Media*, 10(1): 5–6.

Monck, Adrian (2008) *Can You Trust the Media?* Thriplow: Icon.

Montgomery, Martin (2007) *The Discourse of Broadcast News: A Linguistic Approach*. London: Routledge.

Moores, Sean (1993) *Interpreting Audiences: The Ethnography of Media Consumption*. London: Sage.

Morgan, Michael and Shananan, James (2010) 'The state of cultivation', *Journal of Broadcasting and Electronic Media*, 54(2): 337–355.

Morley, David (1986) *Family Television*. London: Comedia.

Morley, David (1980) *The 'Nationwide' Audience: Structure and Decoding*. London: BFI.

Morris, Jonathan S. (2009) 'The Daily Show with Jon Stewart and audience attitude change during the 2004 party conventions', *Political Behavior*, 31: 79–102.

Morris, Jonathan S. (2005) 'The Fox News Factor', *Harvard International Journal of Press/Politics*, 10(3): 56–79.

Morris, Richard (2010) 'Media's most trusted brands', *Brand Republic*, 4 October, available at www.brandrepublic.com/bulletin/brandrepublicnewsbulletin/article/1031677/medias-trusted-brands/ (accessed 2 December 2010).

Mosey, Roger (2000) 'A chance to sidestep spin', *The Times*, 21 July.

Mullen, Andrew (2010) 'Twenty years on: the second-order prediction of the Herman-Chomsky Propaganda Model', *Media, Culture and Society*, 3(2): 367–390.

Murdock, Graham (1990) 'Redrawing the Map of the Communications Industries: Concentration and Ownership in the Era of Privatization'. In Marjorie Ferguson (ed.), *Public Communication: The New Imperatives*. London: Sage.

Nacos, Brigitte I. (2003) 'Terrorism as breaking news: attack on America', *Political Science Quarterly*, 11(1): 23–52.

Negrine, Ralph (1994) *Politics and the Mass Media in Britain*. London: Routledge.

Newman, Ric (2010) *UK Election 2010, mainstream media and the role of the internet: how social and digital media affected the business of politics and journalism*. Working Paper for Reuters Institute for the Study of Journalism.

Norris, Pippa (2000) *A Virtuous Circle? Political Communications in Post-Industrial Democracies*. Cambridge: Cambridge University Press.

O'Connor, Rory and Cutler, Aaron (2008) *Shock Jocks: Hate Speech and Talk Radio*. New York: Alternet Books.

O'Malley, Tom (2009) 'Introduction'. In Tom O'Malley and Janet Jones (ed.), *The Peacock Committee and UK Broadcasting Policy*. London: Palgrave Macmillan.

O'Malley, Tom (2001) 'The Decline of Public Service Broadcasting in the UK 1979–2000'. In Michael Bromley (ed.), *No News is Bad News: Radio, Television and the Public*. Harlow: Pearson.

O'Neil, Deirdre and Harcup, Tony (2008) 'News Values and Selectivity'. In Karin Wahl-Jorgensen and Thomas Hanitzsch (eds), *The Handbook of Journalism Studies*. London: Routledge.

Ofcom (2010a) 'Halt in decline of flagship TV news programmes', 30 June, available at http://media.ofcom.org.uk/2010/06/30/halt-in-decline-of-flagship-tv-news-programmes/ (accessed 17 January 2010).

Ofcom (2010b) *Public Service Broadcasting Annual Report*. London: Ofcom.

Ofcom (2009) *International Communications Market Report*. London: Ofcom.

Ofcom (2007) *New News, Future News*. London: Ofcom.

Ofcom (2003) *Communications Act 2003*. London: Ofcom.

Örnebring, Henrik (2009) 'The Two Professionalisms of Journalism: Journalism and the Changing Context of Work'. Working publication for Reuters Institute for the Study of Journalism.

Outfoxed: Rupert Murdoch's War on Journalism (2004) Documentary from the Disinformation Company.

Palvik, John V. (2004) 'A sea-change in journalism: convergence, journalists, their audiences and sources', *Convergence: The International Journal of Research Into New Media Technologies*, 10(4d): 21–29.

Papper, Bob (2010) RTDNA/Hofstra University Survey, available at www.rtdna.org/media/Salary_Survey_2010.pdf (accessed 2 December 2010).

Paterson, Lindsay, Brown, Alice, Curtis, John and Hinds, Kerstin (2001) *New Scotland, New Politics?* Edinburgh: Edinburgh University Press.

Patterson, Chris (2010) 'The Hidden Role of Television Agencies: "Going Live" on 24-Hour News Channels'. In Stephen Cushion and Justin Lewis (eds), *The Rise of 24-Hour News Television: Global Perspectives*. New York: Peter Lang.

Patterson, Chris and Domingo, David (eds) (2011) *Making Online News: Newsroom Ethnography in the Second Decade of Internet Journalism*. New York: Peter Lang.

Patterson, Chris and Domingo, David (eds) (2008) *Making Online News: The Ethnography of New Media Production*. New York: Peter Lang.

Patterson, Thomas E. (2000) *Doing Well and Doing Good: How Soft News and Critical Journalism are Shrinking the News Audience and Weakening Democracy – And What News Outlets Can Do About it*. Cambridge, MA: John F. Kennedy School of Government, Harvard University.

Peak, Steve and Fisher, Paul (2000) *The Media Guide*. London: Guardian.

Pelling, Rowan (2001) 'Cheer up, Kate Adie: you can go from old trout to bimbo. I should know', *Independent*, 28 October, available at www.independent.co.uk/opinion/columnists/cheer-up-kate-adie-you-can-go-from-old-trout-to-bimbo-i-should-know-646854.html (accessed 17 November 2010).

Perrim, William (2010) 'Media Studies 2.0', available at http://mediastudies2point0.blogspot.com/2010/03/studying-me-dia-problem-of-method-in.html (accessed 18 January 2011).

Petley, Julian (2009) 'Impartiality in Television News: Profitability Versus Public Service'. In Stuart Allan, *The Routledge Companion to News and Journalism*. London: Routledge.

Petley, Julian (2003) 'The re-regulation of broadcasting, or the mill owners' triumph', *Journal of Media Practice*, 3(3): 131–140.

Pew Internet and American Life Project (2009) 'Online politics in 2008', *Pew Internet and American Life Project Report*, available at www.pewinternet.org/Reports/2009/6–The-Internets-Role-in-Campaign-2008/2--The-State-of-Online-Politics.aspx?r=1 (accessed 18 January 2011).

Pew Project for Excellence in Journalism (2010) *The State of the News Media: An Annual Report on American Journalism.* Available at www.stateofthemedia.org/2010/cable_tv_summary_essay.php (accessed 21 October 2010).

Pew Project for Excellence in Journalism (2009) *The State of the News Media: An Annual Report on American Journalism.* Available at www.stateofthemedia.org/2009/narrative_networktv_audience.php?cat=2&media=6 (accessed 21 October 2010).

Pew Research Center for the People and the Press (2010) 'Ideological News Sources: Who Watches and Why'. Washington, DC: Pew Research Center for the People and the Press.

Pew Research Center Project for Excellence in Journalism (2008) 'Journalism, Satire or Just Laughs? "The Daily Show with Jon Stewart," Examined', http://www.journalism.org/node/10953#fn2 Accessed 17 May 2011

Pew Research Center for the People and the Press (2011) 'Beyond Red vs. Blue: Political Typology', http://people-press.org/files/legacy-pdf/Beyond-Red-vs-Blue-The-Political-Typology.pdf Accessed 17 May 2011

Pew Research Center for the People and the Press (2007) 'Today's Journalists Less Prominent Fewer Widely Admired than 20 Years Ago', a Pew Research Center for the People and Press Report, available at http://people-press.org/report/309/todays-journalists-less-prominent (accessed 21 October 2010).

Pew Research Center for the People and the Press (2004) 'News audiences increasingly politicized', 8 June, available at http://people-press.org/report/?pageid=834 (accessed 21 October 2010).

Philo, Greg (1990) *Seeing & Believing: The Influence of Television.* London: Routledge.

Philo, Greg and Berry, Mike (2004) *Bad News From Israel.* London: Pluto.

Philo, Greg and Miller, David (2001) *Market Killing: What The Free Market Does And What Social Scientists Can Do About It.* London: Pearson Education.

Plunkett, John (2010) 'Andrew Marr says bloggers are "inadequate, pimpled and single"', *Guardian*, 11 October, available at www.guardian.co.uk/media/2010/oct/11/andrew-marr-bloggers (accessed 2 December 2010).

Plunkett, John (2009) 'Director General tells BBC bosses to put more older women on screen', *Guardian*, 24 September, available at www.guardian.co.uk/media/2009/sep/24/bbc-ageism-mark-thompson (accessed 2 December 2010).

Porto, Mauro (2007) 'TV news and political change in Brazil: the impact of democratization on TV's globo's journalism', *Journalism: Theory, Practice and Criticism*, 8(4): 363–384.

Prior, Markus (2007) *Post-Broadcast Democracy: How Media Choice Increases Inequality in Political Involvement and Polarizes Elections.* Cambridge: Cambridge University Press.

Pulitzer, Joseph (1904) 'Planning a school of journalism – the basic concept', *North American Review*, May, p. 20.

Quinn, Adrian (2007) 'Contrary to claims, cultures & conventions: an apologia for the Glasgow Media Group', *International Journal of Media & Cultural Politics,* 3(1): 5–24.

Quinn, Stephen and Lamble, Stephen (2008) *Online Newsgathering: Research and Reporting for Journalism.* Oxford: Focal.

Radway, Janice (1984) *Reading the Romance: Women, Patriarchy and Popular Literature*. Chapel Hill, NC: University of North Carolina Press.

Rai, Mugdha and Cottle, Simon (2010) 'Global News Revisited: Mapping the Contemporary Landscape of Satellite Television News'. In Stephen Cushion and Justin Lewis (eds), *The Rise of 24-Hour News Television: Global Perspectives*. New York: Peter Lang.

Randall, Steve (2007) 'Rough Road to Liberal Talk Success: A Short History of Radio Bias'. In *Fair: Fairness & Accuracy in Reporting*, available at www.fair.org/index.php?page=3144 (accessed 29 September 2010).

Raspberry, William (2005) 'Fox's Sandstorm', *Washington Post*, 18 April, available at www.washingtonpost.com/wp-dyn/articles/A61709-2005Apr17.html (accessed 21 October 2010).

Reese, Stephen D. (2010) 'Journalism and globalization', *Sociology Compass*, 4(6): 344–353.

Reith, John (1952) Speech at the House of Lords, 22 May: Hansard col 1297.

Revoir, Paul (2010) '"As shallow as a paddling pool": BBC dumbing down row as *Panorama* reporter attacks channel boss in email', *Daily Mail*, 17 July, available at www.dailymail.co.uk/news/article-1295399/As-shallow-paddling-pool-BBC-dumbing-row-Panorama-reporter-attacks-channel-boss-email.html (accessed 17 January 2011).

Reynolds, Amy and Barnett, Brooke (2003) '"This Just In" … how national TV news handled the breaking "live" coverage of September 11', *Journalism and Mass Communication Quarterly*, 80(3): 689–703.

Robinson, James (2009) 'James Murdoch hits out at BBC and regulators at Edinburgh TV festival', *Media Guardian*, 28 August, available at www.guardian.co.uk/media/2009/aug/28/james-murdoch-bbc-mactaggart-edinburgh-tv-festival (accessed 21 January 2011).

Robinson, Piers (2005) 'The CNN effect revised', *Critical Studies in Media Communication*, 22(4): 344–349.

Robinson, Piers (2002) *The CNN Effect: The Myth of News, Foreign Policy and Intervention*. London: Routledge.

Robinson, James (2010) 'BSKYB: only 1 in 20 back Murdoch takeover, poll reveals', *Media Guardian*, 27 December, available atwww.mediaguardian.co.uk/media/dec/27/bskyb-poll-murdoch-takover?cat=media&type=article (accessed 25 January 2011).

Roper Opinion Poll (2010) 'PBS Roper poll', available at www.pbs.org/roperpoll2010/PBS_Roper_brochure_2.18.10.pdf (accessed 2 December 2010).

Rosen, Philip T. (1980) *The Modern Stentors: Radio Broadcasters and the Federal Government, 1920–1934*. Westport, CT: Greenwood.

Rosie, Michael, Petersoo, Pille, MacInnes, John, Condor, Susan and Kennedy, James (2006) 'Mediating which nation? Citizenship and national identities in the British press', *Social Semiotics*, 16(2): 327–344.

Ryan, Kathleen M. (2009) 'The performative journalist: job satisfaction, temporary workers and American television news', *Journalism: Theory, Practice and Criticism*, 10(5): 647–664.

Ryan, Kathleen M. and Mapaye, Joy (2010) 'Beyond "anchorman": a comparative analysis of race, gender, and correspondent roles in network news', *Electronic News*, 4(2): 97–117.

Ryan, Kathleen M., Lake, Hillary and Mapaye, Joy (2008) 'Talent 24/7: The Changing Nature of On-Air Newswork'. Paper presented at the Annual Meeting of the Association for Education in Journalism and Mass Communication, Chicago, 6 August.

Ryan, Michael (2006) 'Mainstream news media, an objective approach, and the march to war in Iraq', *Journal of Mass Media Ethics*, 21(1): 4–29.

Ryley, John (2009) 'Introduction'. In *20 Years of Breaking News* (Sky News publication).

Ryley, John (2006) 'Never been a better time to be in TV news; television's *Sky News*; in the age of broadband, podcasts and texts, how can the small screen hope to keep up?', *Independent*, 4 September, p. 10.

Samuel, Lawrence R. (2001) *Brought to You By: Postwar Television Advertising and the American Dream*. Austin, TX: University of Texas Press.

Sanders, Karen, Hanna, Mark, Berganza, María Rosa and Carlos, Rey Juan (2008) 'Becoming journalists: a comparison of the professional attitudes and values of British and Spanish journalism students', *European Journal of Communication*, 23(2): 133–152.

Scannell, Paddy and Cardiff, David (1991) *A Social History of British Broadcasting: 1922–1939: Serving the Nation*. London: Blackwell.

Scheheter, Danny (2007) 'Anna Nicole Smith and the media of distraction', *Buzzflash Blog*, http://blog.buzzflash.com/contributors/811 (accessed 23 January 2011).

Scheheter, Danny (1997) *The More You Watch the Less You Know*. New York: Seven Stories.

Schlesinger, Philip (1978/1987) *Putting Reality Together: BBC News*. London: Methuen.

Schlesinger, Philip, Miller, David and Dinan, William (2001) *Open Scotland? Journalists, Spin-Doctors and Lobbyists*. Edinburgh: Polygon.

Schiffers, Steve (2003) 'Who Won the US Media War?', *BBC News Online*, 18 April, avilable at http://news.bbc.co.uk/1/hi/world/americas2959833.stm (accessed 21 October 2010).

Schudson, Michael (1998) *The Good Citizen*. New York: Free.

Schudson, Michael (1995) *The Power of News*. Cambridge, MA: Harvard University Press.

Schudson, Michael and Anderson, Chris (2009) 'Objectivity, Professionalism, and Truth Seeking in Journalism'. In Karin Wahl-Jorgensen and Thomas Hanitzsch (eds), *The Handbook of Journalism Studies*. New York: Routledge.

Shaw, Donald, Hamm, Bradley J. and Knott, Diana L. (2000) 'Technological change, agenda challenge and social melding: mass media studies and the four ages of place, class, mass and space', *Journalism Studies*, 1(1): 57–79.

Shaw, Martin (2004) 'Ofcom and Light Touch Regulation'. In Colin Robinson (ed.), *Successes and Failures in Regulating and Deregulating Utilities*. Cheltenham: Edward Elgar.

Sherwin, Adam (2010) 'Mark Thompson: Britain needs a channel like Fox News', *Media Guardian*, 17 December, available at www.guardian.co.uk/media/2010/dec/17/mark-thompson-bbc-fox-news (accessed 24 January 2011).

Shott, Nicholas (2010) *Commercially Viable Local Television in the UK: A Review for the Secretary of State for Culture, Olympics, Media and Sport*. London: HMSO.

Silverstone, Roger (1994) *Television and Everyday Life*. London: Routledge.

Small, William (1970) *To Kill A Messenger: Television News and the Real World*. New York: Hastings House.

Smith, Laura K. (2008) 'Race, ethnicity, and student sources: minority newsmakers in student-produced versus professional TV news stories', *Howard Journal of Communications*, 19(2): 182–199.

Smith, Maurice (1994) *Paper Lions: The Scottish Press and National Identity*. Edinburgh: Polygon.

Sparks, Colin and Tulloch, John (eds) (2000) *Tabloid Tales: Global Debates Over Media Standards*. Lanham, MD: Rowman & Littlefield.

Spigel, Lynn (1993) *Make Room for TV: Television and the Family Ideal in Postwar America*. Chicago: Chicago University Press.

Springhall, John (1999) *Youth, Popular Culture and Moral Panics: Penny Gaffs to Gangsta Rap, 1830–1996*. Basingstoke: Palgrave Macmillan.

Sreberny-Mohammadi, Annabelle, Winseck, Dwayne, McKenna, Jim and Boyd-Barrett, Oliver (1997) *Media in a Global Context*. London: Bloomsbury.

Starkey, Guy (2006) *Balance and Bias in Journalism: Representation, Regulation and Democracy*. Basingstoke: Palgrave Macmillan.

Starkey, Guy and Crisell, Andrew (2009) *Radio Journalism*. London: Sage.

Steensen, Steen (2008) 'The shaping of an online feature journalist', *Journalism: Theory, Practice and Criticism*, 10(5): 702–718.

Stevenson, Nick (2003) *Cultural Citizenship: Cosmopolitan Questions*. Basingstoke: Open University.

Street, John (2010) *Mass Media, Politics and Democracy* (2nd edition). Basingstoke: Palgrave.

Street, John (2001) *Mass Media, Politics and Democracy*. Basingstoke: Palgrave.

Street, John (1996) *Politics and Popular Culture*. Cambridge: Polity.

Straw, Jack (2010) 'The public gets scared and providing information is vital', *Guardian*, 30 October, available at www.guardian.co.uk/uk/2010/nov/01/jack-straw-public-terror-threat?cat=uk&type=article (accessed 25 January 2011).

Stroud, Natalie J. (2010) 'Polarization and Partisan Selective Exposure' in *Journal of Communication*, Vol.60(3): 556–576.

Stroud, Natalie J. (2008) 'Media Use and Political Predispositions: Revisiting the Concept of Selective Exposure' in *Political Behavior*, 30(3): 341–366.

Sweeney, Mark (2011) 'Jeremy Hunt unveils plan for new national channel', *Media Guardian*, 19 January, available at www.mediaguardian.co.uk/media/2011/jan/19/jeremy-hunt-new-television-channel (accessed 26 January 2011).

Sweeney, Mark (2010a) 'Mark Zuckerberg: Facebook "almost guaranteed" to reach 1 billion users', *Media Guardian*, 23 June, available at www.guardian.co.uk/media/2010/jun/23/mark-zuckerberg-facebook-cannes-lions (accessed 10 January 2011).

Sweeney, Mark (2010b) 'Ofcom slashes cost of ITV and Channel 5 regional broadcasting licences', *Media Guardian*, 1 October, available at www.guardian.co.uk/media/2010/oct/01/ofcom-slashes-regional-broadcasting-licences (accessed 10 January 2011).

Synge, Dan (2010) *The Survival Guide to Journalism*. Buckingham: Open University Press.

Tait, Richard (2007) Cited in 'Does the BBC have a bias problem?', *BBC News Online*, available at http://news.bbc.co.uk/1/low/entertainment/6764779.stm (accessed 24 September 2010).

Tait, Richard (2006) 'What Future for Regional Television News?'. In Bob Franklin (ed.), *Local Journalism and Local Media*. London: Routledge.

Tambini, Damian and Cowling, Jamie (2002) *New News? Impartial Broadcasting in the Digital Age*. London: IPPR.

Tambini, Dominic (2010) 'Ofcom cuts are grave assault on freedom', *Guardian*, Comment is Free, 18 October, available at www.guardian.co.uk/media/2010/oct/18/ofcom-cuts-threaten-freedom (accessed 21 January 2011).

Tanner, Andrea and Smith, Laura (2007) 'Training tomorrow's television journalists: in the trenches with Media Convergence', *Electronic News*, 1(4): 211–225.

Tay, Jinna and Turner, Graeme (2008) 'What is television? Comparing media systems in the post-broadcast era', *Media International Australia, Incorporating Culture & Policy*, 126.

Taylor, Jerome (2009) 'Wanted: TV news presenter. Must be female. Young need not apply', *Independent*, Media Section, 25 September, available at www.independent.co.uk/news/media/tv-radio/wanted-tv-news-presenter-must-be-female-young-need-not-apply-1792901.html (accessed 17 November 2010).

Television Digital News Association (2008) 'Cover Story: 2008 Women and Minorities Survey', by Bob Papper, available at www.rtnda.org/pages/media_items/the-face-of-the-workforce1472.php (accessed 2 December 2010).

Television and New Media (2009) Special Edition on My Media Studies: 10(1).

Temple, Mick (2006) 'Dumbing down is good for you', *British Politics*, 1(2): 257–273.

Thomas, James (2006) 'The Regional and Local Media in Wales'. In Bob Franklin (ed.), *Local Journalism and Local Media*. London: Routledge.

Thomas, James (2003) 'Buried without tears': *The Welsh Mirror* 1999–2003', *Planet: the Welsh Internationalist*, 162 (December): 23–27.

Thomas, James, Cushion, Stephen and Jewell, John (2004a) 'Stirring up apathy? Political disengagement and the media in the 2003 Welsh Assembly elections', *Journal of Public Affairs*, 9: 355–363.

Thomas, James, Jewell, John and Cushion, Stephen (2004b) 'The media and the 2003 Welsh Assembly elections', *Representation: The Journal of Representative Democracy*, 40(4): 281–288.

Thomas, James, Jewell, John and Cushion, Stephen (2003) *Media Coverage of the 2003 Welsh Assembly Elections*. Report for the Electoral Commission.

Thompson, John B. (1995) *The Media and Modernity*. Cambridge: Polity.

Thornham, Sue and O'Sullivan, Tim (2003) 'Chasing the real: "employability" and the Media Studies curriculum', *Media, Culture and Society*, 26(5): 717–736.

Thussu, Daya Kishan (2007) *News as Entertainment: The Rise of Global Infotainment*. London: Sage.

Thussu, Daya Kishan and Freedman, Des (2003) *War and the Media: Reporting Conflict 24/7*. London: Sage.

Tracey, Michael (1998) *Decline and Fall of Public Service Broadcasting*. Oxford: Oxford University Press.

Tsfati, Yariv and Cappella, Joseph, N. (2003) 'Do people watch what they do not trust? Exploring the association between news media skepticism and exposure', *Communication Research*, 30(5): 504–529.

Tuchman, Gaye (1978) *Making News: A Study in the Construction of Reality*. New York: Free.

Tuchman, Gaye (1972) 'Objectivity as strategic ritual: an examination of newsmen's notions of objectivity', *American Journal of Sociology*, 77: 660–679.

Tuggle, Charlie and Huffman, Suzanne (2001) 'Live reporting in television news: breaking news or blackholes?', *Journal of Broadcasting & Electronic Media*, 45: 335–344.

Tuggle, Charlie and Huffman, Suzanne (1999) 'Live news reporting: professional judgment or technological pressure? A national survey of television news directors and senior reporters', *Journal of Broadcasting & Electronic Media*, 43(4): 492–505.

Tuggle, Charlie, Casella, Peter and Huffman, Suzanne (2010) 'Live, Late-Breaking and Broken: TV News and the Challenge of Live Reporting in America'. In Stephen Cushion and Justin Lewis (eds), *The Rise of 24-Hour News Television: Global Perspectives*. New York: Peter Lang.

Tuggle, Charlie, Huffman, Suzanne and Rosengard, Dana (2007) 'Reporting live from the scene: enough to attract the 18–24 audience?', *Journal of Broadcasting & Electronic Media*, 51(1): 58–72.

Tunney, Sean and Monaghan, Garrett (2010) *Web Journalism: A New Form of Citizenship?* Eastbourne: Sussex Academic Press.

Turner, Graeme, and Jinna Tay (eds) (2009) *Television Studies After TV.* London and New York: Routledge.

Ursell, Gillian (2003) 'Creating value and valuing creativity in contemporary UK television: or "dumbing down" the workforce', *Journalism Studies*, 4(1): 31–46.

Ursell, Gillian (2001) 'Dumbing down or shaping up? New technologies, new media, new journalism', *Journalism: Theory, Practice and Criticism*, 2(2): 175–196.

Van Zoonen, Liesbet (2007) 'Audience reactions to Hollywood politics', *Media, Culture and Society*, 29(4): 531–547.

Van Zoonen, Liesbet (2005) *Entertaining the Citizen: When Politics and Popular Culture Converge.* Boulder, CO: Rowman and Littlefield.

Van Zoonen, Liesbet (1993) 'A Tyranny of Intimacy? Women, Femininity and Television News'. In Peter Dahlgren and Colin Sparks (eds), *Communication and Citizenship: Journalism and the Public Sphere.* London: Routledge.

Verkaik, Robert (2006) 'Female reporters paid £6,500 less than men by BBC', *Independent*, Media Section, 8 December, available at www.independent.co.uk/news/media/female-reporters-paid-1636500-less-than-men-by-bbc-427555.html (accessed 17 November 2010).

Volkmer, Ingrid (2010) 'The rise of 24-hour news television: global perspectives', Book Review, *Times Higher Education*, available at www.timeshighereducation.co.uk/story.asp?sectioncode=26&storycode=414095 (accessed 18 January 2011).

Volkmer, Ingrid (1999) *News in the Global Sphere: A Study of CNN and its Impact on Global Communication.* Luton: University of Luton Press.

Wahl-Jorgensen, Karin (ed.) (2007) *Mediated Citizenship.* London: Routledge.

Wahl-Jorgensen, Karin and Franklin, Bob (2008) 'Journalism Research in the UK: From Isolated Efforts to an Established Discipline'. In Martin Loffelholz and David Weaver (eds), *Global Journalism Research.* Oxford: Blackwell.

Wahl-Jorgensen, Karin and Hanitzsch, Thomas (eds) (2009) *Handbook of Journalism Studies.* London: Routledge.

Walker, Andrew (1992) *A Skyful of Freedom: 60 Years of the BBC World Service.* London: Broadside.

Ward, Ian (2008) 'Australia and the Postmodern Election Campaign'. In Dennis W. Johnson (ed.), *Routledge Handbook of Political Management.* London: Routledge.

Wardle, Claire and Williams, Andrew (2010) 'Beyond user-generated content: a production study examining the ways in which UGC is used at the BBC', *Media, Culture & Society*, 32(5): 781–799.

Watt, Nicholas (2010) 'BBC website "needs clearer red lines" to let competitors survive', *Guardian*, 25 July, available at www.guardian.co.uk/media/2010/jul/25/bbc-website-jeremy-hunt (accessed 27 July 2010).

Wayne, Mike, Petley, Julian, Murray, Craig and Henderson, Lesley (2010) *Television News, Politics and Young People: Generation Disconnected?* Basingstoke: Palgrave Macmillan.

Weaver, David and Wilhoit, Cleveland G. (1986) *The American Journalist.* Bloomington, IN: Indiana University Press.

Weaver, David, Beam, Randal A., Brownlee, Bonnie J., Voakes, Paul S. and Wilhoit, Cleveland G. (2007) *The American Journalist in the 21st Century: U.S. Newspeople at the Dawn of a New Millennium.* Mahwah, NJ: Erlbaum.

Welsh Electoral Commission (2002) *Wales Votes?* Cardiff: Electoral Commission.

Wheeler, Mark (2004) 'Supranational regulation: television and the European Union', *European Journal of Communication*, 19(3): 349–369.

Williams, Andy and Franklin, Bob (2007) *Turning Around the Tanker: Implementing Trinity Mirror's Multimedia Strategy*. Report for the NUJ.

Williams, Andy, Wardle, Claire and Wahl-Jorgensen, Karin (2011) 'Have they got news for US? Audience revolution or business as usual at the BBC?', *Journalism Practice*, 5(1): 85–99.

Williams, Kevin (2010) *Get Me a Murder a Day! A History of Media and Communication in Britain*. London: Bloomsbury Academic.

Williams, Kevin (2009) 'The Unbearable Light of the Market: Broadcasting in the Nations and Regions of Britain post-Peacock'. In Tom O'Malley and Janet Jones (eds), *The Peacock Committee and UK Broadcasting Policy*. Basingstoke: Palgrave Macmillan.

Williams, Kevin (2005) *European Media Studies*. London: Hodder Arnold.

Williams, Kevin (2000) 'No Dreads, Only Some Doubts: The Press and the Referendum Campaign'. In Barry Jones and Denis Balsom (eds), *The Road to the National Assembly for Wales*. Cardiff: University of Wales Press.

Williams, Kevin (1999) 'Teaching Journalism in Britain' in Philo, Greg (ed.), *Message Received*. London: Longman.

Williams, Kevin (1997) *Shadows and Substance: The Development of a Media Policy in Wales*. Llandysul: Gomer.

Williams, Raymond (1974) *Television: Technology and Cultural Form*. London: Routledge.

Wilson, Robin and Fawcett, Liz (2004) *Election – Coverage of the 2003 Northern Ireland Assembly Poll*. London: Electoral Commission.

Woodward, Bob (2004) *Plan of Attack*. London: Pocket Books.

Wring, Dominic and Ward, Stephen (2010) 'The media and the 2010 campaign: The television election', *Parliamentary Affairs*, 63(4): 802–817.

Xenos, Michael A. and Becker, Amy B. (2009) 'Moments of Zen: effects of *The Daily Show* on information seeking and political learning', *Political Communication*, 26: 317–332.

Young, Sally (2010) 'Audiences and the Impact of 24-Hour News in Australia and Beyond'. In Stephen Cushion and Justin Lewis (eds), *The Rise of 24-Hour News Television: Global Perspectives*. New York: Peter Lang.

Young, Dannagal G. and Tisinger, Russell (2006) 'Dispelling late-night myths: news consumption among late-night comedy viewers and the predictors of exposure to various late-night shows', *International Journal of Press/Politics*, 11(3): 113–134.

Zaller, John (2003) 'A new standard of news quality: burglar alarms for the monitorial citizen', *Political Communication*, 20(2): 109–130.

Zayani, Mohamed (2010) 'The Changing Face of Arab News Media: Ambiguities and Opportunities'. In Stephen Cushion and Justin Lewis (eds), *The Rise of 24-Hour News Television: Global Perspectives*. New York: Peter Lang.

Zayani, Mohamed (2005) *The Al Jazerra Phenomenon: Critical Perspectives on New Arab Media*. London: Pluto.

Zelizer, Barbie (2004) *Taking Journalism Seriously: News and the Academy*. Thousand Oaks, CA: Sage.

Zelizer, Barbie (1993) 'Journalists as interpretive communities', *Critical Studies in Media Communications*, 10(3): 219–237.

Zelizer, Barbie and Allan, Stuart (2011a) *Journalism After September 11* (2nd edition). London: Routledge.

Zelizer, Barbie and Allan, Stuart (2011b) *Keywords in News and Journalism Studies*. Basingstoke: Open University Press.

INDEX